PRAISE FOR
ROBERT K. TANENBAUM'S
TRUE-CRIME CLASSICS

BADGE OF THE ASSASSIN

"Engrossing. . . . The incredible story of a hit squad sent to kill cops. . . . The accounts of the two murder trials in New York . . . and an intervening chase down to a remote farm in Mississippi . . . are almost as suspenseful as the stalking and capture of the killers."

—*The New York Times*

"Artfully recreated."

—*Library Journal*

"A thriller of a book!"

—*San Francisco Chronicle*

THE PIANO TEACHER

"Compelling . . . horrific . . . a nightmare voyage through two of the most gruesome murders imaginable . . . and an odyssey through a killer's life."

—*Los Angeles Times*

"Fascinating, chilling. . . . A must read!"

—Ann Rule, author of *Empty Promises*

"An important and frightening true story!"

—Joseph Wambaugh

"Stinging, intelligent . . . unusually provocative and satisfying."
—*Kirkus Reviews*

"Tanenbaum and Greenberg meticulously reconstruct the murders so that they read like fiction. . . . Their book is worth seeking out."
—*People*

Praise for Robert K. Tanenbaum's
Butch Karp thriller
TRUE JUSTICE

"Intelligent dialogue, a well-designed maze of political and moral traps, and the charming and incendiary chemistry between Karp and Ciampi. For those who prefer their legal thrillers with plenty of spice and a high I.Q., Tanenbaum remains an essential addiction."
—*Publishers Weekly*

"This is vintage Tanenbaum: each of the deftly drawn characters wrestles with the moral dilemmas raised by the intertwined plots in a believable way, and readers will close *True Justice*'s final page satisfied they've wrestled with those dilemmas a bit themselves."
—*Booklist*

"A keenly intelligent book, many cuts above the usual courtroom procedural."
—Amazon.com

"Deftly handled. . . . Karp and Ciampi are smart, honest, and aggressive."
—*Los Angeles Times Book Review*

Also by Robert K. Tanenbaum

Fiction

Enemy Within
True Justice
Act of Revenge
Reckless Endangerment
Irresistible Impulse
Falsely Accused
Corruption of Blood
Justice Denied
Material Witness
Reversible Error
Immoral Certainty
Depraved Indifference
No Lesser Plea

Nonfiction

The Piano Teacher:
  The True Story of a Psychotic Killer
Badge of the Assassin

ROBERT K. TANENBAUM
& PHILIP ROSENBERG

BADGE OF THE ASSASSIN

POCKET BOOKS
NEW YORK LONDON TORONTO SYDNEY SINGAPORE

POCKET BOOKS, a division of Simon & Schuster, Inc.
1230 Avenue of the Americas, New York, NY 10020

Copyright © 1979 by Robert K. Tanenbaum

ISBN: 0-7434-3298-3

First Pocket Books printing December 2001

10 9 8 7 6 5 4 3 2 1

POCKET and colophon are registered trademarks of Simon & Schuster, Inc.

For information regarding special discounts for bulk purchases, please contact Simon & Schuster Special Sales at 1-800-456-6798 or business@simonandschuster.com.

Cover design by Tony Greco

Printed in the U.S.A.

To my special loves Patti, Rachael, Roger, and Billy.
To Kenny Klein, for his dedication
to excellence, loyalty, and courage.
To the memory of District Attorney Frank Hogan.
RKT

To Charlotte and Mark.
PR

AUTHORS' NOTE

The entire manuscript of *Badge of the Assassin* was written jointly by both authors. Parts One and Two describe events that occurred prior to Mr. Tanenbaum's involvement in the case. In Parts Three and Four, the first person pronoun refers to Mr. Tanenbaum. The authors hope that this transition to the first person does not confuse the reader. They chose this method as the most direct way of narrating events in which one of them was intimately involved.

This book, in a very real sense, is the product of four years of investigative work involving literally thousands of police officers. The authors, however, are solely responsible for the accuracy of all statements contained herein. We have changed the names and otherwise disguised the identities of a number of civilians who testified at the trial or cooperated with authorities in other ways. The following names are *not* real names: Antonia Torres Allen, Howard Allen, Nanny Closter, Jack Franklin, Linda Gill, Hector Grace, Duncan Grant, S. W. Griffin, Irene Grohman, Bernard Hexter, Alexandra Horn, Francis A. Howland, Ruth Jennings, Gloria Lapp, Horace Lukes, Lester Bertram May, Mrs. Mitchell, Jethro Peel, Nana Peel, Christine Rowe, Malcolm Rowe, Grace Russell, Ulysses Tatum, Celia Torres, Nana Tucker, Adela Wine. The character of Horace Lukes is a composite figure drawn from more than one New Orleans police officer. One place name has been changed: the town of Cordelia, Mississippi. All personal and place names not mentioned above may be assumed to be real names.

We wish to express our deep gratitude to a number of people who read and commented on portions of the manuscript, provided us with information, answered our questions, or generously donated editorial advice. In these categories, our thanks go to Richard Beahrs, Bill Butler, L. J. Delsa, Cliff Fenton, Olga Ford, Ken Klein, Frank McCoy, Sammy McGee, Terry O'Reilly, Charlotte Rosenberg, Stuart Rosenberg, Marcy McGaugh, and Michael Warnecke. We are most deeply grateful to Aaron Frosch for his encouragement during one of the most difficult periods in the life history of any book—the time before it is begun. We would like to thank Barbara Welsch for her excellent secretarial assistance and the very capable staff at Star Pack, Inc.—Wanda Huttner, Ernie Hill, and Beverly Bonner—for skillful, efficient, and cheerful work in producing the physical manuscript. We would especially like to thank Jane Rosenman for midwifing the book through labor and delivery. And finally, our deepest thanks to Henry Robbins, whose confidence in the book meant a great deal to both authors, especially the one who isn't always quite so sure.

PART ONE
Scoping Pigs

WAVERLY JONES WAS DEAD BEFORE HE HIT the sidewalk, the bullets tracing a neat line straight down his back as though someone had been trying to bisect him from top to bottom. The first one smashed through his skull, an almost perfect shot, dead center to the back of his head, fired from no more than six inches behind him. If he felt anything, it was only the wallop of impact, for the bullet that seared through his brain was hot enough to cook the tissue as it passed.

He was already pitching forward when the next shot ripped into the back of his neck, severed his spine, and neatly cracked his lower jaw the way impatient hands might snap a pencil. The third shot, about eighteen inches directly below the second, again tore through a vertebra and came to rest in the dead tissue of what had been only thirty seconds before the powerful body of a proud black police officer in the prime of his life.

The bullets came so fast he was still falling when the fourth one hit. Moving upward now, because of the angle of his body, it pierced the tissue of his left buttock and didn't stop until it had ruptured his kidney and diaphragm.

Dead at thirty-two, Patrolman Waverly Jones was the lucky one. His killer worked with the cool precision of a professional executioner. But the second gunman didn't have the first one's skill, and so Patrolman Joseph Piagentini died the way a bull dies in the ring, his body scored and torn with a dozen wounds that left him alive long enough to feel the impact of each bullet, long enough to crawl along the damp, foul sidewalk while bullet after bullet easily outran him. Long enough to plead with his killers, to beg them not to shoot him again.

But they wouldn't stop. The second gunman emptied his long-barreled .38 into Piagentini's body and then stood over him, cursing him for his stupidity in refusing to die.

Meanwhile, the first gunman, the one who had killed Waverly Jones, reached down and unstrapped the leather harness that held Jones's service revolver in its holster. He slid the gun free and studied it for a few seconds, feeling the heft of it in his hand, appreciating it the way a hunter values an animal he has killed. The weapon was now his, the tusk or tooth or talon of his fallen prey.

He thrust the .38 into his belt and strode to where his partner was now stooping over Piagentini trying to pry the gun from the holster of the writhing cop. He watched as the cop's hand made desperate movements toward his hip, like the uncoordinated flailings of a crying baby. Then the second shooter stood upright, the cop's gun in his right hand, his own empty .38 in his left. He pulled the trigger of the service revolver again and again, each bullet sending spasms of fresh pain to Piagentini's tortured brain.

Then the cop's gun, too, clicked empty, and the cop was still alive, his moanings and movements delivering a clear and appalling message to the confused killer. "We are the police," the still living body seemed to say. "You can hate us and revile us, you can come up behind us in the dark of a Harlem night. You can arm yourselves like warriors and shoot us until your guns are empty. But you cannot kill us."

The first gunman saw the look of panic and perplexity on his partner's face. Calmly, he raised his .45 and fired one last shot into the cop's body. Then he and his partner fled as they might have fled a ghost, leaving Patrolman Joseph Piagentini still alive on the sidewalk, still crawling in his own blood toward the shelter of a hedge.

He was alive a few minutes later when a passing stranger saw what he first took to be a clump of clothes, then saw it move, heard it groan. He was alive when the first police car arrived on the scene. And he was alive when they lifted him into the back seat of a squad car that went screaming off toward Harlem Hospital.

He died in the police car.

The next morning the doctor who performed the autopsy took three bullets from his body. Nine others had passed completely through him. In all, the doctor counted twenty-two bullet holes in Joseph Piagentini. He had been twenty-eight years old.

One

NORTH OF THE TRIBOROUGH BRIDGE, THE
Harlem River slices sharply to the northwest, narrowing Manhattan Island down to a tadpole tail of land. At
142nd Street, Fifth Avenue, the dividing line between
the East Side and the West Side, runs up against the
river and comes to a stop. Lenox Avenue, which is
Harlem's name for Sixth, extends northward as far as
147th, and then it, too, runs out of land. Seventh lasts
all the way to 154th, just one block short of the
Macombs Dam Bridge, which leads across the river to
the Bronx and Yankee Stadium.

From the air, the triangle of land bordered on the
south by 155th Street, on the west by the sheer cliff
known as Coogan's Bluff, and on the east by the Harlem
River doesn't look like it belongs to New York. Beyond
it, to the south and west, one can see the huddled tenements of Harlem pressed to each other like subway riders in the morning. But in the triangle itself, known generally as the Colonial Park district, the tenements have
long since been leveled, to be replaced by two distinct
sets of ungainly X-shaped apartment towers.

The southernmost set of towers consists of four

thirty-story apartments that from above look like mammoth jacks left lying on the ground by the children of giants. And well they might, for the land they stand on was once the home of Giants. The Polo Grounds used to be here, and now someone's living room covers the spot where Eddie Stanky rode from third to home on Leo Durocher's back after Bobby Thomson's home run in the '51 playoff.

Just north of the Polo Grounds Project stand seven identical twelve-story towers and a larger eighth one that is really just two of the smaller buildings run together. Although the grounds have been attractively landscaped with hedges, grass, trees, and wide walkways, nothing can disguise the fact that the Colonial Park Houses, as these eight towers are collectively called, are low-income housing. In an effort to pass them off as something else, the architects hoped to create a parklike atmosphere by facing the main entrances of all the buildings inward, so that the project is self-contained, its back turned on Harlem. But Harlem cannot be so easily thrust aside. Like an unpleasant thought the mind tries to reject, it has a way of reasserting itself. Psychoanalysts call this phenomenon the return of the repressed, but the cops in the Thirty-second Precinct had a simpler way of putting it. In Colonial Park, they said, you watched your ass.

Richard Hill had fought in Vietnam and should have known the sound of gunfire when he heard it. But on a spring night twelve thousand miles from where he had done his fighting, the sudden noise caught him off guard and he assumed the explosions were firecrackers. It took a moment for him to realize he was once again on a battlefield. When he did, he reacted like a soldier.

As he passed between buildings 159-14 and 159-20, he glanced to his left, the direction from which the sound of the firecrackers had come. But there were no children playing in the area, no signs of life at all. There was just, on the sidewalk near the bushes, sixty to seventy feet in front of him, a clump of discarded clothes.

Then the clothing moved, shifting on the ground as though there were something alive in it. He watched for a few seconds, until he was certain he had seen it move, then walked toward it, quickening his pace as he drew closer. When he had cut the distance in half he began to hear a terrible moaning, like an animal in pain, like the wind keening through high trees. By this time he was running.

The thought flashed through his mind that there were snipers on one of the roofs. An instinct bred in distant jungles took over and he darted for cover, then raised his head and scanned the rooftops. He saw nothing. In an infantryman's crawl, he inched toward the fallen man, alert for any glint from above that would be the only warning he would get of the sniper's presence.

As he rounded the corner of the walkway, he saw a second body, actually closer to him than the one he had seen before. He crawled to it, saw it was a cop and that the back of his head was missing. He looked for the cop's gun but it wasn't there. He knew he was safe, for a sniper couldn't have taken the gun, so he ran toward the other cop. The walkie-talkie one of them had been carrying lay on the ground between them. Hill grabbed for it, punched at the button that would make it work, and shouted an alarm. "May Day! May Day! Two cops shot!" he called. Then he dropped the box and ran to the second patrolman, the one whose cries he had been hearing all along.

Joseph Piagentini was still moving, still trying to crawl to the clump of bushes at the edge of the sidewalk. He didn't know the shooting had stopped.

Hector Grace, a beer-bellied, forty-five-year-old gypsy-cab driver, had taken his wife out for dinner before going on the night shift. He dropped her off in the back of the project and waited in the cab for a light to go on in the apartment window, their signal that she was safely inside.

He heard shots and saw, not far from where his wife had just walked, the flashes of gunshots, a quick bright series of flares in the near darkness. He saw two cops go down, then two men running along the sidewalk toward him, pistols in their hands.

He didn't follow them with his eyes once they were beyond his cab, didn't even wait for the light to come on in his living-room window. He gunned the engine and raced from the project, squealing the tires in a hard right onto Eighth Avenue. He was looking for a cop, heading south toward the precinct house but praying he would find a patrol car sooner than later.

He was in luck. At 145th and Eighth he spotted a green-and-white cruiser, pulled up beside it, and told the officer what he had seen and heard. The siren flashed on even as the cruiser was screeching into the U-turn that would take it back uptown to Colonial Park.

Mike Warnecke reached for the radio to report the call. "Jesus, that's our sector," his partner Bob Alvino muttered under his breath, in the back of his mind the realization already taking shape that but for a chance call that had drawn them from their sector only minutes before, it would have been he and Mike lying in their own blood on the sidewalk.

"They was sitting on that car," someone shouted from the crowd of thirty or forty curious and angry blacks clustered behind the barricade of sawhorses and ropes that had been set up to quarantine the crime scene.

Bill Butler, the blond, thick-bodied thirty-one-year-old detective who had just caught what was going to be the longest and most difficult case of his career, scanned the crowd, knowing that somewhere in it was a witness. For an instant he thought of holding them all, questioning them until they produced the man who called out that he had seen the killers sitting on the white Mustang. But Butler had been in the Thirty-second Precinct long enough to know it wouldn't work. Pressure from the police would only deepen the silence. So he turned his back on the crowd, ordered a nearby patrolman to secure the Mustang, then stood at parade rest, waiting. Behind him, voices in the crowd whispered hoarsely but offered him nothing more.

An Emergency Services crew arrived with its generator truck and began stringing the high-powered lights that would illuminate the parking area like a fairground. While fifteen or twenty detectives circulated through the crowd, prowling the lawns, shrubs, and walkways in search of evidence, at least as many uniformed men began canvassing the project for potential witnesses. Kneeling on the ground, a detective from Forensic was tracing outlines on the sidewalk where the bodies had been found. He drew a circle for Waverly Jones' head, a long ellipse for his body, then wrote the name JONES in large square letters across the chest. He stood up, stepping carefully around the bright puddle of blood that still gleamed red under the powerful lights.

Butler watched him silently, then crossed the parking area and approached Carl Lacho, the Forensic Division's fingerprint expert. He ordered Lacho to dust the exterior of the Mustang and of the two other cars parked nearby. "We should get a break on this," Lacho told him. "It rained a couple of hours ago, so any lifts we make are going to be fresh."

About fifty yards from where Butler and Lacho were conferring, a forty-nine-year-old self-employed upholsterer named Jack Franklin circled furtively around the parking lot until he felt reasonably safe from observation. With a small, almost imperceptible hand movement, he caught the attention of one of the detectives. "I see them," he whispered when the detective had come close enough.

"What did you see?"

"I seen them running. That's my car over there. I was unloading and I seen them running this way."

The detective flipped open his memo book, took Franklin's name and address. "Okay, start from the beginning," he said.

"Like I say, I'm unloading the back and I hear these

shots. So I look up and I seen these guys running right over there." He motioned with his hand.

"Two guys?"

"Three."

"You sure of that?"

"They was right over there."

"Okay. What else?"

"They had guns. And they run up that way. And that's all I seen."

The detective was skeptical. "Did you get a good look at them?" he asked. "Would you be able to recognize them?"

"You know it. I seen them real good. They was brothers, y'know—I mean they was black," he corrected for the benefit of the white officer. "They was running kinda stooped down. Short fellas."

"About how tall?"

"The bigger one, he was maybe say about five-one. The other two was shorter, say maybe four-eleven."

The detective gulped. "How tall am I?" he demanded, to gauge if the witness had any concept of height.

Jack Franklin studied him carefully for a few seconds, then announced, "Five-eleven."

Right on the money. The detective closed his notebook and told Franklin the police would be in touch with him to make an identification when the killers were apprehended.

At the same time that Franklin was having trouble convincing the investigating officers he had seen the killers, an eighteen-year-old Parks Department worker named Duncan Grant was having just as much trouble convincing them he had seen nothing. Grant had been sitting in front of building 159-38 when the gunmen ran by. "I saw them coming and I got under that bench man. I'm telling you they had guns!" he said shrilly.

"But you did see them?" the detective questioning him insisted.

"Yeah, when they first come around the building. But they was too far away."

"How about when they got closer?"

"I just told you, man, I was under that bench. One of them says, 'Be cool brother, we ain't after you,' but I wasn't taking no chances."

"Could you identify them?"

"Their feet maybe. I could identify their feet. What do you want from me, man?"

Unsatisfied with the answers he was getting, the detective took Grant to the Thirty-second Precinct for further questioning.

While all these was going on outside, the team of patrolmen assigned to canvass building number 159-20 was making headway of its own. They had just entered the lobby and were crossing toward the elevator when the car opened and two teen-age black girls stepped out. As soon as they saw the cops, the girls exchanged nervous glances. "We didn't see anything!" one of them blurted out. She tried to get back into the elevator but one of the patrolmen grabbed the door. Both girls were handcuffed and taken to the Thirty-second Precinct for questioning.

So far, then, in the first minutes of the investigation, the police had turned up five witnesses, including Hector Grace, the gypsy-cab driver who had followed Patrolmen Warnecke and Alvin's radio car back to the murder scene after notifying them of the shooting. Grace claimed to have gotten a fairly good look at the gunmen, but the other four witnesses were of doubtful worth—a kid who wouldn't talk, a guy who had seen three midgets, and a pair of terrified and incoherent sixteen-year-old girls. It wasn't much to go on.

Still, Bill Butler knew he had his first break in the case. It wasn't a clue, it wasn't anything that would help him find the killers. But the fact that the back-shooting butchers who killed Waverly Jones and Joseph Piagentini had taken the cops' guns meant they were after trophies and they weren't about to throw them away. Sooner or later those two Colt .38 Police Specials would be found. And when they were, they would tie the murderers to their deed like an umbilicus.

"We're in a war," Edward J. Kiernan, the truculent president of the Patrolmen's Benevolent Association, announced the moment he arrived at Harlem Hospital. As the elected leader of the city's thirty thousand uniformed cops, the gray-haired, craggy-faced PBA president had more than enough cause for outrage. Just two days earlier, on Wednesday, May 19, 1971, Patrolmen Thomas Curry and Nicholas Binetti were parked on 112th Street in front of District Attorney Frank Hogan's apartment building while the cops assigned to the D.A.'s regular security detail took a late dinner break. Spotting a late-model yellow maverick heading west on the one-way eastbound street, they attempted to flag it down and were ignored. The Maverick turned south on the service road that parallels Riverside Drive and sped off. Curry and Binetti gave chase.

They caught up with the vehicle just north of 106th Street and pulled alongside. As they signaled for the car to pull to the curb, the driver suddenly ducked his head and the passenger to his right opened fire with a .45-caliber submachine gun, pumping a couple of dozen rounds through the doors and windows of the green-and-white patrol car. Curry, who was on the passenger side, was the most critically wounded, taking slugs in the face, shoulder, chest, and leg. One bullet passed through his optic nerve. Binetti was hit eight times, virtually ripped from the steering wheel by the tremendous pounding. Their bullet-riddled car careened on past the yellow Maverick, sliced murderously across the uptown lane of traffic, and came to a crashing stop at the foot of a statue in the narrow strip of park between Riverside Drive and the service road.

Curry fell from the car and was lying unconscious on the grass when the first police cars responded to the scene. Binetti managed to gasp out a description of the car and part of the license number before he, too, passed out. Both were taken to Saint Luke's Hospital, where their conditions were listed as critical. It was only the fifth month of the year, but Curry and Binetti were the twenty-ninth and thirtieth officers wounded in the line of duty in 1971, compared to forty-five in all of 1970. Already five cops had been killed, and for a while it looked like Curry would be number six. But early Friday evening the hospital announced that his condition had stabilized. Then, barely two hours after the bulletin on Curry was released, Waverly Jones and Joseph Piagentini became the sixth and seventh police officers to die in the line of duty since the start of the bloodiest year New York's cops had ever seen.

"It's open season on cops in this city," Kiernan told the reporters clustered around him in the spacious hospital foyer. "I refuse to stand by and permit my men to be gunned down while the Lindsay administration does nothing to protect them. Accordingly, I am instructing them to secure their own shotguns and to carry them on patrol at all times."

"Do you think that will make a difference?" one of the reporters asked skeptically.

"I don't know," Kiernan answered after a long hesitation. "But we'll do whatever is necessary. If we have to patrol this city in tanks, that's what we'll do. This is a war. I want all of my men to understand that in any situation in which they have to draw their weapons, they are to shoot to kill."

Just three blocks away, in the detective squad room on the second floor of the Thirty-second Precinct station house, Police Commissioner Patrick V. Murphy was holding his own press conference, which was attended by Mayor John V. Lindsay. The commissioner released copies of two identical letters that had been hand-delivered earlier that evening to the *New York Times* office on 42nd Street and to the office of radio station WLIB, a black-owned soul music station in Harlem. The letters were dated May 19, 1971, the date of the Curry-Binetti shooting, and each was accompanied by a license plate matching the partial number Binetti had given.

The typewritten messages read:

Here are the license plates sort [*sic*] after by the fascist state pig police. We send them in order to exhibit the potential power of oppressed people to acquire *revolutionary justice*. The armed goons of this racist government will again meet the guns of oppressed Third World peoples as long as they occupy our community and murder our brothers and sisters in the name of American law and order; just as the fascist marines and army [who] occupy Vietnam in the name of democracy and murder Vietnamese people in the name of American imperialism are confronted with the guns of the Vietnamese Liberation Army, the domestic armed forces of racism and oppression will be confronted with the guns of the Black Liberation Army, who will met [*sic*] out in the tradition of Malcolm and all true revolutionaries real justice. We are Revolutionary Justice.

In answer to direct questions, the commissioner said that at that time he had seen no evidence of any connection between the shooting on Wednesday and the double murder at Colonial Park, which he characterized as "an organized attempt . . . deliberate, unprovoked, and maniacal." When told that Edward Kiernan had "ordered" his men to secure their own shotguns, Murphy smiled at the phraseology but refused to get involved in a verbal battle with the PBA president. "Police officers will carry regulation firearms," he said diplomatically, declining to comment further. Clearly, he seemed troubled by the possibility that his department might quickly degenerate into a posse of thirty thousand enraged and vengeful vigilantes.

The press conference had just ended when Commissioner Murphy's fears began to be realized. As they left the ancient four-story brick station house, the commissioner and the mayor found their way to their waiting limousine barred by about twenty-five or thirty angry patrolmen clustered on the sidewalk. Most of the men had been to the hospital already, and then had drifted back to the precinct, their mood a volatile mixture of grief, outrage, and resentment.

Lindsay and Murphy sidled down the four concrete steps to street level, passing silently through the crowd, nodding glumly until forced to stop when the cops closed ranks.

"Jonesy and Joe are dead," someone shouted. "What are we gonna do about it?"

"What are *you* gonna do about *us*?" another cop challenged. His question was echoed by half a dozen other voices.

"I don't know about you guys," a powerfully built patrolman on the top step of the stoop growled from behind the mayor and the commissioner. "But the next time I go out there I got my shotgun with me."

"That's not the answer," Murphy said softly, without turning, the pious banality of his words making no impression at all on the men. "Those two patrolmen were ambushed from the back. Shotguns wouldn't have done them any good."

"That's them," someone shouted brutally. "I gotta be able to protect me."

Murphy shook his head and merely repeated, "That's not the answer." Lindsay said nothing. Together, the mayor and the commissioner edged to the curb and were met at their car by a tall, boyish-looking patrolman who strode forward until he was eyeball to eyeball with the mayor. "We're targets," he said, his voice more plaintive than angry. "Every day we go out there we're targets. They don't fear us or respect us. Maybe if we carried shotguns, maybe if we got tough with them . . ."

His voice trailed off, the sentence unfinished, unfinishable. Mayor Lindsay and Commissioner Murphy disappeared into the idling limousine, which immediately sped off, leaving the cops to mutter among themselves on the street.

One of the cops on the sidewalk was Bobby Alvino, who already was having waking nightmares. The Colonial Park project was his sector, and the bullets that killed Piagentini and Jones would have killed him if it hadn't been for the dumbest luck. At 9:45 he and his partner Mike Warnecke had been patrolling on the Harlem River Drive north of the project when they spotted a late-model yellow Maverick with two teen-age black males in the front seat. Warnecke checked the plates against the partial number on the small strip of paper taped to the dashboard—the single letter and three digits that had been all Nick Binetti had managed to say.

"Those aren't the plates," he announced flatly, but Alvino said, "They would've got rid of the plates. Let's toss them."

In response to their signal, the yellow Maverick eased off the Harlem River Drive onto Eighth Avenue and pulled to the curb at 159th just in front of the drugstore in the corner building of the project.

The kids and the car checked out clean. "Okay, beat it. Sorry to trouble you," Alvino snarled, not particularly meaning it as an apology. While Warnecke jotted a note on the incident in his log, Alvino looked around and wondered if his partner was thinking the same thing he was. If the Maverick had been the car they were looking for, their service revolvers wouldn't have done them much good against a .45 submachine gun. The thought of it sent a shiver down his spine. "Let's get the hell out of here," he snapped. "I don't like it."

He had driven less than a block when a call came in on the radio—a domestic disturbance on 144th. It was in the Dora sector, not the Paul, but Alvino was looking for something to get his mind off the yellow Maverick and what might have been waiting for the two of them when they walked up to it. "Let's take it," he said.

Warnecke was thinking the same thing and his hand was already on the mike.

A half hour later, when a call came in about another domestic disturbance at 159-20 Colonial Park Houses, a radio car from the John sector had to respond. That was why Bob Alvino and Mike Warnecke were alive, why Joe Piagentini and Waverly Jones were dead. That was why Alvino was having nightmares standing on the sidewalk in front of the Thirty-second Precinct station house on 135th Street.

Inside the station house, Bill Butler was questioning witnesses. Ruth Jennings and Gloria Lapp, the two teen-age girls picked up in the lobby of building 159-20, told their story while standing over the shoulder of a police artist, helping him sketch the killers.

Both girls were sixteen years old, high-school class-mates. Ruth was small and sweet-faced, with wide oval eyes, pretty only by comparison with Gloria, who often came by to visit on a Friday night. Ruth's parents, religious and overprotective, considered her too young to date, and Gloria, who was painfully shy and very much overweight, rarely was asked out, so they were sulking around the apartment with nothing to do. A little after ten o'clock Ruth's father suggested a drive to City Island for a late supper. Bored in the apartment, wanting to talk out of adult earshot, Ruth and Gloria decided to wait in the parking lot out back until Ruth's parents were ready to go.

On their way out, in the lobby, the two teen-age girls passed two cops on their way in, a black one and a white one. The black one was tall and handsome. "He's cute," Ruth said when the elevator doors had closed on the cops. Gloria mumbled noncommittally, pretending not to have noticed.

They followed the walkway down to the back of the building, stepping over the puddles that an evening shower had left in the pitted sidewalk. As they lounged against the front end of a car angle-parked in one of the numbered spaces, they noticed, only a few feet away to their right, a young black man no more than twenty years old nervously pacing the sidewalk. Despite her belligerent indifference to boys, Gloria got a good look at him. "He was tall," she said, "had black attire, black hat, close-cropped Afro, a slight mustache and slight goatee." The artist's pencil flew as she spoke.

Stopping at the hedge that lined the sidewalk, the slender young man tore off a few leaves to gnaw on as he passed back to a white Mustang parked at the curb.

Another man, perhaps a year or two older, perched motionless on the left front fender of the Mustang, his hands under his thighs. His body faced the girls but his head was turned to the side as he stared over his right shoulder in the direction of the project building. Gloria described him as "shorter, about five-ten to five-eleven, and kind of stout, about 175 pounds." Because he kept his head turned, she saw him only in profile.

Ruth and Gloria waited in the parking lot ten or fifteen minutes. "What's keeping them? How long does it take to get dressed?" Ruth asked at last. She stepped away from the car, brushed her skirt off, and walked quickly down the sidewalk past the two men. Gloria hurried after her. They turned left at the walkway leading toward the front of the building and stopped under the window to the Jennings apartment. Ruth called up, got no answer, called a few more times. "They must be on their way," Gloria said. "C'mon, let's go back."

As she turned, she noticed the two police officers she had seen in the lobby. They had come out the back door and were crossing along the sidewalk to their car, with the two young black men now behind them, the tall, nervous one in back of the black cop Ruth thought was cute, the heavier one who had been sitting on the car stalking the white cop. There was a noise and the policemen pitched forward, both of them, and then there were only the two black men, arms rigid, firing into the cops' bodies. Between the explosions Gloria heard the white cop moaning, begging, "Don't shoot me, don't shoot me, I got a wife, I got two little kids, don't shoot me."

Gloria ran, with Ruth beside her, two frightened girls following the same path Piagentini and Jones had taken less than a half hour before on their way into the building. The cop's piteous cry was still in their ears, but the shooting went on and on.

"Yes," Ruth Jennings said, leaning forward for a better look at the sketch. "That's him, that's what he looked like."

Gloria Lapp studied the sketch pad mutely. Two cold, coal black eyes stared back at her from under the visor of a black applejack cap. The forehead was high and clear, the mouth cruel. She nodded her head with her eyes closed tight, but couldn't make the killer's face go away.

Two

THE BABY TOOK THE BOTTLE AND SETTLED back to sleep, drinking unconsciously. Diane watched her jealously, envying her serenity. She stroked her cheek, marveling at the warmth of it, then crossed the room to peek at Deborah, who was two now, almost three, the grown-up daughter.

The clock in the kitchen said 12:30. Thank God, she thought. Joe's tour ended at twelve and he was on his way home. She lit a low fire under the stew and decided to wait for him in bed.

At the bottom of the stairs she was startled by a loud knocking on the front door. Then she smiled to herself as she crossed the living room, thinking she had locked the screen door again. But the knocking wasn't on the screen. Amused, she laughed lightly; it was like Joe to forget his keys.

As she passed the front window she saw a police car, dome light flashing, parked on the far side of the street. She quickened her pace, curious for Joe's explanation. But when she opened the door the smile fell from her face and she leaped backward, reflexively slamming the door on the black-clad figure outlined against the night. She threw on the chain lock, ran for the phone, and started to dial the police emergency number. Then she stopped herself and set the phone down carefully, trying to think.

The police were there already. There was no need to call.

Like someone in a trance, obeying commands she does not understand, Diane went back to the door and opened it slowly. Reverend Arnold stepped in, two police officers with him. Not the Deer Park police. City police.

"Mrs. Piagentini, please come with us," Reverend Arnold said softly, his voice low and warm. "We have to take you to Harlem Hospital."

She didn't ask why. She knew.

"I . . . can't," she stammered. Her eyes went to the staircase. "The children."

"Someone will be coming to look after the children," one of the officers said. "They'll be here in just a minute. Please, Mrs. Piagentini."

She was backing away from them, shaking her head, as though she were afraid they would take her against her will. The minister moved toward her, his hand reaching for hers. From the corner of the kitchen, Argus eyed him suspiciously but didn't move. The other dogs, taking their cue from his strange stillness, backed off. In March, she and Joe had bought four German shepherds, the start of the dog-breeding business she hoped would grow fast enough to let him quit the force. So far, the kennels weren't even finished in the back yard.

She reached for the phone, groping for it without taking her eyes off Reverend Arnold. She dialed and let it ring a long time. "It's Diane," she said. "You have to come over right away. Something's happened to Joe."

She followed Reverend Arnold down the walkway, the wisteria, just coming into flower, brushing at her elbow as she reached the drive. The house was set well back from the street, but the front yard had never seemed so long to her. They crossed to the patrol car, but Diane hesitated as Reverend Arnold held the door for her. Three houses down, she saw a light come on on the front porch and watched as Elaine, in a bathrobe, hurried down the three wooden steps to the yard, then ran across the lawns to the Piagentinis' house, clutching her robe closed.

Knowing the children were not alone, Diane slid into the back seat of the patrol car, which wound its way to the expressway. Instead of driving straight to the city, it got off the highway at Queens Village. Twice Diane tried to ask how bad he was hurt but she stopped herself both times, afraid of their answer. She knew it was bad or they wouldn't have come for her like this. The thought that he was dead didn't once cross her mind.

When the car stopped, she made a conscious effort to orient herself but didn't realize where she was until the door opened. They were in front of her parents' house and a patrol car was there already. She wondered how they knew where her parents lived. Then her father slid into the back seat beside her but said nothing, which was his way. She sat stiffly, her anguish as sharp as pain, refusing comfort, and in truth he offered little other than what his presence brought.

With the siren off but the dome light twirling colors into the still night, the patrol car sped on, crossing into Manhattan, racing north to Harlem, as silent as a dream. Police cars, press cars, and limousines crowded Lenox Avenue in front of the immense rectangular hospital, but they left a narrow passage to the emergency entrance on 136th Street. As the patrol car looped into it, Diane reached for the door handle, but her father stopped her with a touch on her arm.

"He isn't alive, you know," he said.

She ran from him, her vision blurred, her mind numb as she stumbled past an empty green-and-white patrol car parked just beyond the ambulance bay. Three hours earlier, her husband had died in the back seat of it.

Inside the hospital, breathless and trembling, she heard her name being whispered by people she didn't know. "Is that his wife?" "Piagentini's wife?" "Diane, isn't it? Someone check, see if her name is Diane."

A man in a lightly striped suit stepped through the crowd. "Mrs. Piagentini? This way please."

"I want to see my husband."

He nodded as though he understood.

There were uniformed cops all around, new ones showing up all the time. They always came like that, from everywhere in the city, and it was after midnight now, the end of the tour—the four-to-midnight tour, Joe's tour—so that hundreds more would be rushing uptown to join those already at the hospital. They had come to give blood, for they knew it was their blood that had been spilled that night. And they had come to keep a vigil, to wait until the verdict was in.

But why were they just standing in glum, speechless knots? Why weren't they going off in ones or twos with a nurse, coming back pale and unsteady with sleeves rolled up? A terrible intuition told her he didn't need their blood. *He's dead, isn't he?* she wanted to ask, just cry the question out loud and let one of the uniformed men answer it.

Instead, she followed the man in the striped suit down a gray tiled corridor away from the crowd. As she walked, hope seeped back with each step. Deep in the bowels of the building he stopped and pushed open a door for her. She stepped past him quickly, expecting to see her husband, injured but asleep, breathing lightly in a hospital bed. But the room was a reception area of some kind, filled with middle-aged men in suits who stopped talking when she walked in.

A small, precisely dressed man with thinning white hair and the blank face of a high-school principal stepped forward and approached her. This was the commissioner, Patrick V. Murphy. As he walked toward her, two men peeled from the group he had been with and fell into place behind him. None of their faces told her anything.

"I want to see my husband," she said while the commissioner was still half a dozen steps away.

"Not right now, Mrs. Piagentini," Murphy said. His voice was soft, even gentle, and she hoped it meant that Joe was all right, that he was being operated on, that . . . anything except what she knew it meant.

"I want to see him," she repeated, in exactly the same tone she had used before. Her voice calm and sounded almost cold in her ears, but inside she could feel she was starting to lose her grip.

One of the commissioner's aides said, "Mrs. Piagentini, your husband is dead. They did everything they could for him."

Her straight brown hair, parted in the center, fell on both sides of her long, oval face, framing dark eyes that gleamed with the pale sorrow of a Giotto madonna. She closed her eyes and held them closed, and when she opened them she looked straight at Murphy, as though the commissioner had the authority to countermand what his aide had said. "I want to see him," she said again. This time her voice was shrill and peremptory, her need to be with her husband urgent.

"I'm sorry, Mrs. Piagentini. A little later perhaps." The commissioner said something else, something about a sedative, but she was no longer listening.

"Why did you bring me here if you won't let me see him?" she demanded angrily. "I have to go home to my children, they need me, my God, my God."

She turned to run from them, but the commissioner motioned with his head in what struck her as a prearranged signal, and an aide reached out a hand for her. She heard them talking about sedatives again, but she pulled free and fled through the door. She raced down the corridor, looking for a way out, a way back to her fatherless children.

Her footsteps, running, were still audible through the open door, when an aide rushed out after her. The commissioner followed a good ten yards behind his aide, who managed to overtake the fleeing widow just as she entered the broad foyer by the hospital's main entrance and found herself facing about half a dozen reporters and as many photographers. The aide called her name and she turned, her face scarred with tears. "Make them go away," she cried. "Please don't let them take my picture."

The aide held up a hand to stop the photographers and crossed the foyer to her. "The commissioner has something to say to you," he said almost insolently.

Behind him she could see Murphy scurrying across the marble floor. Miscalculating the distance that still separated them, she turned to walk away, but the commissioner's hand darted out, catching her forearm just above the wrist as he fell in step beside her. Precisely at that instant photographers' bulbs exploded through the lobby.

She wrenched herself free and ran from the hospital. The caption on the picture in the *Daily News* that morning read, "Diane Piagentini Being Escorted from Hospital by Commissioner Murphy after Viewing Her Husband's Body."

Three

ON MONDAY, MAY 24, JUST THREE DAYS AFTER the shooting, Gloria Lapp's father called Bill Butler at the Thirty-second Precinct. "My girl's seen the killer," he said.

"I know," Butler answered. "We told you Saturday, if you think she needs police protection, we can arrange it. Want me to set it up?"

"That's not what I mean," the heavy-set man growled into the phone.

"Yeah, okay, what is it?" Butler said, not understanding.

"I mean, she seen him today."

"Where?" the detective's excitement registered in his voice.

"The subway. Hundred-sixty-eighth."

"When? Just now?"

"No. This morning."

Butler hung up the phone and hurried to the Lapps' apartment in the Polo Grounds project. There Gloria told of seeing the taller of the two gunmen—the one who had paced between the Mustang and the hedge, sucking leaves, the one she had gotten a good look at in the fifteen minutes before the murders. On her way to school Monday morning, she was switching from the Independent train to the IRT when he passed within a few feet of her.

"Are you sure it was him?" Butler asked. For some reason he didn't understand, witnesses to crimes often report seeing the perpetrator shortly after the incident. Perhaps the killer's face was so deeply etched in her consciousness she couldn't help seeing him wherever she looked.

"I'm not *sure* it was him," Gloria Lapp answered, as though mere certainty could not possibly express the strength of her conviction. "It *was* him."

Butler nodded, convinced. "Did he recognize you?" he asked.

Until that moment the thought that the killer might have seen and recognized her hadn't fully come home to her.

"No, I don't think so," she answered hesitantly, suddenly afraid, trying to bring back the picture of his face as she saw him in the subway, trying to read it for a sign of recognition. And then it struck her that he was a strong and wily man, capable no doubt of utterly concealing his shock of surprise at their second encounter. Had he recognized her as a witness to the killings? Was he sizing her up, looking for a telltale sign that would warn him she could identify him? Had she given herself away?

These thoughts terrorized the simple, trusting girl, who had no confidence at all in her power to dissemble.

"You hadn't ought to frighten the child like that," Mr. Lapp muttered sorrowfully. "She saw him. What more do you want?"

"No, nothing more," Butler said, rising.

Back at the Three-two a few minutes later, he lined up a squad for stakeout duty at the 168th Street subway station the next morning. In the back of his mind he knew it was a long shot, but not any longer than Gloria Lapp's seeing the killer getting on the train in the first place. Take any man on the subway at 8:30 in the morning, he told himself, and the chances are he's on the same train at the same time every morning. There is a certain feeling a cop gets when it seems that a case is starting to break his way, and Butler had that feeling.

Besides, the news waiting for him in the squad room made the need for a solution all the more urgent. At just about the time Gloria Lapp's father had called, two notes had been delivered simultaneously to the *New York Times* and radio station WLIB, just as had happened after the Curry-Binetti shooting on May 19th. A copy of these notes was immediately forwarded to the Thirty-second Precinct and was waiting on Butler's desk when he walked in. It read, in part:

Revolutionary justice has been meted out again by righteous brothers of the Black Liberation Army with the death of two Gestapo pigs gunned down as so many of our brothers have been gunned down in the past. But this time no racist class jury will acquite [*sic*] them. Revolutionary justice is ours!

Every policeman, lackey or running dog of the ruling class must make his or her choice now. Either side with the people: poor and oppressed, or die for the oppressor. Trying to stop what is going down is like trying to stop history, for as long

as there are those who will dare live for freedom
there are men and women who dare to unhorse
the emperor.

All power to the people.

Butler threw the note onto his desk with mixed feelings of rage and humiliation, as appalled by the arrogance of it as he was stung by the insult. *Like trying to
stop history? Bullshit!* He almost leaped from his chair
and nervously paced the office for a few minutes.
Then, to calm himself, he forced himself to think ahead
to the morning, when the tall gunman would walk into
a trap set by a sixteen-year-old girl at the 168th Street
subway station. So much for history!

It was already well into the evening, and for the first
time in three days there seemed to be a break in the
tempo of the investigation, which up to that point had
been random, directionless, nonstop. Now, abruptly,
everything was on hold for a few hours. The lull gave
Butler a chance to realize he was exhausted. Slumping
back into his seat, he debated with himself whether to
drive home or sleep on one of the cots upstairs on the
third floor, then decided that he had to get home even
though the fifty-mile drive up and back would cost him
about two hours that could be better spent sleeping.
He pulled himself from behind his desk, went to the
file for a copy of the artist's rendering of the tall gunman, and then left for the night. The sketch was on his
dashboard as he drove, on the night table next to his
bed as he slept.

In the morning he passed out copies of the artist's
sketch to the six detectives who met him at the station

house. Each of them studied the picture carefully, memorizing it anew, even though they all had seen it before and would never forget the lean, hard face. Then, using a diagram of the subway station, Butler gave orders for the deployment of his squad.

By 7:30 the seven detectives—including Butler, who stationed himself in the token seller's booth—were all in position, eyes scanning the thin but steady stream of passengers from behind a copy of the *Daily News*, from a head bent over a broom, from under the visor of a battered baseball cap. Two of the detectives were wearing business suits, two wore wind-breakers and work pants, and the last two had on coveralls borrowed from Transit Authority maintenance men.

Around 8:20 Butler saw Gloria Lapp enter the station on her way to school. She had a token in her hand, didn't stop at the booth, didn't see him. By this time riders were pouring down the stairs in rush-hour profusion, spilling onto the platform and forming small dense herds at the points where the car doors would open. Watching their faces was like trying to count snowflakes, but Butler and the other detectives in the station knew the gunman could not have passed unnoticed before their eyes. Although the sketch they were working from was imprecise, like a blurred snapshot, they would have spotted him as surely as if he wore the mark of a murderer branded into his face.

When he hadn't appeared by 9:00, the tension of expectant confidence began to give way to sour disappointment. By 9:30 the pulse of the station had slowed markedly; there were fewer riders and they moved without haste. Occasionally a late-for-work secretary flew past, heels clattering noisily on the steel steps. The trains came fully five minutes apart. At 10:00 Butler accepted the fact that the killer was not following a routine, that his appearance now would be only a matter of chance. Still, he waited.

At 10:30 he gave up and called off the stake-off. The men hurried back to the Thirty-second Precinct, where they just had time to exchange their work clothes for dark suits before leaving the station house with all the other uniformed officers and detectives who had gathered there. Funeral services for Waverly Jones were scheduled to start in Harlem at 11:30.

Questioned by reporters after the funeral, Police Commissioner Murphy promised an "early solution" to the brutal double murder. When asked if the Black Panther Party or any other radical group were involved in either of the preceding week's two shootings, Murphy said there was no proof of such involvement, although he did concede that this was one of the possibilities "under investigation."

Largely for political reasons, the department persistently downplayed the racial aspect of the case, for the Lindsay administration prided itself on having kept New York City free of ghetto rioting and other manifestations of interracial hostility. Indeed, City Hall was so alarmed by the angry and anguished sentiments being freely voiced by the city's cops—and especially by their elected representative, PBA President Kiernan—that at times there actually seemed to be more concern about what the cops would do than about what was being done to them. Manhattan Borough President Percy Sutton, one of the most influential black political figures in the city, issued a statement roundly denouncing what he characterized as "emotional calls for shotgun justice." From other black spokesmen came similar pronouncements warning that the community would not tolerate police militancy. Commissioner Murphy fell right in line with these sentiments when he announced that henceforward radio patrol cars in high-crime areas would be followed by unmarked backup units. Instead of describing this new procedure as a measure to protect cops from being lured into ambushes, he explained that it "would counteract possible overreacting by policemen."

Ironically, in this area the police department's thinking closely paralleled the theories of revolutionary terrorism that undoubtedly activated the killers. According to those who rationalize murdering policemen, shooting a cop in the back is a revolutionary act because it provokes police retaliation, which in turn "educates the masses" to the true nature of the oppressive system under which they live. In real life, though, it turned out that the police department and the Black Liberation Army had underestimated both the cops and the ghetto community. In the tense days that followed the Colonial Park killings, there was a lot of angry rhetoric but not a single instance of police "overreaction." And Harlem, instead of turning on the cops, condoled with them and tendered its sympathy. On 125th Street, when a four-year-old boy cocked his finger and squealed bang-bang at a cop on foot patrol, he got a hard slap across the mouth from his mother and the cop got an apology. "Maybe something good can come out of all this," the patrolman said later. "They know we're hurting and they're being nice to us. It feels good not to be called a pig every day. I hope it lasts."

The stake-out was repeated on Wednesday, the day Joseph Piagentini was buried, and again on Thursday and Friday, each day with dimmer hopes. On the following Monday the seven detectives, who by this time needed no briefing and reported straight to the subway station before checking in at the precinct, approached the assignment with feelings of numb desperation which they managed to temper with self-mocking optimism. "Well, we know he doesn't go to work," one of them said. "Maybe he was going to get his unemployment check. Monday's his day."

But it wasn't.

The stake-out went on for two more weeks—with no luck, no hope, and no results. Then, in the predawn hours of Saturday, June 6, the dying investigation suddenly came alive again. Four heavily armed black men attempted to rip off the Double M, an after-hours bottle club in the Bronx. The lookout, who was stationed on the street directly in front of the entrance to the second-floor "social club," wore a Colt .45 tucked in his belt. The other three went upstairs ready for war: the first with a double-barreled sawed-off shotgun in one hand and a 9-millimeter Browning automatic in the other, the second with a shotgun and a .357 Smith and Wesson Magnum. The third man, who seemed to be the leader, menaced the tipsy patrons with a .45-caliber M3A submachine gun.

He ordered everyone, men and women, to strip. When one man was slower than he should have been, the machine gun sent a string of bullets ripping over his head into the wall behind him, filling the corner of the room with plaster dust and leaving an ominous row of ugly woundlike holes. The man quickly undressed and threw his clothes onto the pile.

While the machine gunner guarded the line of naked hostages, his two accomplices began rifling the clothes for wallets and jewelry. The lookout on the street, alarmed by the sound of gunfire, raced upstairs. "Get your dumb ass back to the street," the machine gunner barked at him. "You ain't doing no good up here."

The lookout turning sullenly to leave. "Yeah, well just be quick, man," he muttered, shaking his head. "You sure made a lot of noise."

Enough noise that a radio patrol unit, passing two blocks away, stopped to gauge the direction from which the sound had come. Knowing the neighborhood, the patrolmen guessed that a ripoff was in progress at the bottle club. They called in for backup and raced to the scene, arriving just as the lookout reached the bottom of the steps and opened the rotting wood door. "Shi-i-i-it!" he gasped, loud enough for the cops outside to hear him. Taking the steps four at a time, he charged back up to the club. "There's pigs out there," he shouted. "You sure done it this time."

"How many?" the machine gunner asked coolly. The other two stopped their search through the clothes and grabbed their weapons.

"I don't know. Two. I don't know," the lookout stammered.

The machine gunner walked to the window and looked out, saw a green-and-white patrol car directly beneath him. He couldn't see the cops in it but would have opened fire anyway except that at that moment another car skidded around the corner and pulled to a stop about twenty yards from the first. Seconds later there were two more cars and then a fifth, making the odds far too heavy.

"Okay, folks," he said, turning from the window, "stay cool and put your clothes on. Sorry about the inconvenience."

The cops outside took covered positions behind their cars. Then they waited, guns trained on the doorway. When no one came out, the patrolman who had first heard the shots decided to go in. His partner and another team followed while the six remaining cops covered them with drawn guns. The lead patrolman threw open the door and dropped low in a crouch, motionless for a moment until he was certain the stairway ahead of him was clear. Slowly, he inched his way forward and started up the steps, ready to answer a burst of gunfire at any second. The six men on the street left their positions and fell in behind the first four.

Upstairs they found twenty-five or thirty black people, most of them well dressed, in their forties or fifties. They weren't drinking and they weren't sitting at the tables, but were standing together on one side of the room. It looked odd, but the cops didn't know what to make of it.

"What's going on here?" one of the patrolmen demanded.

"Beats me," a goateed gentleman in a tomato-red suit answered. "We just mindin' our own business."

"We heard shooting," the cop said, by way of explanation.

For a moment no one answered. Then a woman said, "No, there wasn't no shooting."

At the same time a man said, "Yeah, some dudes tried to rip us off. But they gone now."

The customers exchanged nervous glances. The cops looked at each other. Then the man who had been slow undressing said, "No way. The cats you lookin' for ain't gone. It's him. And him. And him. And him."

There was a chorus of concurrence from the crowd. The four men were cuffed without a struggle. Under a tablecloth in a corner of the room the police found the two shotguns, the submachine gun, and the three hand guns. All the weapons except the machine gun were taken back to the precinct. The machine gun was rushed to the ballistics laboratory at the Police Academy on 20th Street, where ballistics experts discharged about two dozen rounds into the Academy swimming pool, dove in to recover the bullets, then ran comparisons with the slugs found at the scene of the Curry-Binetti shooting. They matched perfectly.

All four of the men arrested at the Double M Club had criminal records; three of them were known to be members of the Black Panther Party, while the fourth was a petty stickup artist. Of special interest to the police was the one with the machine gun, who called himself Dharuba. His name was Richard Moore and he was one of the "Panther 21," although he had jumped bail and hadn't stood trial with the others.

At a line-up held a few hours after the arrests, witnesses to the May 19th machine gunning on Riverside

Drive identified Moore as one of the men they had seen in the yellow Maverick. But the eye-witnesses from the Colonial Park project were equally positive that neither Moore nor any of his three accomplices at the social club resembled Piagentini's and Jones's killers.

Later an informant told police that Moore had written the Curry-Binetti letter two days after the shooting, that Moore's common-law wife had typed it out, and that a nineteen-year-old camp follower had delivered it. On the evening it was delivered, according to the informant, Moore was drinking wine and celebrating at a friend's house when an associate, who later was to serve as lookout during the ill-fated social-club stickup, rushed in to say he had just heard on the radio that "some brothers offed two pigs in Harlem." Moore undoubtedly expected that within a day or two the newspapers would be carrying a defiant revolutionary message from the killers like the one he had sent. When no such message appeared by Monday morning, he corrected the error by composing the letter himself.

With the arrest of Richard Moore, the Curry-Binetti case was partly solved. But the investigation of the murders of Piagentini and Jones was back to zero. Even in the terrorist circles in which Moore moved, no one seemed to know the identity of the killers.

And that is the way it stayed through the summer. On the day after the killings, the police department set up two special phone numbers and promised that all information would be kept confidential. The Patrolmen's Benevolent Association offered a reward. Dozens of detectives were assigned to the case and literally hundreds more volunteered their time, working in off-duty hours to track down the leads that poured in over the phone.

Through May, June, July, and into August, over a thousand calls came in on the special numbers. Each one was laboriously checked out. Sometimes they said simply, "The guys that shot the cops are at the corner of Eighth and Forty-third," in which case a radio car would be sent immediately. sometimes they were more promising: "There's a dude name-uh Shorty shoots pool up on Lenox, like around Hunna-thirtieth. He got hisself a po-lice gun." One call led to a man who turned out to be the director of a federal poverty program. The detectives who went to question him learned that on twenty-two separate occasions over the past three months someone had harassed him by calling an undertaker and asking that a hearse be sent to his home to pick up his body.

Sometimes a woman would have a fight with her lover and then call in to inform on him. Or someone who simply wanted to collect the reward would finger a friend he had quarreled with, an acquaintance he had a grudge against, even a total stranger. Neighbors phoned in to report that the people living down the hall from them were militants, were probably involved, and in any case bore watching. And so it went. Every lead, no matter how seemingly inconsequential, was investigated. In the end it turned out that they all had one thing in common. They led nowhere.

In the spring of 1971, the New York City Police Department did not have in its possession any systematically classified data about the activities of militant radicals. There were M.O. files on burglars, armed robbers, known gamblers, rapists, forgers, extortionists, and dozens of other criminal categories, but up until that point terrorists activities carried out by self-proclaimed revolutionaries were handled on a case-by-case basis.

Day after day, while detectives were running down the latest batch of bogus tips, a team of fingerprint experts downtown in the Bureau of Criminal Identification was going through the police department's massive file of prints, drawer by drawer and card by card, comparing them with the one clear fingerprint Carl Lacho had lifted from the left front fender of the white Mustang. Because the police department does not keep palm prints on file, the palm print found next to it was useless for the time being. Among laymen it is commonly believed that if a single latent fingerprint is put in at one end of a computer, the name, address, and criminal record of its owner comes out at the other end. In fact, however, a latent print has no value unless it can be compared with another print. To make matters worse, there is no way to tell which finger or even which hand, left or right, is represented by an isolated print. As a result, the fingerprint specialists at BCI had to check the print lifted from the Mustang against each of the ten inked impressions on each of the hundreds of thousands of cards in the department's archives. One detective, James Bannon, a twenty-two-year veteran who has since retired, made so many comparisons that even four years later he still knew that print by heart, still recalled its hieroglyphic patterns of jumbled lines as clearly as one remembers a familiar face.

But, like the cops out on the street, the detectives who

worked on the case bent under the goose-neck desk lamps at the old headquarters on Centre Street came up empty. The days grew longer and city hotter, but for Bill Butler and the hundreds of other detectives on the case, all clocks had stopped. For them it was still the night of May 21. The thousands of hours they had put into the investigation disappeared as completely as though they had never happened, like time spent in stalled traffic, like prison time. The weeks passed unmarked, with nothing to show for them except the slow and accumulating drain of energy and confidence. As the summer wound down, there wasn't one thing the detectives knew that they hadn't known on the night of the killings. Not a single clue had been turned up, not a single lead developed.

Four

IN THE COURSE OF ALMOST EIGHT YEARS IN the San Francisco Police Department, George Kowalski had been cited for bravery three separate times. He was in his early thirties, with a powerful body and striking good looks, a dead ringer for the actor Kirk Douglas.

On the night of August 27, 1971, Kowalski had been a sergeant barely five weeks and had caught the night-shift patrol supervision in the seamy Mission District. Alone in his radio car, he cruised past run-down clapboard houses and all-night bodegas that spilled dirty pools of yellow light out onto the deserted sidewalks. Though a supervisor now, he drove at patrolling speed, eight years of habit dying slowly. When he reached Sixteenth he turned left, heading west between rows of great square factories and gray brick warehouses. At Vermont he glided under the elevated freeway, the drone of its Friday-night traffic like the growl of one immense engine that powered the city.

A red light stopped him at the corner of Folsom and Sixteenth. It was just short of midnight and except for the dark sedan to his left, speeding north on Folsom, there wasn't a car or a pedestrian in sight. If he had been driving patrol he would have had his partner with him, someone to talk to, but as a supervising sergeant he drove alone and often found time to reflect that a sergeant's stripes conferred very little authority in an otherwise empty car.

The dark sedan—it was an Oldsmobile, '65 or '66, he guessed—still hadn't reached the intersection. When Kowalski first noticed it, it seemed to have been going a lot faster but now it slowed to a crawl and shifted to the curb lane as though to make a turn. But instead of taking a right onto Sixteenth, it slid into the intersection directly in front of Kowalski's radio car.

Then he saw it. The passenger window was down and a black man in the passenger seat was looking straight at him over the barrel of a submachine gun.

Kowalski dove for the floor, reaching for his gun as he did, expecting to hear bullets exploding through glass and metal, expecting that they would find him where he hid. He had just time enough to wonder what it would feel like to be shot. But there was only silence. He waited for what seemed a long time—probably no more than five or ten seconds, long enough in any case for him to be surprised he was still alive. Then, knowing that the machine gunner, like a hunter in a duck blind, would be waiting for his target to rise into range, he lifted his head slowly until he could see over the padded lip of the dash.

The Oldsmobile was inching forward across the intersection, barely rolling. The passenger was struggling with the gun, which obviously had jammed. His hands seemed to be fighting with each other and he wasn't watching what he was doing, for his eyes were fixed on the windshield of Kowalski's car. For a second the sergeant and the man with the machine gun stared at each other in an equal exchange of rage and hatred. Then the Olds took off up Folsom.

Kowalski slammed his foot on the accelerator with the ferocity of a man trying to kill a snake. His tires screamed in response as his Plymouth leaped into a turn and charged after the fleeing Oldsmobile. The sergeant reached for his radio and broadcast a Code 33—an emergency call to clear the channel so he could direct other units in the chase. Ahead of him, at first almost a block, then quickly closing to about fifty yards, the dark sedan sped on. When it crossed Fifteenth Street, the passenger threw the hopelessly jammed machine gun to the back seat and pulled a wood-handled Colt .38 revolver from his waistband. He leaned out the window and got off three wild shots in the direction of Kowalski's radio car. At Fourteenth the driver threw the car into a hard right turn that knocked the gunman tumbling back in through the window. A few seconds later his head reappeared and he fired twice more. But the car was bouncing too erratically on the cobbled road and the shots didn't even come close to the cop.

At Alabama the driver took another right, hurtling the Olds over the Southern Pacific tracks. For a moment the car seemed to hang in the air. When it hit the pavement the tires spun treacherously, then bit. The Olds gained speed as it climbed Alabama.

Behind it, Kowalski had less luck with the tracks. His Plymouth, lighter than the Olds, took them like a hurdler but came down hard, splay-legged. For a few seconds the backend swayed like a tree in a storm, and then Kowalski felt it sink and he knew he had blown a rear tire. It would steer but it wouldn't make any speed. Ahead of Kowalski, the Olds opened space, bounded over the crest at Fifteenth, and kept climbing, disappearing from sight.

Patrolmen Pete Gurnari and Bobby Rames heard Sergeant Kowalski's frantic shouts over the open channel. "On Alabama, moving south. They passed Fifteenth. Intercept! Intercept! I'm losing them!" Gurnari, who was driving, reached down to unstrap the leather flap that held his revolver in his holster. Rames yanked the shotgun from its clip under the dash and pumped a shell into the chamber.

Their car sped east on Sixteenth, heading for Alabama. In front of them they could see the intersection and knew the Olds hadn't passed yet. Driving straight toward them on Sixteenth was a gray sedan, bumping toward the intersection with the clownish nonchalance of something from a Saturday-morning cartoon show. As it passed under a streetlight, Gurnari could see its occupants clearly, a bald-headed man and his stubby wife, their heads bobbing carelessly like carnival balloons, grinning complacently.

The charging Oldsmobile wiped the smiles from their faces. it was doing between sixty and seventy when it streaked into the intersection, caught their sedan just behind the rear door, and sent it spinning like a coin on a table. There was just enough to see the couple's mouths drop simultaneously in uncomprehending surprise before their heads disappeared from view, tossed about in the whirling car like marbles in a can. The Olds drifted sideways for a while and then died on Alabama just past the intersection, its front tires against the curb.

Rames and Gurnari leaped from their cruiser, guns ready, just as the passenger door of the Olds flew open and a slender black man tumbled out, firing even before he hit the pavement. Still, quick as he was, he got off only one shot before the two patrolmen sent him diving back into the car with return fire from Gurnari's revolver and Rames's 12-gauge. Crouched like a soldier in combat, Gurnari then raced toward the civilian car in the middle of the intersection. "Stay down, stay down!" he shouted in warning, hoping for their own sake that the couple was unconscious, that they wouldn't stagger to the street, too dazed to be alarmed by the gunshots.

Meanwhile, George Kowalski had been a full block behind the Olds when he heard the impact of the collision, had been halfway up the hill toward Sixteenth when the shooting started. He reached the intersection, grabbed his shotgun and climbed from the car just as another cruiser pulled in from the west. "Watch it, they're armed!" he shouted to warn the newcomers. Rames and Gurnari didn't need to be told.

Inside the Olds, only the driver was visible, a skinny, boyish black man who was frantically trying to get the engine restarted, the sweat standing on his forehead like sequins.

Sergeant Kowalski moved up next to Rames, who glanced across to him, saw the stripes on his shoulder, and said nothing, awaiting orders. Rames's cruiser stood between them and the Olds, offering cover.

"Let's move in. Take the front, I'll take the back," Kowalski said.

The two cops stepped from behind the cruiser and began circling in opposite directions, Rames taking a path that carried him to the west curb of Alabama, Kowalski moving to his left, toward the opposite sidewalk directly behind what their reports coyly refer to as "the suspect vehicle." They heard the engine kick over and start, they saw the driver desperately working the gear shift, trying to force the wrecked transmission into reverse. Then Kowalski saw the head of the second man rise above the seat on the passenger side. "Look out! He's getting up!" he shouted, warning Rames. At the same time he fired his shotgun through the rear window, sending a hailstorm of glass shrapnel into the car. The head disappeared again but the driver, unconscious of everything around him, went on wrestling with the gearshift.

By this time Rames had been joined on the sidewalk in front of the Olds by Bob Quinn, a nineteen-year veteran who had been in the cruiser that arrived when Kowalski did. Crouched low, almost crawling, Rames and Quinn advanced until they were just even with the headlights of the Olds, then crept alongside the car to the front door. Rames, in back of Quinn, reached around him and gently slid his hand into the handle, positioning his thumb on the lock button, not wanting to make a sound that would give him away until it was time, knowing the gunman could fire through the door straight into Quinn's chest.

Rames squeezed the button but nothing happened. The door was locked. He glanced at Quinn, who nodded his readiness. Then, in what seemed on simultaneous movement, Rames thrust his hand in through the open window and yanked on the inside handle while Quinn leaped to his feet as the door flew back.

A black man lay on his back across the front seat, his head at the door. In his right hand he held a pearl-handled .45, which he raised as the door opened so that the barrel of it was in Quinn's eyes. But Quinn was too fast for him. His left hand flashed out and grabbed the gun while his right, which held his revolver, smashed downward into the gunman's face, metal cracking bone. The black man's hand fell to the floor. As Quinn bent into the car to drag his limp body to the street, Rames leaned in over him, his shotgun reaching in across the street until it seemed almost to touch the driver's cheek.

The man and woman in the car hit by the fleeing Oldsmobile at Sixteenth and Alabama were badly shaken but not seriously injured. If they considered themselves lucky to have come out of it so well, Tony Bottom and Albert Washington—the driver and his machine-gunning partner—were luckier still. Bottom, whose head apparently hit either the windshield or the steering wheel, suffered a broken cheekbone but no other damage, although his face remained swollen for weeks. Washington, too, had suffered a broken cheekbone when Quinn disarmed him. In addition, the shot Kowalski fired through the rear window had caught him in the face. Its force spent penetrating the glass, it caused only a superficial wound.

The real miracle was that Washington wasn't killed

the instant Rames and Quinn opened the door. When he raised the muzzle of his .45 to Quinn's face, it was only the veteran officer's amazing restraint that kept him from getting off a point-blank shot that would have splattered the interior of the Oldsmobile with the contents of Albert Washington's head.

Washington and Bottom were booked for attempted murder. In addition to the pearl-handled .45 taken from Washington's hand at the moment of his arrest, police also found a .38-caliber Colt revolver on the floor in front of the passenger seat and a .45-caliber submachine gun on the floor in back, its butt end down, a long lethal clip sticking straight up like the handle of a dagger.

The .38 found on the floor had one live cartridge in firing position and five expended cartridges in the chamber—evidence of the five shots Washington fired at Kowalski's car during the chase. After the collision Washington apparently realized he had only one shot left in the revolver and borrowed Bottom's .45 for his abortive attempt to shoot his way out. The gun held six live rounds and one expended shell.

In addition to the weapons and bullets already enumerated, the police also found the following items. In the machine gun: a clip containing twenty-nine rounds of live .45 ammunition. On the floor in front of the back seat: a clip containing twenty-five additional rounds. In Albert Washington's pockets: seven loose .38-caliber shells; a cellophane bag containing fifteen rounds for the .38; another cellophane bag with thirteen rounds of similar ammunition. In Tony Bottom's pockets: a clip for the .45 automatic containing seven live rounds. In a leather pouch secured by leather thongs to Tony Bottom's belt: fifty-nine rounds of .45-caliber ammunition.

In all—three weapons and 168 rounds of ammunition. The Black Liberation Army was mobilized for war.

Forty-five hours after the attempted machine gunning of Sergeant Kowalski, the terrorists launched their next attack. At exactly 9:41 P.M., nine armed men entered the small two-story brick cottage that served as the local precinct house in the Ingleside district of San Francisco, a pleasant, racially mixed, middle-class community in the southwest corner of the city. Their leader carried a 12-gauge shotgun. A second man held a pistol in one hand and a homemade bomb in the other. The others were armed with either rifles or side arms or both. The plan was to kill the officers on duty and then level the building with the bomb.

Five days before the raid—four days before his arrest—Tony Bottom had conducted a reconnaissance of the Ingleside station house. Carrying a phony driver's license and social-security card for identification, he filed a complaint about a stolen bicycle. Then he wandered about inside the station house unnoticed for almost half an hour. In that time he was able to learn all he needed to know about the interior of the building and to leave without attracting any attention.

What he learned was that the ground floor of the station was virtually deserted except for the few officers on desk duty and a small staff of civilian clerks. The desk officers worked in an enclosed area behind a waist-high counter and a sheet of countertop-to-ceiling bulletproof glass. The door to the enclosure, however, was kept open.

Fortunately, on the night of August 29 it was closed—a result, no doubt, of the increased security consciousness of San Francisco police after the unprovoked attack on Sergeant Kowalski. Because of the confusion that prevailed during the raid, it is difficult to reconstruct exactly what happened, but a few details stand out clearly.

The assault team entered the station house unnoticed and apparently split into two groups, one proceeding directly to the steel door that opened into the desk area, the other sliding past the glassed-in counter to cover the corridor that led back into the building. When the leader of the first group found the door locked, he immediately raced to the counter, heading for the porthole in the bulletproof glass. On the other side of the partition, Sergeant John Young, fifty-four years old, reacted quickly. The sound of muffled footsteps had already caught his attention, and he had looked up in time to see four armed black men running past the counter toward the back of the building. Without a moment's hesitation, the heroic sergeant leaped from his desk and bolted toward the counter in a desperate race to get the open porthole closed before the attackers could reach it.

He was seconds too late. A blast from a 12-gauge shotgun thrust through the porthole as Young reached it caught him high on the chest, dead center, smashing through his collarbone and killing him even before he hit the floor. Behind the fallen sergeant, Irene Grohman, a civilian clerk, sat frozen at her typewriter, unable even to scream. Then someone fired a 9-millimeter rifle at her. The shot caught her in the upper arm, passed through the muscle as cleanly and as painlessly as a hypodermic needle, and flew under her chin like a shiny, swift insect. Only then did she dive for cover, disappearing safely behind the steel desk just as a rain of deadly metal from the rifle and the shotgun reached it. She lay there crying softly, even after the shooting stopped.

The attack ended as abruptly as it had begun. The crude but powerful bomb, its fuse accidentally stripped from the metal casing in a fumbling attempt to get it lit, was abandoned on the stationhouse floor. Someone shouted, "Let's get the fuck outta here," there were footsteps, then a silence broken only by the sound of Irene Grohman sobbing.

In the modern prison attached to the San Francisco Hall of Justice, Tony Bottom postured arrogantly in front of his fellow inmates, spouting radical rhetoric, correcting their "ideology," and attempting to raise the revolutionary consciousness of prisoners awaiting trial for such "reactionary bourgeois crimes" as robbery and assault.

The principal target for his educational efforts was his cellmate, Bernard Hexter, a twenty-five-year-old small-time dope dealer who had long ago made his peace with the system. Streetwise and cynical, Hexter knew his niche in the bizarre and sordid underworld of narcotics trafficking; he had, moreover, no scruples to prevent him from working for the Man. Often he had served as an informant, and as a result never had faced heavy time despite an impressively long arrest record.

It took Bottom less than a week to drive the sleepy-voiced and usually imperturbable drug dealer up the cell wall. "Shit, man," Hexter moaned when he had had enough, "I don't want to hear one more sound out of your mouth about this revolution, hear?"

Bottom shook his head sadly. "Conditions has gotta change," he said.

"Right on. But you ain't gonna change 'em."

"And you are?" Bottom challenged.

Hexter laughed and lay back on his cot. "No, man, we ain't talking about me," he answered mockingly. "We talking about you. And what I'm saying is it just beats me cold where you're coming from. Revolution is revolution and talk is talk. And you, nigger, ain't nothing but talk."

Bottom snorted derisively. "Hexter, that is ignorant," he said. "If I am all talk, then what am I doing here?"

Hexter bounced to a sitting position, sensing the opening he had been waiting for. "You are here," he crooned, "for b-a-a-d driving. And for not knowing how to work a grease gun. Fuck, man, even your jive-ass Mao See-tong would be running a Chinese laundry if he didn't know how to work no grease gun!"

For a full minute Bottom said nothing, stung. "In a revolution," he stammered at last, with something less than conviction, "we have to accept some tactical defeats. But that don't change . . ."

Hexter cut him off. "It changes this," he said. "It changes whether I gotta be preached at by a nigger that can't even shoot a man when that's what he gotta do."

Bottom sidled up to Hexter's cot and sat next to him. "There are some things that is none of your business," he whispered conspiratorially. "Like what I done and what I ain't done. But as ignorant as you are, Bernard, maybe you can relate to this. The piece I got busted with was once the property of a pig that got hisself offed in New York. I took it off him. Can you relate to that?"

He stood up and strutted across the cell, then turned to face Hexter. "Now you tell me, man, is the Black Liberation Army talk or is it action?"

Hexter stared at him hard. "Are you saying you killed a pig in New York?" he asked.

Bottom smiled and leaned back on his elbows. "I'm saying what I'm saying."

By the next morning Hexter had made up his mind to cash in the information. After breakfast he went to the prison library, signed out a book, and took it to a corner table where he could count on being unobserved. While pretending to take notes on his reading, he wrote the following letter:

> *Dear Inspector McCoy.*
>   *You know that when I tell you something you can count on it. & I know that you will do what you can. My cell mate is Tony Bottoms, who was busted for trying to grease a cop. He says he took the piece he was busted off a cop that was killed in New York city. That is all he said to me. He also related he was in the black liberation army and once before he told me he was a general in it.*

Hexter signed the letter, folded it into an envelope, and addressed it to Inspector Frank McCoy, the cop he had been stooling for ever since he first started trading information for time six years earlier.

The letter reached McCoy's desk a few hours later. It was Labor Day, but Frank McCoy wasn't enjoying the holiday. For the past ten days, he had been working almost nonstop, trying to get a lead on the murderous band that already had killed Sergeant Young and attempted to machine gun Sergeant Kowalski. Convinced that the two incidents were related, McCoy was not surprised by Bernard Hexter's note, with its suggestion of a coast-to-coast cop-killing conspiracy. He immediately punched up the extension number of the San Francisco Police Department's ballistics section. "Why the hell didn't you guys tell us those guns were wanted in New York?" he demanded.

"It's news to me. Where'd you get that?" the ballistics clerk answered defensively.

"Never mind. Just check it out. I'll stay on the line."

"I'll get back to you," the clerk countered.

Five minutes later, having thumbed through the eight-page mimeographed list of wanted weapons, the ballistics clerk rang McCoy's extension. "No dice, Inspector," he said. "I don't know who's been telling you stories, but those guns are clean."

McCoy slammed down the phone, angry and disappointed. Hexter's information made sense, and in six years Hexter had never lied to him before, at least not on anything big. Still, there had to be a first time. Ballistics said Hexter was wrong—the gun wasn't the New York gun, and that was that.

Or it would have been if Frank McCoy hadn't been the kind of cop he was. A huge, massively powerful man—six feet, four inches tall, well over two hundred pounds—his every step automatically called up images of a defensive end rampaging through the enemy backfield. But, in what almost seemed a deliberate attempt to be paradoxical, he spoke softly, using almost none of the profanity that in police circles does heavy duty as all-purpose adjectives. He dressed in well-tailored three-piece suits that made him look if not exactly dandified, then at least dapper. And he prided himself on mastering every detail of every case he worked. It was as though someone had put the mind of Hercule Poirot in the body of a tough street cop. Once Frank McCoy got his teeth into something, he stuck to it like a tick to a dog.

He contemplated the telephone on his desk less than a minute and then bolted from the office, charging through the maze of corridors that led to the prison facility adjoining police headquarters. It took prison officials, short-staffed because of the Labor Day holiday, over an hour to arrange a meeting between McCoy and Hexter. When the fidgety dope dealer finally was led into the tiny six-by-eight conference room, he found the inspector standing next to the small square table, seeming to fill all the available space. "Sit down, Bernard," McCoy ordered.

Hexter slid into one of the two straight-backed chairs next to the table. He saw a copy of the note he had written in the inspector's meaty hand.

"Is this your idea of a joke?" McCoy demanded, holding the note before Hexter's eyes.

"It's straight, what can I tell you?" Hexter answered, his voice betraying his nervousness.

The inspector dropped the note on the table and turned away. He and Hexter went back a long way together, and over the years each had done the other some good. McCoy's voice was low, almost sorrowful, and he kept the threat, if there was one, heavily veiled. He said, "I've always trusted you, Bernard. So far it's worked out for you."

Hexter knew that another cop might have slammed him into the concrete wall to make the same point, but McCoy's way was even scarier. The worst sin a guy who plays both sides can commit is to burn a cop with a bad tip. But Hexter didn't back down. "Look," he stammered, "I got this from Bottom. The other one, the Old Man . . ."

"Washington?"

"Yeah, Washington. He don't say nothing. But Bottom got a mouth. He says he got the piece off a pig in New York. Check it out, what else can I say?"

"I did check it out."

Hexter didn't bat an eyelash. "Then check it again," he said with laconic insolence, gesturing with both hands. "What the fuck do you want from me?"

Hexter's cockiness told McCoy what he had come to find out. The whole of the young informant's twenty-five years had been spent with wise-asses like Tony Bottom, and he wouldn't have lived even that long if he hadn't known how to size them up. Hexter believed Bottom, and that was good enough for McCoy.

Without a word, McCoy turned and walked from the room, motioning for the guard to take Hexter back to his cell. As he strode through the windowless fluorescent-lit corridors that led back to headquarters, he made a conscious effort to sift through everything he had learned since Bottom and Washington were arrested at the corner of Sixteenth and Alabama.

The car they had been driving at the time belonged to neither of them. It was registered to a twenty-year-old black named Samuel Lee Pennegar, who had bought it from a used-car dealer in Vallejo on August 5. Pennegar had no criminal record at all—didn't even exist in police files. But Washington and Bottom were a different story. Information on them already had begun trickling in from police departments around the country. So far Albert Washington had been traced back to Denver, where he first appeared in 1965. Apparently he worked there in a meat-packing plant for a while, and then as a farm laborer at a ranch outside Denver in mile-high San Luis Valley. A week before Christmas 1965 he walked into a Steak and Burger restaurant in Denver and tried to open the unattended cash register. When a waiter spotted him and yelled for help, Washington pulled a gun and shot him. He was arrested and sentenced to twelve to twenty years in a Colorado prison.

While in prison he began the process of self-education that transformed him from an incompetent stickup man into a revolutionary theorist. In addition to studying radical literature, he also dabbled in law and Eastern religions. He began to practice meditation, and soon reported that during his meditative sessions he heard voices that gave him counsel and advice. With the help of these inner voices and law books borrowed from the prison library, he prepared the briefs that won him the right to a new hearing on his armed-robbery conviction. In a bizarre proceeding, he served as his own attorney while pleading insanity convincingly enough to win a reversal of his original conviction. He was then committed to the Colorado State Hospital at Pueblo pending retrial.

In November 1970 he escaped from Pueblo. He was then thirty years old, but his hair already had begun to turn gray, his walk was a slow-gaited shuffle, and his posture a premature stoop. His fellow inmates called him the Old Man.

Two months after his escape, on January 28, 1971, Washington was stopped by the police in Salt Lake City for running a red light. In the car with him were a Puerto Rican named Francisco Torres and a black named Lester Bertram May. Washington naturally had no valid driver's license, having spent the past five years either in prison or as a fugitive, and the fake license he carried turned out not to be good enough to fool the Salt Lake City cops, who immediately arrested him on a charge of giving false information. After searching his car and finding a loaded gun in it, they added a charge of possession of a loaded firearm in a motor vehicle. Francisco Torres and Lester Bertram May were booked on the same weapons charge and as accomplices to the giving of false information.

At the station house the Salt Lake city police learned that Washington had escaped from a Colorado mental institution, where he was being held pending retrial for an armed robbery in which he shot and critically wounded an unarmed civilian. They also discovered that the Colorado warrant on him had been drawn in such a way that it was good only in the state of Colorado and could not be used as a basis for extradition from another jurisdiction.

Whether they could have held him until another warrant was drawn is not at all clear, but certainly they had an obligation not to treat lightly the arrest of an armed, dangerous, and unstable man. Unfortunately, though, they didn't see it this way. Washington, Torres, and May were cut loose.

There the record ended. Seven months later Albert Washington was arrested for attempting to kill Sergeant George Kowalski with a .45-caliber submachine gun.

The biography of the man arrested with him, Tony Bottom, presented a sharp contrast to Albert Washington's life story, for there was in Bottom's record nothing to match Washington's history of violent and erratic behavior. Bottom had gotten in trouble with the law only twice, both instances occurring in 1969, when he was only seventeen years old. After that, he seemed to have straightened himself out.

Almost twelve years younger than Albert Washington, Bottom was born in Oakland in 1951. His parents were divorced when he was either seven or twelve years old—the records are contradictory on this. But there is no ambiguity about the fact that he spent his early years in an acrimonious home environment. After his parents' divorce, Tony went to live with his mother but continued to see his father. Apparently he did not suffer financial hardship, for his father owned his own business, seems to have been successful, and from all indications was generous in his support of his ex-wife and their three children.

Tony's troubles started when his mother remarried. Unable to get along with his stepfather, he began to fall behind in his schoolwork and was soon brought to the attention of the juvenile authorities. In 1969 he was arrested for burglary and sentenced to four months at a northern California boys' ranch. The arrest came just as Tony's mother and stepfather were planning to move to Salt Lake City. They moved anyway, leaving Tony behind to serve out his time.

When he was released from the ranch at the end of the summer, he took an apartment by himself in San Francisco. Within a matter of weeks he was picked up again by the police, this time on a charge of conspiracy to commit burglary and transfer of marijuana. He was sentenced to three years probation. Up to this point he seems to have been no different from thousands of other boys who get in trouble with the law without really breaking their ties to straight society or committing themselves to lives of crime. Indeed, the judge who sentenced him to probation for his second offense undoubtedly was taking into consideration the fact that Tony had enrolled in San Jose City College for the fall semester.

A tall skinny kid, well over six feet in height but under 170 pounds, with boyish good looks and a clever, quick-witted mind, he successfully completed his freshman year at San Jose, even though his father and stepfather had cut off all financial support and he was forced to earn his own way through school. At various times he worked as a gas-station attendant, as a dishwasher, and as a trainee with the phone company.

Early in his sophomore year he gave up the struggle, dropped out of school, took a job as a social-work counselor for the California Department of Human Resources. Compared to the other jobs he had held, it paid well—slightly over a hundred dollars a week. He moved to an apartment on Divisadero Street in San Francisco, not far from the teeming rock-and-acid Haight-Ashbury district. Living with him was a pretty eighteen-year-old stenographer; between her income and his, they were able to save some money.

He stayed with the Department of Human Resources

only five months, quitting suddenly without giving notice on April 22, 1971. From then until his arrest behind the wheel of Samuel Lee Pennegar's bullet-riddled Oldsmobile at the corner of Sixteenth and Alabama, there is no record of criminal activity, no record of employment.

Strange, Frank McCoy thought as he arrived at his office and threw himself into the swivel chair behind his desk. Bottom and Washington seemed to have nothing in common, except perhaps the chance occurrence of Salt Lake City in both their biographies. Yet there was no indication that Bottom had ever gone there to visit his family, no indication that Washington had been more than passing through. Neither had any discernible ties to New York.

Nevertheless, a date stuck in McCoy's mind—April 22, the day Bottom quit his job. The New York cop-killings, he remembered, had happened in May. What kind of man, he wondered, would travel three thousand miles to murder a stranger?

He reached for the phone and dialed the main switchboard number of the New York City Police Department. He identified himself, told the operator that he had information relating to the death of a New York City police officer, and asked to speak to the detective in charge of the case. The operator didn't know who that was. Neither, of course, did McCoy. She couldn't help him unless he knew whom he wanted to speak with. Perhaps if he knew the precinct?

"Damn it, lady," McCoy snapped, "do you people have so many cops killed you can't keep track of them?"

"I'm doing the best I can, sir," the operator whined. "If you'll just tell me who you wish to speak with?"

"Anyone."

"Anyone?"

For about half an hour McCoy's call was shuttled back and forth through a dozen different departments and offices, most of them closed because of the holiday. McCoy was just beginning to feel like the whole world had suddenly turned into a cross between a Kafka story and a Lily Tomlin routine when the long trail of telephone connections finally reached Bill Butler's desk in the Thirty-second Precinct.

"This is Inspector Frank McCoy, San Francisco Police Department," McCoy muttered wearily.

"Yes, sir," Butler responded crisply, his voice snapping to attention. In New York an inspector is high-level brass, out-ranking a captain, whereas in San Francisco the term is simply the equivalent of detective.

"You had two men killed this summer," McCoy said. "Are you missing any guns in the case?"

Bill Butler felt his heart stop, then start again, like a cold underchoked engine. "All of them," he gasped hoarsely. "What've you got?"

"A forty-five and a Colt Special."

A Colt Special was a policeman's gun.

"Give me the number on the Colt," Butler said.

He had been waiting a long time for this call—three months that felt like three hollow, empty, desperate years.

Slowly, the soft, almost toneless voice at the other end of the line tolled off the sequence of numerals—one, seven, seven, five, nine, eight—while Bill Butler held his breath, each digit ticking in his head like the countdown at the end of the championship game.

It was Waverly Jones's gun.

Five

BILL BUTLER WAS THE FIRST ONE OFF THE 707 when it landed at the San Francisco airport. He strode quickly down the debarkation telescope and followed the signs to the waiting area, where he scanned the lounge for a face that looked like a cop's.

The tall man in a three-piece gray suit walking toward him looked more like a retired football player who had gone into banking. But he reached out his hand and said, "Detective Butler? I'm Frank McCoy."

"Bill," Butler corrected. They shook hands warmly and Butler said, "I'm glad to meet you, Inspector. I can't even begin to tell you . . ." His voice trailed off.

McCoy laughed softly. "I'm not making any guarantees," he said. "All I know is we've got your gun. Did you get the prints we sent?"

"Our people were working on them when I left," Butler answered. "We found some pretty good latents in the area. They'll give me a call as soon as they get a match."

On the long ride from the airport to the Hall of Justice in downtown San Francisco, McCoy filled Butler in on the case. "We've got Bottom and Washington open and shut on an attempted homicide on one of our sergeants," he said. "We think Bottom, possibly both of them, may also have been involved in planning an attack on a station house that went down after they were arrested. We lost a good man in that one, shotgunned in the chest. And from the looks of it, that's just the tip of the iceberg. As far as ballistics goes, we got the three guns in the car when Bottom and Washington were popped. There's the one from your case, the Police special they took off—"

"Waverly Jones."

"Right, Waverly Jones. Now we're tracing the records on the other two, a forty-five automatic and a grease gun, but so far it's zip. The grease gun has to be hot so we can forget about that, but if the forty-five was bought anywhere we'll be able to trace it. Should have it in a couple more days. Now what about Bottom and Washington? Are you people doing backgrounds on them?"

"I just got your call yesterday," Butler answered apologetically, impressed by the San Francisco detective's cool efficiency. "We put some men on it. If they find anything, they'll let us know."

"They will," McCoy said confidently. "If these dudes have ever been in New York, you'll have them. They're not the kind of cats that can show up anywhere without getting a record. So far we've traced Washington back to Denver, but that's as far as we could get. Bottom's local stuff, from Oakland, nothing to tie him to New York. But he's got a big mouth. He's on a revolution trip, goes around telling everyone he's a general in the Black Liberation Army. He's easy to talk to because if you approach him right he'll brag about everything. That's how I found out about his involvement in the

Ingleside attack. I say to him, 'Jesus, did you hear about that thing at the Ingleside Station? It's gotta take some pretty big balls to walk into a police station like that.'

"And Bottom says, 'They had it planned pretty good.'

"So I say, 'C'mon. How you gonna plan a thing like that? Who's gonna case a police station?'

"And he tells me he did it. He looked me right in the eye and said, 'That's what you know. I set the whole thing up. But you can't touch me on it. I was in here when it went down.' Just like that. He even gave me the name he used, said he went in and filed a stolen-bicycle report. Sure enough, it checked out."

McCoy stopped speaking, as though he still couldn't comprehend the arrogant recklessness that would lead a man to boast to a cop that he had engineered a cop-killing.

Butler took advantage of the silence to ask a question that had been preying on his mind. "We sent out an alarm on Jones's gun. Piagentini's too. Didn't you get them?"

McCoy glanced from the road to Butler for only a second. Then his eyes went back to his driving. "Yeah," he said softly. "We got them."

"What happened?"

"That's what I couldn't figure out at first. Turns out it's just a dumb mistake—funny now, but it wouldn't have been funny if we hadn't caught it. See, there's six numbers on the handle of the gun, right?"

"Right."

"And off to the side there's a letter."

"Yeah, that's the model designation."

"Right. So the alarm you sent out had the whole

thing. C, one, seven, whatever it was. And our property office logged the gun in under just the numbers. Can you believe that?"

Butler shrugged. "Well, we got it anyway," he said without conviction.

For a few miles they drove in silence, both men contemplating the fragility of the system they worked in. If Bottom hadn't bragged to Bernard Hexter about taking a gun off a pig in New York, Waverly Jones's revolver would have lain forever collecting dust in the San Francisco Police Department's property office, as irretrievable as if Bottom had thrown it into the Harlem River the night Jones and Piagentini died.

"Is this your first time in San Francisco?" McCoy asked, to have something to say.

"Yes," Butler answered, prompted to look around. In his mind's eye he had an image of San Francisco as a picturesque village of quaint houses nestled on precarious hills, but the reality he saw was disappointing. They were approaching the city on the Bayshore Freeway from the south, so that the hills looked unimpressively flattened and the skyline was dominated by the black slab of the Bank of America building and the pyramidal skyscraper he recognized from television as the Transamerica Building. The skyline was just a smaller and less impressive version of New York's. "Is that the Golden Gate Bridge?" he asked, spotting the tops of two suspension towers rising just above the horizon.

"No, that's the Oakland Bay Bridge," McCoy explained. "Actually, it's longer than the Golden Gate." Then he added, "You'll be here a while. I'll give you the whole tour."

Instead of driving directly to the Hall of Justice, McCoy turned to the west when they reached the complicated set of interchanges in the Division Street area, their route then carrying them just north of the neighborhood where George Kowalski had exchanged gunshots with Tony Bottom and Albert Washington. Soon they were off the highway and on city streets.

"There's something I want to show you," McCoy said as they cruised between rows of ill-kept stucco houses on Divisadero. "Don't look too hard," he cautioned, pointing, "but the third house in is where Bottom lives. We think they're using it as a headquarters. I've got a photo surveillance man in the house across the street."

Butler's head wheeled from one side to the other, trying to take it all in. Up to this point, the Black Liberation Army had been only an abstraction in his mind—a crude pencil sketch, a few partial fingerprints, some mutilated bullets. But suddenly it was becoming vividly real, as real as the images captured through the telephoto lens of the unseen detective hiding behind the drapes of a bay-windowed room to his right.

"Have you got anything yet?" he asked.

"So far maybe half a dozen faces. We've put a name on one of them. We're working on it."

Inside San Francisco Police Headquarters, a square, featureless building in white granite that stood at the corner of the starkly utilitarian Hall of Justice complex, Butler was introduced to two members of McCoy's team, Ed Erdlatz and John McKenna. Erdlatz looked to be no older than his mid-twenties. Slender, with a wiry, athletic body, he was a son of the former Navy football coach. McKenna was in his mid-thirties, five-ten and portly.

"I suppose you want to question the suspects?" Erdlatz asked.

"No," Butler said. "We don't want them to know I'm here." He thought he heard a collective sigh of relief from the three San Francisco cops.

Before he left New York, Butler and representatives of the district attorney's office had decided that Bottom and Washington should not be told they were suspects in the Piagentini-Jones murders until the Colonial Park witnesses could be flown out to San Francisco for a line-up. Once it became known that Bottom and Washington were being investigated for the New York homicides, their militant associates would disappear underground. There was no proof yet that Bottom and Washington were the actual killers.

The San Francisco police saw the issue in exactly the same way, although their interest, of course, was in the nine men who attacked the Ingleside station and murdered Sergeant Young. In the eighteen hours since Butler told McCoy he was coming to San Francisco, McCoy, Erdlatz, and McKenna had all had their fingers crossed, hoping the New Yorkers wouldn't barge onto the scene and make a lot of noise, scaring Tony Bottom's colleagues out of range of the cameras on Divisadero Street.

With Butler's announcement clearing the air of all traces of tension, the four detectives were ready to get down to work. McCoy pulled a large manila envelope from an almost empty file drawer and joined the others, who had seated themselves around a long conference table in the detectives' wardroom. Opening the envelope, he slid out a stack of about a dozen eight-by-ten surveillance photographs and passed the first one to Butler. It showed a sturdy, well-muscled black man no older than his early twenties, caught by the lens as he strode down the street away from Bottom's apartment. He wore his hair in a medium-length Afro. Under the magnifying glass McCoy supplied, he seemed to be grinning with the satisfaction of some inner secret. As a whole, his round, boyishly handsome face suggested an openness that was hard to square with his presence at a field headquarters of the Black Liberation Army.

A second picture showed the same young man with a woman, perhaps a year or two younger than he. The mood in this one was quite different, and his features were so altered by the change in emotion that at first Bill Butler thought the San Francisco detectives had made a mistake when they told him it was the same man. "I know," McCoy said. "We had to spend hours with it under the magnifying glass before we could be sure. Believe me, it's the same guy."

In this picture the man and woman were standing on the stoop in front of Bottom's apartment, side by side, his arm around her shoulder. He seemed to be pulling her toward him in an embrace which she resisted. The round lines of his face in the first picture had hardened here almost into a square, his features all pulled taut by the tension in the underlying muscle. His lips, uncommonly thin, were compressed into a straight, narrow line, like the lightest brush stroke of a practiced calligrapher, and his dark eyes glowed on the white photo stock with hypnotic intensity.

The woman in the picture was just a shade shorter than the man—perhaps around five-ten. She wore tight-fitting jeans and a tank top that left no room for doubt about the sheer power of her Amazonian body. With her wide hips accentuated by the sideways twist of her upper body, her broad shoulders, and her sturdy arms, she seemed like a woman who would have no trouble handling the scowling intensity of her companion. As he studied her face under the magnifying glass, Bill Butler knew he would never forget it. It was a large, homely face, solemn and ferocious, its lips thick and sensuous, its nostrils wide and flared, the nose more full than flat. But the tiny dark eyes were as out of proportion as a whale's and seemed almost lost in the broad expanse of her high, flat cheeks, her incredibly high forehead.

The third picture showed a young man in the black shirt and black leather jacket that were worn as uniforms by the Black Panther Party. But he was too light-skinned to be called black and struck Butler as probably Puerto Rican or Chicano. His hair, though, was in a wide Afro that made a perfect circle enclosing the circle of his round, full-cheeked face. He had heavy, arching eyebrows over dark, round eyes, and a droopy mustache that gave him the slightly comic appearance of the Hollywood version of a Mexican bandit.

"This is the only one we've got a make on," McCoy announced as Butler examined the photo. "Remember, I told you Washington was arrested with two other men on a gun rap in Salt Lake city? This is one of them. His name is Francisco Torres and he told the Salt Lake City Police he's from New York. Your people will have to check that out. Anyway, he's got a minor record out here—some kind of disorderly conduct at a demonstration a few years back, 'sixty-six or 'sixty-seven. He was in the air force till 'sixty-nine, in Nam and then at Peterson Air Force Base, which is just outside Denver. So we're starting to get some kind of geographical pattern on them. Anyway, he did time in the stockade at Peterson for some kind of a radical thing. They tried to take over the base. Apparently he held a colonel at gunpoint, which has gotta tell you something."

Butler nodded and passed to the next picture in the stack. Another hour was spent going through the remaining photographs, the last of which was a small, square color snapshot that was obviously not from the Divisadero Street series. It shows a young black man, perhaps in his teens, his face smirking benignly above the top of a bulky turtleneck sweater. He had a wide, full-lipped mouth that seemed almost to stretch as far as his thick sideburns, a broad nose, and light eyebrows over bland, uninquisitive eyes. Flashlit from the front, the picture seemed flat, without modeling.

"The Department of Motor Vehicles sent us this," McCoy explained. "It's the driver's license picture of a guy named Samuel Lee Pennegar. The Olds Bottom and Washington were driving is registered to him. We don't know a thing about him. He hasn't shown up at Divisadero Street, and as far as we know he has no record here—at least under the name. In any case, the address he gives on the license is a fake. There's a couple living there, name of Russell. The wife's got a son by another marriage who's a militant. I showed them the picture but they don't know who he is. The husband thought he had seen him around the neighborhood, but that's all I could get."

McCoy stacked the photos and slid them back into

the manila envelope. "Not much to go on, is it?" he muttered under his breath.

But Bill Butler didn't see it that way. "It's a start," he said. "It's something."

The news that greeted Bill Butler shortly after he arrived at San Francisco Police Headquarters early Wednesday morning was devastating. In New York, Detective Vinnie Scalice of the Latent Fingerprint Section had been up all night, poring over Bottom's and Washington's fingerprints, minutely comparing them with the latents found at the scene of the killings.

Unlike an inked print, a latent print, representing perhaps no more than a quarter of a square inch of skin surface, does not have an obvious top and bottom; it may come from any portion of the finger, from the tip down to the first joint. Each latent, therefore, had to be turned this way and that, moved up and down, left and right, so that it could be compared with the entire area of the twenty fingers depicted on the fingerprint cards of Albert Washington and Tony Bottom. The process is something like cracking a code, something like doing a jigsaw puzzle. And the results in this case were irredeemably negative. "If Bottom or Washington were at Colonial Park that night," Scalice told Butler, "they didn't leave their fingerprints."

Butler's head felt like it was swimming as he hung up the phone. He didn't even want to think about the worst of the possibilities that suddenly opened before him. If Bottom and Washington were the wrong men, all bets were off and the investigation was back where it had started. No, worse—because until now Butler had been absolutely convinced that the killers who stole the dead cops' guns wouldn't part with them. Find those service revolvers and you find the murderers, he had told himself a thousand times.

But what if the unbreakable chain of possession had been broken? Then there would be no hope left unless Bottom or Washington could be induced to reveal who had given them Waverly Jones's gun.

Thank God there were other possibilities. Maybe the fingerprints had nothing to do with the case. A limitless number of innocent people could have touched those cars and left those prints. Then Bottom and Washington still might be the men he had been tracking all these weeks. Only the eyewitnesses could say for sure.

It was a comforting hypothesis, but at the same time a frightening one. It would mean going to trial with no fingerprint evidence, with only possession of the gun and the testimony of a few witnesses. The best of them, the two teenager girls, Ruth Jennings and Gloria Lapp, were scared kids who could be annihilated by a good defense attorney, and in any case they both admitted they hadn't had a good look at the killer who sat on the Mustang. The taller one, the one who paced between the Mustang and the bushes, they had seen quite well, and the sketch done on the basis of their description looked more than enough like Tony Bottom to leave Butler room for hope. But if Albert Washington was the second killer, the one who put twenty-two bullet holes into the body of Joseph Piagentini, right now it looked like he could beat the case. The best witnesses couldn't identify him and the fact he had been perched on the white Mustang exactly where someone else's fingerprints had been found would count heavily in his favor.

All in all, then, it might be better in the long run if the second killer were still at large. That would leave open the possibility of a match with the prints from the Mustang.

Maybe the man they were looking for was Francisco Torres, who was apparently from New York, who might have known Washington from Denver, who was arrested with him in Salt Lake City, who was photographed entering Tony Bottom's apartment in San Francisco. Or perhaps it was the unidentified chameleonlike man whose face appeared, so different from one time to the next, in two of the surveillance photos. Or even the elusive and mysterious Pennegar, who supplied Bottom and Washington with a car the night they went out to machine gun a cop.

Or it could be none of them.

Over the next few days pieces of the puzzle started coming together fast, giving all the detectives involved a sense of progress but in fact doing little to clarify the situation.

From the Bureau of Criminal Identification in New York came word that Francisco Torres wasn't alone among the small group of Divisadero Street suspects having ties to New York City. Albert Washington had been born there on February 28, 1940. At the age of fifteen he moved out of his family's apartment in the Bronx to live by himself. Two years later, in 1957, he was arrested in Manhattan and placed on probation, but because of New York State laws protecting juvenile offenders, the record forwarded to Butler in San Francisco did not indicate the specific charge. In any case, a few weeks after he was put on probation, Washington was brought back to court—apparently for violating the terms of probation, for no new charges were lodged against him. He was sent to Bellevue Hospital for psychiatric observation, as a result of which he was committed to Rockland State Hospital, where he remained for more than three years. In 1960 he was transferred from the upstate facility at Rockland to Creedmoor State Hospital in Queens, apparently so that he could be closer to his family.

After seven months at Creedmoor, the slender twenty-year-old was released to the custody of his family on what was euphemistically called a "convalescent leave." Although the terminology seems to suggest some sort of outpatient status for a person who is not considered cured, the fact is that hospital authorities lost all contact with him. There is no record of any further treatment or any efforts to keep tabs on the young man's progress during this period of "convalescence." Nothing more was heard from him until 1963, when he walked back into Creedmoor and voluntarily committed himself for drug addiction.

This time he stayed six months. When he got out, his parents sent him to live with an uncle in South Carolina, hoping that if he got away from the city he could straighten himself out.

The experiment didn't work. When Albert got his hands on his uncle's .25-caliber automatic pistol and used it for target practice in the house, the uncle called his brother in New York and said he had had enough.

Albert was put on the next bus north, and apparently the pistol went with him. Incensed when he discovered the theft, the uncle made another long-distance call that resulted in Albert's arrest on a concealed-weapons charge the moment his bus pulled into the Port Authority Terminal on Eighth Avenue. After observation at Bellevue, he was sent to Creedmoor for the third and last time.

On October 14, 1964, Washington escaped from Creedmoor and apparently headed west, for there are no further records of his activities until his arrest in Denver fourteen months later.

The next five years of Washington's story were already familiar to Butler—commitment to Pueblo, escape, arrest in Salt Lake City. But now he had a tantalizing piece of new information that forced him to rethink his earlier conclusion about Washington's involvement in the Colonial Park killings. Five months after Washington and Francisco Torres were picked up and then released in Salt Lake City, Washington's name again appears in police records—this time back in his native New York. He and two other men, both known members of the Black Panther Party, were arrested on June 18, 1971, after an armed robbery at a savings-and-loan institution in East Harlem. On August 5, after spending almost seven weeks in the run-down and overcrowded New York City jail known as the Tombs, Washington was freed when his five-thousand-dollar cash bail was posted by a man who identified himself as Gabriel Torres. Thereafter, nothing further was heard of Washington until he was arrested in San Francisco with Tony Bottom.

A raucous concerto of names and dates drummed at Bill Butler's brain as he finished reading the report and threw it to the desk he had been assigned in San Francisco Police headquarters.

Gabriel Torres. Was it just coincidence that the man who bailed Washington out of the tombs bore the same surname as the man arrested with him in Salt Lake City? Were Gabriel Torres and Francisco Torres the same man? Why had anyone considered it worth five thousand dollars to get Washington out of jail? And where would any of these young punks get that much cash?

June 18, 1971, the day Washington was arrested for the savings-and-loan stickup in Harlem. Here was the first evidence putting either of the two suspects in New York in 1971. Albert Washington had been there a mere four weeks after the Colonial Park killings.

August 5, 1971, the day Gabriel Torres bailed Washington out of the tombs. On the very same day, three thousand miles to the west, Samuel Lee Pennegar purchased the '65 Olds that Washington soon would use in his attempt to kill Sergeant George Kowalski.

The connections suggested by these coincidences began to become clear within a matter of days. McCoy, Erdlatz, and McKenna had been showing the Divisadero Street pictures as well as mugshots of Bottom and Washington to a number of key San Francisco detectives in the hope of uncovering additional information. The tactic paid quick dividends when a veteran inspector attached to a robbery detail recognized two of the faces. From his own files he drew a series of photographs taken on July 21 during a bank robbery at the Fidelity Savings and Loan in downtown San Francisco. Triggered by a teller, a set of four bank cameras had captured the entire robbery on film.

Of the three armed men who held tellers and bank customers at gunpoint, one was a new addition to McCoy's slowly growing picture gallery. His two accomplices, though, were no strangers to the detectives working homicide. The one holding the automatic pistol inches from the frightened young teller's collarbone was Tony Bottom. Francisco Torres stood in the middle of the floor, keeping watch with a sawed-off shotgun. The robbery netted $9,400 and answered some of Bill Butler's questions. Perhaps the Fidelity Savings and Loan company had unwittingly supplied the money for Pennegar's car, for Torres's air fare to New York, and for Albert Washington's liberation from the Tombs.

As the investigation inched along, the case began to look like a misfocused picture. Sharp details stood out clearly toward the edges, but the crucial center was still an unresolved blur. Butler grew impatient for the arrival of the witnesses from New York and the line-up that would tell him definitely where he stood. Ten days passed, and still the only word from home was that the district attorney's office was having trouble finding a date convenient for all the witnesses. "Bottom and Washington aren't going anywhere anyway," Butler was told. "Sit tight."

In fact, he was too busy to sit tight. On September 16, a tedious, brain-numbing search through the records of innumerable firearms dealers in northern California disclosed the name of the owner of the pearl-handled .45 automatic that Officer Bob Quinn had ripped from Albert Washington's hand. On April 15, 1971, the S. W. Griffin Gun Shop in San Jose had sold the weapon to Francis A. Howland of San Francisco. A background check on Howland produced little information: he was twenty-three years old and he had no criminal record. McCoy immediately dispatched a squad car to pick up Howland and bring him to the Hall of Justice for questioning. When the lanky, unshaven black man was led into the room, McCoy introduced himself and Detective Butler. Howland failed to pick up on the fact that there was no such rank as detective in the San Francisco Police Department. In weight, height, and general body build, Howland bore a definite resemblance to Tony Bottom, but neither McCoy nor Butler regarded him as a suspect since Bottom already had implicated himself with his statements to his cellmate.

"Mr. Howland, do you own any guns?" McCoy asked.

Howland pursed his mouth, considering the question. "No, I don't believe I do," he said slowly.

"A forty-five automatic? Pearl handle?"

"That does have a ring of familiarity," Howland conceded, nodding. "Tell me more."

He seemed to be baiting the cops deliberately, but Butler was in no mood for playing cat-and-mouse. "On April fifteenth," he said, keeping his voice low, "you purchased a pearl-handled Colt forty-five automatic at Griffin's Gun Shop in San Jose. Where is it?"

Howland snapped his fingers and grinned from ear to ear. "I'm glad you reminded me, Officer," he said genially. "It slipped my mind. Yes, yes, yes, I recollect it very well. Now that you mention it." He paused and stared straight into Butler's eyes. "But I seem to have forgotten what your question was."

"Where is it?" Butler repeated.

"Of course," Howland answered with elaborate civility. He explained that there had been a number of robberies in his neighborhood in the spring, that he bought the gun for his own protection and then put it away without ever using it. As far as he knew, it was still in his closet, but if it wasn't there it might have been ripped off. He said that his "digs" were the scene of almost nightly parties, and that any of his numerous guests might have helped himself to the contents of the closet. Pressed for a list of his friends, he reeled off about twenty names, including the name of Tony Bottom.

Butler and McCoy were sure Howland was lying. They assumed he bought the gun for Bottom because he had no record and Bottom did. Long before the cops came knocking on his door to take him down to the Hall, he must have known that Bottom had been arrested with it. His only interest was in protecting himself from a charge of trafficking in firearms. In that he succeeded.

The two detectives, though, had no reason to be disappointed with the interview. They hadn't expected any helpful answers from Howland, but by getting his story on record they closed off one possible line of defense in case it should turn out that the pearl-handled .45 was the gun used to kill Waverly Jones. Now it would be impossible for Howland to take the stand and testify that he hadn't given Bottom the gun until after the Colonial Park killings. Any cop who has ever prepared a case for trial knows that details like this won't help him win a conviction. But they may keep him from losing it.

• • •

The phone in Bill Butler's hotel room rang just after dawn, waking him from a sound sleep. It was Friday, September 17.

"Yeah," Butler said, sitting upright in bed in the hopes that a wakeful posture would make his voice sound more alert.

"Billy? It's Rod. We've got a problem."

Rod Lankler was an assistant district attorney assigned to the homicide bureau in New York District Attorney Frank Hogan's office. On Thursday evening he had gone to a concert, followed by dinner and a few drinks at a friend's house. A slightly punctilious minister's son who believed all the adages about early to bed, Lankler had been trying to get away from the party since before midnight but found himself unable to escape until almost 1:30. On his way home, feeling sleepy and out of sorts, his eye was caught by the headline on Friday morning's *Daily News*: "Slain Cop's Gun Found; Nab 2."

Below it, in smaller type, a secondary bulletin declared, "Tie Coast Pair to Ambush Here."

The accompanying copyright article, filed by *News* reporter Edward Kirkman from the Patrolmen's Benevolent Association's summer camp in Tannersville, New York, credited "high police sources" with disclosing that "the .38-caliber revolver taken from slain patrolman Joseph Piagentini [*sic*] and a .45-caliber automatic believed used" in the double cop-killing had been recovered in California. The article went on to say that at that very moment two suspects in the Piagentini-Jones killings were in custody in San Francisco and were being questioned by New York City detectives.

Bill Butler listened to Lankler's excited retelling of the story in the *News* and rattled off a string of appropriate expletives. By letting Kirkman in on the secret, the unnamed police source also tipped off Tony Bottom, Albert Washington, and any of their friends who might conceivably be affected by this intelligence.

Butler dressed without showering and raced to the Hall of Justice, arriving just after 7:00. Frank McCoy was waiting for him in the office.

"Goddamn it, Bill," McCoy fumed. "What's going on here? We held off questioning them so they wouldn't know they're suspects in your case. I thought we had an agreement on that. Now anyone connected with Washington or Bottom is going so far underground we're going to have to strip mine the city to find them."

There was no answer Butler could give. "I just hope it's not too late to get them to talk," he said.

By 7:30, he and McCoy were at the jail, urgently demanding an immediate opportunity to question the two prisoners. A potbellied middle-aged lieutenant in the Corrections department who wore his necktie tucked into his shirt, G.I.-style, tried to stall them off with the usual bureaucratic excuses. Inmates weren't interrogated until after breakfast; if they started making exceptions, there would be chaos; the prison was understaffed, didn't have the manpower to treat everyone as a special case. McCoy, though, was in a towering rage and wouldn't take no for an answer. "I'll get them myself," he roared, flinging open the office door. "You want to stop me, go ahead and try!"

He was already twenty yards down the long corridor by the time the frightened lieutenant waddled from behind his desk and stuck his head meekly through the door, as though he half expected the gigantic inspector to be lurking in wait for him on the other side of it. When he realized McCoy had no intention of returning, he turned helplessly to Butler, who had been standing unobtrusively to the side.

"Is he serious?" the lieutenant asked, his voice halfway between wonderment and whining.

Butler shrugged expressively.

"Well, then, you stop him," the lieutenant conceded. "Tell him to go to the interrogation room. I'll have the prisoners there in ten minutes."

Five minutes later, McCoy was already on his second cigarette in the tiny eight-by-ten interrogation room when the door opened and a young white man who looked to be no older than twenty-five stepped in. His collar was unbuttoned, his tie knotted but pulled loose in the accepted style of radical lawyers.

"Inspector McCoy? Detective Butler?" he said, smiling coldly. "I represent Mr. Bottom and Mr. Washington. My clients know their rights, and at this time they are not willing to talk to you about the New York homicides."

He stopped talking and seemed to be waiting for a reply. But Bill Butler had nothing to say to him. McCoy dismissed him with a gesture that was the closest either of them could come to expressing what he felt.

The irretrievable loss of an opportunity to question the two suspects—especially the boastful and garrulous Bottom—wasn't the only bad news that hit Butler that day. Late in the afternoon a telephone call from a robbery detail in a San Francisco business district summoned him and McCoy to a downtown precinct. "I think some of your boys were working today," a blond inspector announced cheerfully, obviously well pleased with himself.

Just hours earlier, shortly after noon, five armed men had held up the Cortland Avenue branch of the Bank of America. When the film in the bank's camera was developed, the blond inspector immediately recognized one of the bank robbers from the pictures McCoy, Erdlatz, and McKenna had been circulating. "Is this your man?" he asked triumphantly, handing a picture to McCoy.

A young black man stood at the teller's window, leveling a shotgun through the open grate. He wore a large, soft hat that hid his hair and threw his eyes in deep shadow, but there was no mistaking the cool, faraway smile. It was the unidentified man from the Divisadero Street pictures, whose almost magical ability to change his features with each change of mood and expression had for a few days fooled McCoy and the others into thinking he was two men.

"How much did they get?" Butler asked.

"The bank will give us the final figure by tonight," the blond inspector responded. "Right now it looks like it was over twenty thousand."

McCoy and Butler exchanged glances, both thinking the same thing. The Black Liberation Army robbed banks when it was ready to move. The last job traced to them had been followed by the release of Albert Washington from jail in New York, the purchase of a car, and the attempt to murder Sergeant Kowalski. Twenty thousand dollars would bankroll a lot of attacks.

And there was another possibility, in a curious way

every bit as distressing as the prospect of more blood-shed. If the mysterious, grinning gunman was in any way involved in the Colonial Park killings, he, too, would have heard that Bottom and Washington were already being questioned in the case. The bank rob-bery, coming just hours after an anonymous police source's ill-considered disclosure, might mean that the BLA was socking in a cash reserve so that it could run and hide. Either way, whether it was planning to take the offensive with more assaults or whether it was heading underground, the photos from the robbery were an ominous reminder that the enemy was still calling the shots.

Although neither Butler nor McCoy would say so, even to himself, the second possibility was the one that bothered them more. At this stage they would have welcomed a shootout. It was a feeling few civilians would understand but most cops shared. They wanted the Black Liberation Army out in the open, where police bullets might cast the deciding vote that would settle the politics of cop-killing once and for all.

Six

THE PLANE BEARING THE WITNESSES FINALLY arrived late Tuesday afternoon. Except for Rod Lankler, the nervous young assistant district attorney who had spent six uncomfortable hours tightly strapped in his seat fretting about the limitless number of ways in which things could go wrong, the contingent reached San Francisco airport in high spirits. For Ruth Jennings and Gloria Lapp, neither of whom had ever been farther than an afternoon's bus ride from New York, only the prospect of the line-up scheduled for the next day dimmed the excitement of being flown to California as guests of the government. They were chaperoned by Olga Ford, a veteran black detective whose gentle motherliness with the two confused and dazzled girls would have surprised those who knew her only as one of the toughest cops in Harlem, male or female.

In addition to Lankler and the three females, the party also included gypsy-cab driver Hector Grace, who folded his hands over his immense stomach, tipped back his head, and fell loudly asleep the moment the plane was airborne out of Kennedy; Duncan Grant, the young Parks Department laborer who had been dragged along despite his insistence that he could not identify the gunmen who ran past him; Detective Nick Cirillo, who planned to stay with Butler in San Francisco as long as needed after the line-up; and Detective George Simmons, a twenty-three-year veteran attached to the ballistics section of the police department's Forensic Division.

On Simmons's lap for the entire cross-country flight was a black leather satchel. Inside it, carefully wrapped and labeled, were three of the deformed bullets which had been taken upon autopsy from the bodies of Joseph Piagentini and Waverly Jones. Ever since the first microscopic examination of the bullets found on the scene, the police had known that three separate guns were used in the killings—two .38s and a .45. Waverly Jones had been felled with four slugs from a single .45-caliber weapon, but Joseph Piagentini had been shot with bullets whose markings indicated that they came from two distinct .38-caliber weapons. In addition, a badly deformed .45 slug taken from his back indicated he had been shot at least once by the same gun that killed his partner. Because the law requires that evidence be preserved in an unbroken chain of custody, Detective Simmons had no intention of letting the black satchel out of his sight for even a single second.

While the witnesses were being delivered to their hotel, Butler took Lankler and Cirillo to the Hall of Justice for a briefing session attended by San Francisco inspectors McCoy, Erdlatz, and McKenna. In the evening the entire New York party, including the four witnesses, went to dinner at Trader Vic's.

The next morning, while Cirillo and Ford remained at the hotel, charged with the responsibility of getting the witnesses to the line-up by eleven o'clock, Butler and Lankler went ahead to the Hall of Justice, where Frank McCoy had already started the procedural steps that would get Bottom and Washington delivered from the jail to the line-up room at headquarters. Erdlatz and McKenna were scouting the jail cells for six black men between the ages of twenty and thirty, between five feet ten and six feet two inches in height, to serve as stand-ins at the line-up.

The line-up room itself was a bare room approximately fifteen by twenty feet in size. There was no raised stage for the suspects, no darkened auditorium for the witnesses, who would view the line-up from an adjacent room through a porthole-sized one-way mirror set into the wall. One at a time, each of the eight men in the line-up would approach the mirror, first hatless and then wearing a black applejack cap similar to the one the witnesses saw on the taller of the two gunmen at Colonial Park.

Shortly before eleven, tense from waiting, Lankler and Butler proceeded to the line-up room, where they paced nervously without talking, like actors prowling backstage before the opening-night curtain. After a few minutes the fretful stillness of the room was broken by the arrival of the six stand-ins. Lankler sized them up and concluded they were close enough to the two suspects in age and general body build. "You know how it works," he cautioned them. "Just follow orders, do what you're told, and don't let on that you're having a good time."

The six men nodded glumly and Lankler went off to check on the witnesses, leaving Butler behind with the stand-ins. Ten minutes passed in silence. Then the door opened and Butler turned to it. The automatic smile of recognition that flickered across his face as Inspector McCoy entered the room vanished instantly in the confusing emotions that washed over him. Behind McCoy were Albert Washington and Tony Bottom, both in handcuffs. They were followed by two uniformed Corrections officers. he felt a sudden shock of surprise at finding himself at last in the same room with the two killers. He had seen their pictures literally thousands of times, and he recognized them at once. Yet he fell prey to an inexplicable perplexity as he realized he hadn't been prepared for what they would look like. In front of him stood two bland and smiling young men, their hands manacled behind their buttocks, their eyes peering curiously about with detached amusement. He had been expecting monsters, and this pair looked incongruously harmless.

Albert Washington wore striped jeans, sneakers, and a floppy gray cardigan sweater over a red T-shirt. He seemed to be bending forward from the waist, for the cuffs that bound his wrists behind his back accented the natural stoop of his posture. Even motionless, his body suggested a pensive man caught in the act of contemplative pacing. Bottom seemed much taller—perhaps only an inch or two in measured height, but he stood rigidly erect, his shoulders pulled back, his head held high. The moment the Corrections officer behind him unlocked the handcuffs, his long arms fell loosely to his sides and his bearing lost at once the look of almost military crispness. Nevertheless, he still stood tall and straight, grinning idiotically, nodding an almost imperceptible greeting to each of the six black men in the room. He wore wrinkled cotton trousers and a red-and-white striped sport shirt. His hair was elaborately plaited in corn rows.

Although both suspects were in generally excellent physical condition, each still bore marks of the pounding he had taken at the time of his arrest. Washington's smashed cheekbone had not yet completely healed; his light skin, gray-looking with the pallor of confinement, was slightly discolored below the left eye. Bottom's jaw, broken in the collision, was still swollen, giving his face a soft roundness that made him look all the more boyishly innocent.

Butler took one look at Bottom's hair and knew he would have to do something about it. All the witnesses had described two men in medium-length Afros. Clever son-of-a-bitch, Butler thought. He crossed the room to where the two suspects were standing and addressed Frank McCoy. "Inspector," he said, "I'd like a word with Mr. Bottom if it's all right with you." Although Butler, not McCoy, was in charge of the line-up, he didn't want Bottom knowing that. It would put him on guard and make him less amenable to suggestion.

McCoy nodded his concurrence.

Butler walked a few steps away and motioned for Bottom to join him. The lanky suspect shrugged quizzically and strolled to where the detective stood. "Yeah?" he asked, his voice an equal mixture of challenge and curiosity.

"Mr. Bottom," Butler began, looking straight into

the taller man's eyes, "we've got a problem here and we'd like your cooperation."

Only Bottom's bewilderment kept him from telling Butler to go to hell. Instead, he said, "What are you talking about, man?"

"Well, look," Butler said, gesturing toward the others in the room as though the point were obvious. Bottom looked but didn't know what he was supposed to see.

"Those are the stand-ins for the line-up," Butler explained. "They've all got their hair combed out."

Bottom looked again but still didn't understand. "So what?" he asked.

"So, you're gonna stand out like a sore thumb, see what I mean? When you go into a line-up it's not a good idea to do anything that calls attention to yourself. Didn't your lawyer tell you that?"

Bottom pondered, suspecting there was a trick in it. But he failed to see it. "Okay, what do I do?" he asked.

"Comb it out. I'll get you a comb," Butler answered. He borrowed a wire-toothed Afro comb from one of the stand-ins.

At the one-way mirror through which the witnesses soon would be studying him, Tony Bottom combed out his hair. It took him fully five minutes to undo the intricate braiding, and when he was finished he stepped back from the mirror and studied himself for a long time. Then he nodded his approval and walked away from the glass, satisfied with his appearance—but no more satisfied than Bill Butler, who studied him hard, seeing him for the first time the way he looked the night he shot Waverly Jones in the back.

• • •

Hector Grace went first.

"If you'll just stand here, Mr. Grace," Lankler said, leading him to the window, "we're ready to begin. This is one-way glass. You'll be able to see the men in the next room, but they won't be able to see you. They will be looking into a mirror. There will be eight men in the line-up. They will approach the mirror one at a time. They will each do this twice, once bare-headed and once wearing a hat. If you recognize anyone at all, whether it's from the night of May twenty-first or from somewhere else, please let us know, even if you only *think* you recognize him. If you want to see any of the men again, just ask. Are there any questions?"

Grace shook his head and Lankler asked him to give his answer verbally for the benefit of the tape recorder that was taking down everything said in the witness room.

One by one, each of the eight subjects approached to within four feet of where the gypsy-cab driver was standing. They stared directly at him for an uncomfortably long period of time, then turned to the left and the right. After each of the eight men had passed before the glass once, Lankler said, "Now you will see the same men in the same order again. This time each one will be wearing a hat. Is that clear?"

Grace said it was, and the parade resumed.

"All right, Mr. Grace, did you recognize any of those men?" Lankler asked when it was all over.

He was surprised to hear the paunchy cab driver say yes, for he had been watching him closely and had seen no sign of recognition.

"Could you tell us which ones? Do you remember them by number or would you like to see them again?"

"No, I don't have to see them again," Grace announced crisply. "Number four and number five."

Number four and number five were stand-ins.

Lankler cautioned the witness against discussing his identification and summoned a police officer to escort him from the room. A minute later the officer returned with Gloria Lapp.

The shy, heavy-set girl was obviously nervous, even frightened. She held her hands interlaced at her waist and picked at her fingers. For the most part she kept her eyes lowered, but even when she raised them they failed to meet Lankler's. Trying to put her at ease, the assistant D.A. repeated the instructions he had given Hector Grace but laid particular emphasis on the security afforded by the one-way glass.

When the first subject approached the mirror, Gloria studied him with an intense concentration Lankler hadn't thought her capable of. "No," she said softly, "that's not him."

As the second man strode toward her she stepped back, seemed to fall away from the glass as though she were afraid he would walk right through the wall and be upon her. For a second or two her lips moved soundlessly, and then, in a barely audible voice she said, "That's him, that's him."

Lankler closed his eyes to hold on to the moment. Then he began to question her. He wanted it all down on the record.

Number two was Tony Bottom.

"That's whom?" he asked.

"That's him," she repeated. "Are you sure he can't see me?" Tony Bottom was staring straight at her.

"Absolutely."

"Can he hear us?"

"No."

Gloria Lapp took a deep breath for courage and stepped closer to the window. Bottom stood barely three feet away, pondering his own image in the mirror, but his eyes seemed to be focused somewhere behind the glass, as though they were locked on the girl. To Lankler, his face seemed relaxed, almost insolently at ease. But for Gloria, who had watched him kill, his eyes had a hypnotically menacing power. For what felt like a shockingly long time, her gaze was riveted to his in terrified fascination. Then Bottom turned to offer his profile and the spell broke.

"That's the man who killed the police officer," she gasped. "That's him."

"Which police officer?"

"The black one. He was walking to the bushes and sucking on the leaves. The other one was sitting on the car. Then when we heard the shots he was standing over the black police officer and shooting him. He had on a hat, but that's him."

"Are you positive?"

"I'm not positive," she said, using the same turn of phrase she had used with Butler the Monday after the killings. "It *is* him."

"All right," Lankler said, keeping his voice cold and mechanical to give her no clue that would corroborate her identification. "Now there are going to be six more men. I want you to look at them carefully and tell me if you recognize any of them."

She didn't.

When it was all over, Bottom's lawyer, who had been standing next to Lankler all along, asked permission to question her.

"Do I have to?" she asked, sounding suddenly very childish.

"No, you don't," Lankler answered. "It's entirely up to you."

"Then I'd rather not."

The lawyer began to protest, but Lankler cut him off. A uniformed officer escorted Gloria from the room and returned with Ruth Jennings.

Barely five feet, two inches tall, in a flower-print gathered skirt that made her look even smaller, she was seventeen years old but would have had trouble convincing anyone she was a day over fifteen. She had an oval face with an attractive though slightly wistful smile and dark eyes that sparkled from behind owlishly oversized glasses.

For the third time, Lankler explained the ground rules. Ruth nodded after each sentence, her mouth pursed and her forehead furrowed with concentration. She'll make a good witness from the stand, Lankler thought. Calm and self-possessed. The prosecution would need her to bolster Gloria, who was sure of her identification but unsure of herself. Ruth Jennings didn't seem the type that would crumble under cross-examination the way Gloria Lapp might.

As he had done with the other witnesses, Lankler stood behind Ruth at the one-way glass. He was scrupulously careful to avoid the possibility of an inadvertent look or gesture that might be construed as coaching.

Ruth studied the first subject carefully but said nothing. When he turned to offer his profile, she looked back over her shoulder to Lankler and said matter-of-factly, "That's not him." Like a model of the runway, the man held the pose for a few seconds, then pivoted to present his other profile. Ruth regarded him absently, her mind already made up. Then he walked away from the mirror.

As the second subject approached, Ruth's posture stiffened slightly with the effort of refocusing her attention. For a moment she stared at Tony Bottom with no reaction at all. Then her eyes darkened and a quizzical expression crossed her face. She cocked her head to the side, ran the tip of her tongue across her lips, and at one point turned toward Lankler as though she were about to speak. But then she changed her mind and turned back to the window. He had to stop himself from asking her what she had been going to say.

Lankler could feel his stomach knotting as the seconds passed and Tony Bottom ran through the poses. The tension grew excruciatingly, and then Bottom had his back to the window and was walking away, his shoulders hunched now, his stride an insolent bounce, as though somehow he knew what was taking place on the far side of the wall.

"No," Ruth Jennings said slowly, drawing the syllable out. "That's not him either."

Rod Lankler felt like he had been hit in the stomach.

Six more subjects passed before the mirror. As she had done with the first, Ruth quickly but thoughtfully rejected each of them. "I'm sorry," she said when it was all over, for it was impossible for her not to know they had been counting on her.

"Don't be," Lankler said. "All we want is truthful answers. There was no one there you recognized?"

"No," she answered, her eyes lowered toward the floor.

Lankler nodded. Remembering her hesitation when she saw Bottom, how close a thing it had been, he asked, "Was there anyone there that looked like anyone?"

Ruth raised her eyes and looked straight at the assistant district attorney. "The guy in red," she said. "Number two, in the shirtsleeves."

Lankler asked, "The man in red? Number two?"

"In the shirtsleeves."

"You think he looks like one of them?"

"Yeah," she said. "Except . . ." Her voice trailed off. "Yeah," she repeated.

Bottom's lawyer cut in. "I'm sorry, I didn't hear. Except what?" he asked.

Ruth hesitated, considering, then answered slowly as she tried to get the difference perfectly clear in her mind. "No," she said, "the guy's face was darker. It was harder. It was slim hardness. You could, you know, you could see the jaw, the jawbone real good."

The lawyer said, "I see. So it's not him, is that right?"

Ruth said, "No. It looks like him, though."

The final witness was Duncan Grant. "I told you, man, I didn't see nothing," he snapped after Lankler had recited the instructions. "All I seen was these dudes running."

"I realize that," Lankler said, "You just do the best you can."

Duncan Grant grinned. "I'll be sure to do that," he said.

He watched the line-up without comment and without reaction. When the last subject had retreated from the window he announced that number five "could be" one of the killers.

"What do you mean, 'could be'?" Lankler asked.

"Means could be," Grant said. "I'm not saying it's him. I'm saying it could be, though."

Number five was a stand-in.

Bill Butler didn't get much sleep that night, sick with a nervousness so intense it felt like physical fear. He had a gut-deep conviction that the two men arrested after the Kowalski shootout were the killers of Jones and Piagentini, but the line-up left him with a terrifying dread that no one would ever be able to prove it to a jury. After the line-up, Ruth Jennings had told him she thought the number two subject was the killer, but she hadn't been willing to say so because she wasn't certain. His face looked different from the way it looked at Colonial Park, she said; there was a puffiness she hadn't seen in May. Butler realized, of course, that all that prevented her from making an identification was Bottom's facial swelling, which hadn't fully subsided. But it didn't help to know that, for the hard and inescapable fact was that she was on record as saying that Bottom was not the killer.

As a result, everything depended on Gloria Lapp, and that in turn meant that the whole case hinged on the ballistics tests George Simmons would be performing in the morning. No ballistics test was needed to establish that the Colt .38 Police Special found in the Olds Tony Bottom had been driving was Waverly Jones's service revolver; the serial number alone confirmed that. The trouble was that the ammunition for the .38 had been in Albert Washington's possession. Bottom had been carrying shells for a .45, which left the prosecution facing a very tough paradox. It had two suspects—Bottom and Washington—and two major pieces of evidence—possession of Waverly Jones's gun and an eyewitness identification. But the gun apparently belonged to Washington, whereas the witness had picked out Bottom. A jury would have a hard time making sense out of that unless there was something to bolster Gloria Lapp's identification. With Ruth Jennings ruled out as a supporting witness, that left only one possibility. The .45.

Butler drove George Simmons to the Hall of Justice first thing in the morning. They were met there by Inspector Erlatz, who led the two detectives to the ballistics laboratory, where the two guns and the ammunition seized at the time of the arrests were waiting for Simmons in a locked cabinet.

The veteran ballistics specialist started with Waverly Jones's gun, the Colt .38 Police Special. He loaded it with a single shell which he removed from the cellophane bag Albert Washington had been carrying in his pocket on the night of August 27. After rotating the chamber until the shell was in firing position, he secured the barrel of the gun to the opening at the top of the vertical water tank the San Francisco Police Department used for test firings. Then he pulled the trigger. There was a sharp explosion, followed by a dull thump. Butler, Erdlatz, and two members of the San Francisco Ballistics Unit watched while Simmons freed the gun from the restraints and retrieved the shell, which now bore the barrel markings of Waverly Jones's revolver.

The process was repeated with the pearl-handled .45 Patrolman Quinn had stripped form the hand of Albert Washington. This time Simmons used one of the shells from the leather pouch Bottom had worn tied to his belt.

Simmons began the comparisons by mounting the recently fired .38 shell on the left-hand stage of a comparison microscope. From his black valise he selected one of the two .38 slugs he had brought from New York and mounted it on the right-hand stage. He adjusted the eyepiece and rotated the bullets carefully, taking fully fifteen minutes to satisfy himself that the two pieces of scarred metal before him had not been fired from the same gun.

In another quarter of an hour he had reached the same conclusion with respect to the second .38 shell he had brought with him. The finding was neither surprising nor disappointing, for the scenario worked out by the police had the gunman who killed Piagentini first emptying his own gun into the writhing body, then resuming the attack with the gun he yanked from Piagentini's holster, firing continuously until he was joined by Waverly Jones's killer. The negative findings of the comparison, therefore, simply established what had been suspected all along—that Waverly Jones's gun had not been used on the night of the killings.

Simmons carefully wrapped all three .38-caliber bullets labeled the new one, and filed them away in his evidence case. Then he took a deep breath, arched his back, and rubbed the back of his hands over his eyes, which ached like tired muscles. Reluctantly, with the dread a scientist feels as he begins the crucial experiment that will either prove or disprove a hard-won theory, he reached into the case for the .45 caliber shell a medical examiner had removed from the body of Waverly Jones.

For a moment he held it in his hand, examining it with his naked eye. The silvery white lead had flattened on impact against Jones's spine, so that it now flowed back over the copper casing like ice cream melting over a cone. Over the years Simmons had studied thousands of bullets, but he had never worked on a cop-killing before. He swallowed hard to drive back the wave of physical revulsion that swept over him, for the few ounces of twisted metal in his hand were as loathsome to him as if the seared tissue of his brother officer still clung to the bullet's scarred and cratered surfaces. He mounted it on one stage of the microscope, the test-fired .45 slug on the other, and bent forward for a look.

Even before he had a chance to align the two bullets with each other, he had his answer. So many hours had been spent studying the fatal bullets that he knew the scratches on them by heart. Beyond any possibility of doubt, the test-fired slug was a perfect twin of the one he had taken from his evidence case.

Simmons rotated the test slug on the stage until the markings of the two bullets were perfectly aligned, so that even an amateur at ballistics could see they had been fired from the same gun. Then he leaned back to let the others look. Ed Erdlatz and the two officers from San Francisco Ballistics took turns studying the exhibit. As the last of them stood up and stepped back, he said, "Congratulations," but he said it so softly it was barely even a whisper.

Bill Butler stepped forward and bent over the dual eyepiece. For a moment his eyes had difficulty adjusting to the two separate images on the illuminated stages. Then it was clear to him.

"Those bastards," he said. "Those fucking bastards."

PART TWO
Masks Fall Off

Seven

THE SAN FRANCISCO LINE-UP PRODUCED mixed results. Bottom was clearly the man the police had all along been calling the Number 1 shooter, the one who killed Waverly Jones. Just as clearly, the Number 2 shooter was still at large, for Albert Washington's fingerprints didn't match the partials found on the white Mustang and none of the witnesses had picked him out. It was going to take a whole new investigation to track down the vicious gunman who had emptied two revolvers into the body of Joseph Piagentini, and the only leads the police had so far were names of a few associates of the pair that had tried to machine gun Sergeant George Kowalski.

Two of these associates were named Torres, and they may or may not have been the same man. A Francisco Torres had been arrested with Albert Washington in Salt Lake City in January 1971. A Gabriel Torres bailed Washington out of the Tombs six months later. In filing the bail application, Gabriel Torres listed his address as 425 East 105th Street, a low-income housing project just a stone's throw from the East River in Spanish Harlem. That was where

Bill Butler started as soon as he returned from San Francisco.

For its own inexplicable bureaucratic reasons, the New York City Housing Authority maintains permanent records of all residents in all the thousands of publicly funded dwelling units over which it has jurisdiction. The logbook for the Woodrow Wilson Houses at 425 East 105th listed twelve families by the name of Torres. One of the entries was particularly interesting. In 1949 a two-bedroom apartment on the ninth floor had been rented to a couple named Torres and their two-year-old daughter Antonia. The log then showed the birth of a son Francisco later that year, the birth of a son Gabriel in 1951, and the births of two more children over the next three years. Mrs. Torres and her two youngest children still lived in apartment 9A.

Butler asked for and got permission to put a twenty-four hour stake-out on the Torres apartment. Of the two men he now new to be brothers, the one he wanted most was Francisco, the blackjacketed Panther who had been photographed outside Tony Bottom's apartment on Divisadero Street and who stuck up the Fidelity Savings and Loan with Bottom in July. But there was no evidence that Francisco was in New York and Butler was willing to settle for Gabriel, who so far had not been tied to Bottom but who had a clearly documented connection to Albert Washington.

On October 8, the fifth day of the round-the-clock surveillance, Detectives Eddie Evans and Al McPherson spotted a chubby Puerto Rican girl in her mid-twenties leaving the Woodrow Wilson Houses. An hour and a half earlier, when she went in, the elevator indicator had stopped at nine. The two detectives watched her pass without moving from their bench on the project grounds. They were wearing old clothes and had been passing a quart bottle of beer wrapped in a paper sack back and forth between them.

"*Mira, mira,* I know that chick," McPherson said, affecting a Spanish accent.

An old man who had been sitting alone at the far end of the bench all day couldn't help overhearing. "That's Antonia," he said helpfully. "Used to be Antonia Torres. Used to be she lived here. She's married now. Visiting her mamma."

"*Gracias, amigo,*" McPherson said. He offered the bottle to the old man, who reached for it eagerly, smiling a gap-toothed smile.

McPherson and Evans rose from the bench, and the old man handed the bottle toward them.

"Keep it, *viejo,*" McPherson said. "*De nada.*"

Picking up their pace as they left the project grounds, the two detectives caught up with Antonia Torres as she reached First Avenue. They held back, watched her climb into a '66 Dodge parked at a meter, and then hurried to their own car two blocks farther up the avenue. They tailed her to an apartment building in an overwhelmingly Spanish neighborhood in the Crotona Park section of the Bronx. Then they reported back to the Three-two.

A Department of Motor Vehicles check disclosed that the car she was driving was registered to a Howard Allen with a Crotona Park address. By running Allen's name through various record bureaus, the detectives learned that he worked as a teller in a Manhattan branch of the First National City bank and that Antonia

Torres was his wife. Butler put a second stake-out on the Allen apartment.

At 4 P.M., October 14, the eleventh day of round-the-clock surveillance, Detective Tommie Lyons spotted Francisco Torres entering his sister's apartment. He immediately called in for backup. Four teams of detectives raced to Crotona Park to sit on the apartment and make sure Francisco Torres would still be there by the time Butler got uptown with a federal warrant for his arrest on a bank-robbery charge.

By 7:00, sixteen detectives had gathered in a makeshift command post in a police van parked around the corner from Washington Avenue where it couldn't be seen from the Allen apartment. Twelve others were deployed inside the apartment building, covering exits, corridors, and staircases. Francisco Torres was not known to be violent but he traveled in circles that were, and the police knew they had to be ready for anything. Inspector Edward Jenkins had already arrived to take charge of the operation when Butler showed up with the warrant at 7:15. After a five-minute conference with Butler and Sergeant Robert Maas, Jenkins selected thirteen men to go in after Torres—himself, Maas, Butler, Lyons, Evans, McPherson, Lee Higham, Matt Nichols, Joe Kiernan, John Gaulrapp, Merrill Nanton, John Forget, and Joe Tidmarsh. Butler asked for permission to be the first one in and got it.

Lyons was sent to reconnoiter the interior of the building. "There's two sets of fire stairs, one at either end of the building," he reported back a few minutes later. "The Allen apartment is on the fifth floor, three doors down from the north stairs. There's an elevator in the center of the building. I had the super turn it off so that's not gonna be a problem. There's no fire escapes. And we got a break on the layout. Front door opens straight into the living room, no entranceway. Living room's off to the left. You can see the whole room from the door. There's a corridor goes back to the kitchen, john, and bedroom, but it's dead straight ahead of the front door. Clean line of fire."

Inspector Jenkins nodded appreciatively. "You used to live here or something?" he asked.

"I had the super show me the same apartment on the second floor."

"Nice work. Let's just hope he doesn't call Torres and tell him company's coming."

"Can't. I thought of that already, left two guys with him."

"Then what are we waiting for?"

The detectives divided into two teams in the lobby. Butler, Maas, Nanton, Lyons, Evans, and Tidmarsh climbed the north fire stair. Inspector Jenkins led the remaining men up the south stairway. Tiptoeing single-file, their revolvers drawn, the two assault squads converged on apartment 5C from opposite directions. When the columns had closed to within five feet of the door, Butler held up his right hand in a signal to halt. Proceeding alone, he positioned himself in front of the door, took a deep breath, and felt for the knob. As his fingers circled around it, the other men crept in behind him. There would be no signal because there was no need of one. When Butler shouldered through the door, the others would pour in after him. They had been warned to keep cool, but it was even money that any-thing that moved might be shot.

For fully thirty seconds no one drew a breath. Then the gun poised by Butler's left ear dropped to his side, his right hand came away from the doorknob and hovered above his shoulder in a needless signal for silence as he seemed to strain to hear something on the other side of the wall. He stepped away from the door and motioned for Inspector Jenkins to join him about ten yards down the corridor, leaving the others where they had been standing.

"There's kids in there," Butler whispered, his voice urgent with distress.

"What d'ya mean kids?"

"I could hear them. Little kids, a couple of them, I don't know. And I think there's a baby too."

The inspector considered for a long time. "What do you think?" he asked.

"I think I don't want to take out a bunch of kids."

Jenkins nodded. With hand signals, he called Sergeant Maas away from the door to join the conference. "Listen, Bob," he whispered, his arm around the sergeant's shoulder. "Bill says he heard kids in there. If we drop any kids it's gonna be an awful mess. What d'ya say we try and talk Torres out?"

"It's worth a shot," the sergeant agreed.

Using hand signals, he redeployed the men away from the door. Gaulrapp was sent to the van for a bullhorn. He was back upstairs in a matter of seconds. The inspector flipped the switch and raised the horn to his lips.

"Francisco Torres, this is the police," Jenkins barked through the bullhorn, which sent his voice booming through the narrow corridor like thunder. "We know you're in there. We have a warrant for your arrest. We know there are children inside, but we'll shoot if we have to. Come out with your hands above your head. No one will be hurt."

Half a minute passed with no response. Then there was the sound of a dead bolt sliding in a lock. Bill Butler crouched to fire as the door swung slowly back. A foot and a half in front of him stood Francisco Torres, hands high above his head. With more strength than he knew he had, Butler lunged forward, grabbed Torres by the shoulder, and jerked him forward with such force that he reeled into the opposite wall of the hallway. Joe Tidmarsh caught him as he came off the wall, spun him around, and locked the cuffs on.

In front of Butler, grouped like a family portrait in the center of the living room, stood Antonia Torres Allen holding a year-old child. Next to her was Gabriel Torres. Then Howard Allen. Then, with three small, frightened children peering from behind her legs, stood a scowling, broad-shouldered black woman Bill Butler knew he had seen before.

Leaving the prisoners to be booked by other detectives, Butler and Merrill Nanton drove across the Bronx to Gabriel Torres's apartment on Anderson Avenue, just around the corner from Yankee Stadium. A young woman opened the apartment door and studied them apprehensively.

"Mrs. Torres?" Butler asked.

"Yes."

"Mrs. Gabriel Torres?"

She held a tiny infant, red-faced and precariously asleep, cradled along her left arm. With her right hand she was buttoning her shirt, The door stood open barely three inches. She said, "Yes," again, this time with a touch of impatience in her voice, which she nevertheless kept soft so as not to wake the baby.

"I'm Detective Butler. This is Detective Nanton. May we come in?"

"I'm just putting the baby to sleep."

"I'd rather not talk in the hall," Butler said. "If you want to put—him?"

"Him."

"If you want to put him down, that's fine, we'll wait. We only need a few minutes of your time."

She glanced suspiciously from one cop to the other, then nodded resignedly, stepping back from the door to let them in. But she didn't put the baby down. "What is it?" she asked.

Simply out of habit, Butler took in what he could of the small apartment as he started to speak. The furniture was bare and comfortless, a cheap pine dining table, straight wood chairs. There was a threadbare couch that probably opened out as a bed and a small black-and-white television at the center of the floor, its plug trailing behind it to the wall. The volume was turned way down, barely audible, and the picture danced faintly, rolling vertically every few seconds. "Your husband has been arrested," Butler said.

The color drained from Celia Torres's face and her hand tightened around the baby, pulling him against her. His mouth opened and he started to make a sound but quickly subsided back into sleep. "Where is he?" she asked.

Nanton told her where Gabriel had been taken and when she could see him, but her mind seemed far away and it wasn't clear she was following. "You can reach me or Detective Butler in the morning at this number," he said, handing her a card. Both detectives noticed she hadn't asked what crime her husband had been charged with.

"If you can give us just another minute, Mrs. Torres," Butler said, reaching into his pocket. "We have a couple of pictures we'd like you to look at."

He handed four snapshot-sized photos to her. She looked briefly at the first two. Her face registered confusion. "Why are you showing me these?" she asked. "That's my husband and my brother-in-law."

Butler stepped to her side and removed the top pictures. "All right, thank you. Now who is this?" he asked.

"I don't know."

"You've never seen him before?"

"No."

It was Albert Washington.

"Okay. This is the last one. Can you tell us who this is?"

"No."

"You're positive?"

"I told you. I've never seen him before."

It was Tony Bottom.

Butler thanked her, took the last picture from her hand, and turned to leave. She hesitated a moment, shifted the infant in her arm, then stepped past the two detectives to lead them to the door.

When the door closed behind him, Butler stopped in mid-step and held up a finger to silence Nanton. He leaned toward the door to listen, having already made up his mind to put a stake-out on the apartment if he heard voices. But there was nothing, not even the sound of the lock clicking closed, not even the sound of her receding steps. It was as though she were standing on the other side of the door waiting. As though she expected the cops would be back.

The broad-shouldered woman arrested in the Allen apartment was Alexandra Horn, who gave a home address in Denver, Colorado. Like Howard and Antonia Allen, she was charged with harboring a fugitive and constructive possession of a weapon, the latter deriving from the sawed-off shotgun found under a bed when the apartment was searched. Bill Butler knew her already, for he had seen her in the Divisadero Street surveillance photos, where she was pictured in front of Bottom's apartment struggling against the embrace of the unidentified man with the smoldering eyes and the thin, tightlipped smile.

"Look, she knows something. She's been in too many places," Butler said. "I've gotta squeeze her till she cracks. For Chrissakes, don't let her walk on this."

It wasn't yet nine in the morning and this was the first the young Bronx County assistant D.A. had heard of the case. "Well, what do you want from me?" he asked.

"Name her as a material witness, get a high bail, I don't care. Just keep her locked up, that's all. I don't want her out until she tells me what she knows."

The D.A. looked at the report in front of him and shook his head. "Harboring a fugitive?" he said dubiously. "What kind of bail can I ask that she can't meet?"

"I don't care how you do it," Butler said. "There's two cops dead. You hold on to her." He hadn't slept all night, and anger and tension were audible in his voice.

"I'll do what I can," the young lawyer said, promising

nothing. But he was a good man, better than his word, it turned out. With impassioned pleading at the arraignment later that morning, he convinced a skeptical but cooperative judge to set bail on Alexandra Horn at $150,000.

For two weeks, she was put through an unalterable routine of rugged questioning. A police van picked her up every morning at the Rikers Island prison and delivered her to the New York County courthouse in lower Manhattan. There Bill Butler, Olga Ford, and assistant district attorney John Keenan, chief of the D.A.'s homicide bureau, grilled her for hours at a stretch. Between interrogation sessions, she was left under police guard on a wooden bench in a corridor outside the homicide bureau offices. Sometimes a whole day would pass during which no one would question her, in which case she would be kept waiting on the bench from morning until night while a steady stream of detectives and assistant prosecutors bustled along the hallways, slowing to study her insolently as they passed. Sometimes the questioning went on without interruptions for nine hours of tense combat. At six o'clock the Corrections Department van took her back to her cell on Rikers Island, a grim and solid fortress on a ten-acre rock in the East River, where she got a few hours of rest before the next day's session.

Day after day, the routine never varied. Like a machine running in tracks, the interrogators shifted tactics predictably, sometimes wheedling, coaxing, insinuating, sometimes badgering her at the tops of their voices. She was told she would be kept in jail until the case was solved, she was told she wouldn't see her children again for years. And then they asked her the same questions. What did she know about the men in the photos that were thrust in her face dozens of times each day? Where had she been in May? Where had the men been?

And always Alexandra Horn had the same answers. She knew nothing, absolutely nothing. She would sit rigidly in a chair, her powerful arms folded tightly under her full bosom, refusing to speak at all; she would loosen her volcanic rage in flaming streams of obscenity; she would slump with fatigued resignation and mutter her responses in a barely audible voice. But the answers never changed. She didn't know Bottom, she didn't know Washington, she didn't even know the Torres brothers, with whom she was arrested.

Through it all, Butler never doubted for a single instant that she was lying. Through sheer persistence she might have forced him to believe her when she denied knowing Bottom and Washington, if only she hadn't stubbornly insisted that she didn't recognize the pictures of Francisco and Gabriel Torres. That act of defiance whetted his appetite for the truth and assured that Alexandra Horn could do no better than a draw in a war of wills that Butler was prepared to wage indefinitely.

In many ways, the arrest of the Torres brothers confused the investigation more than it clarified it. On October 15 Francisco Torres was put in a line-up at the district attorney's office. Gloria Lapp and Ruth Jennings did not recognize him as the man they had seen sitting on the fender of the white Mustang, but Hector Grace identified him as one of the gunmen he had seen running along the sidewalk. Yet his fingerprints did not match the prints found on the Mustang, and the police did not believe him to be the second killer. At the end of October, John Keenan threw up his hands. "We've got something, let's go with it," he announced. "Let's put what we've got in front of the grand jury and indict Bottom for murder. Maybe that's what we need to shake things up."

The veteran prosecutor stopped his pacing and turned to gauge Bill Butler's response. Keenan had been in on the case from the beginning, for in New York it is standard practice for members of the district attorney's office to respond to the scene of all homicides involving members of the police force. Thus, John Keenan had been at Colonial Park while Joseph Piagentini's and Waverly Jones's blood was still wet on the sidewalk. Until a suspect was in custody, however, he had taken a back seat to the police. Now that Tony Bottom was identified as a suspect, it became Keenan's job to call the shots.

A small, slender man in his mid-forties, rumpled, nervous, and utterly incapable of sitting still for more than a few minutes at a time, Keenan had been in the district attorney's office since shortly after his graduation from Fordham Law School. In Manhattan, where the legendary Frank Hogan had been district attorney since 1941, Keenan had risen as far as an assistant prosecutor could go. In 1966, his successful prosecution of the widely headlined Wylie-Hoffert murder case had won him a brief celebrity in the public mind and a higher and more lasting regard within the D.A.'s office.

Although the young lawyers who worked under him tended to make fun of his bouncy, flamingolike walk and his nervous habit of compulsively combing and recombing his thinning, sand-colored hair, they were warm in their appreciation of his considerable talents. He was brilliant without being flashy. Theatrics were for defense lawyers, he maintained; prosecutors should rely on thorough knowledge of the law combined with mind-bending preparation of each case. "The defense can pull rabbits out of hats," he used to say. "If they bamboozle only one juror, they win. We need all twelve. Any time a prosecutor is surprised by something that happens in a courtroom, it means he hasn't been doing his homework."

Unquestionably the best trial lawyer D.A. Hogan had, Keenan was not only a superb courtroom tactician but also a master legal strategist. In addition, he was a superlative teacher. Despite his congenital impatience, he never allowed himself to become too harried or too preoccupied to explain his handling of a case to a younger colleague.

Butler glumly nodded his acquiescence to Keenan's decision to go ahead with the grand jury presentation of the evidence against Bottom. Although an indictment against Bottom would in no way foreclose the continuing search for the second killer, Keenan's refusal to wait any longer was an unmistakable indication that the district attorney's office wasn't hopeful that a new break in the case would be coming soon. If not a rebuke of the police, it was clearly an admission of despair, for in a crime with multiple perpetrators it is always better to indict them together.

"Maybe if we put the Horn woman under oath she'll open up," Keenan suggested, making an effort to sound optimistic.

"You believe that?" Butler asked skeptically.

"No."

"Then what are you kidding yourself for?"

"You mean you don't think I should put Horn in the grand jury?" Keenan asked.

"Tell you the truth, I don't give a shit," Butler snapped petulantly. He went to the window and watched the slate sky darkening to black. "Aw, fuck it," he said, turning to face Keenan after a long silence. "Put her in. She's not gonna help us, she's not gonna hurt us. Put in the other one too, what've we got to lose?"

Keenan's attention perked up. "What other one?" he asked.

"The wife, Gabriel's wife. Celia Torres."

"She hasn't even been questioned since the night they were arrested," Keenan objected. "I don't mind fishing, but are we fishing for anything?"

Butler shrugged. "I wish to Christ I knew," he said. "Let's put her in, though. I got a funny feeling about that woman."

Eight

CELIA TORRES CRACKED LIKE AN EGGSHELL.

On the morning of October 27 a police officer served her with a subpoena to appear before the grand jury. The officer waited while she made a phone call from her apartment. A half hour later her mother arrived to take care of the baby, and the officer drove her downtown to the Criminal Courts building, where she was taken to a waiting room in the district attorney's office. An hour passed, then another. Olga Ford joined her on the bench, identified herself as a police officer, and tried to engage her in conversation. Celia listened sullenly but said nothing.

Ford then told her she would be questioned under oath about events that took place in May. She would be questioned about the identity of a number of individuals, about whether she knew them. If she lied or concealed anything it would be perjury and she could be sent to jail.

"You have a baby, don't you?" Ford asked.

Celia nodded dumbly, frightened.

"How old?"

Celia didn't answer.

"A month, isn't it? Three weeks, something like that?"

"Three weeks."

Olga Ford smiled maternally. "If you go to jail," she said softly, making a threat in the form of friendly counsel, "you won't be able to see your baby. You realize that, don't you?"

When Celia was brought into John Keenan's office for questioning, she said nothing, not so much refusing to answer as failing to, as though she were literally struck dumb. As uncommunicative as Alexandra Horn, there was nevertheless a clear difference, for Celia's silence lacked truculence and determination. Keenan asked her if she wanted anything to eat, coffee, or a soft drink. She shook her head. He stepped to the door and leaned out, motioning for Olga Ford to join them in the office. Then Keenan left the two women alone for a few minutes and the detective again reminded the frightened girl about her baby.

When Keenan returned, Celia began to talk. Her story started in late April, when Alie Horn, whom Celia had never met before, knocked on the door of Celia's apartment on Anderson Avenue in the Bronx, just a two-minute uphill walk from Yankee Stadium. "She said she was a friend of Francisco, that's my brother-in-law, Gabriel's brother. But I knew that already. We hadn't seen Francisco for a couple of years. He was in the Air Force, in Vietnam, and then when he got out he was in Denver. But he used to write to Gabriel. He used to mention her in his letters. He was in the Panthers, he joined it in Denver. And she was in the Panthers too. I think they were living together."

Keenan asked if she had been told to expect a visit from Alexandra. Celia shook her head.

"Where was Francisco, your brother-in-law, at this time?"

"I don't know. Maybe Denver or California, somewhere out west I think. I don't know."

"Was your husband home at this time?"

"He was at work. This was in the afternoon. He had a job then at the Ford plant. In Tarrytown."

"I'm sorry, please go on," Keenan apologized.

Alie's visit lasted a few hours. It was purely social. Alie said simply that Francisco had written asking her to look up his brother while she was in New York. Over the next two weeks Celia and Gabriel Torres saw Alie Horn two or three times for no more than an hour or so on each occasion. Then, one afternoon in late April, Alie arrived unannounced at the Torres apartment with her three children. It was clear she intended to stay. "She didn't really ask," Celia said hesitantly. "It was just that she was there. I don't remember what was said about it, maybe nothing I guess. But she was a friend of Francisco's, know what I mean? Like Francisco was Gabriel's older brother and if Francisco wanted her to stay with us then that was okay with us. So that's about how that happened. Anyway, she was there a couple of days and she got this phone call and she said she had to go meet someone at the Panther headquarters. That's downtown in Harlem, like One hundred and twenty-fifth Street I guess. So she brought this guy back to the apartment. He was an older man. She called him Noah."

"Noah what?"

"I don't know. Just Noah. And we called him the Old Man."

"Do you mean to tell me you never heard his last name?"

"No one used last names. They all used different names, we all called them two or three different things. Like sometimes they called my husband Gilbert, so it was like that. But I can tell you who he was because you have his picture."

From the photographs she had been shown on the night her husband was arrested, she identified Noah as Albert Washington.

"Well anyway, so he moved in too. I mean, not in with us, in our apartment. We already had, like, Alie and her kids, there were three of them, so one more wouldn't have made no difference. But Noah was kind of, like he was always off by himself, you know what I mean. So I don't think he would have liked it, with the kids and all those people. But what he did was he took an apartment in the building. You know the neighborhood, don't you? Well, there's always empty apartments, vacancies. All the time. So it was no problem."

A few days later—Celia put the date somewhere around the beginning of May—Gabriel's brother Francisco arrived at the Anderson Avenue apartment. He had two men with him. One of them Celia knew only as T.B., but she identified him from photos as Tony Bottom. The other was called both Herman and Jonas.

The Torres living room became a combination barracks, command post, and school. Discussion groups, usually led by Albert Washington, were held there daily. The topics under study were revolution, urban guerrilla warfare, and "community self-defense," a Black Liberation Army euphemism for ambushing cops. In the evenings the self-proclaimed soldiers often got high on grass, drunk on cheap red wine. Of the five men, only Gabriel Torres worked, but the others—all of whom, Celia learned, had flown to New York from California—did not seem to lack for money. "They paid for their food and like that," she said. "They didn't stay with us because they were broke, they could've got their own places if they wanted to. Francisco wasn't staying with us anyway, he was at Gabriel's sister's. And so was Jonas most of the time, except a couple of nights maybe he slept in the living room. But T.B. was there all the time. And Noah, like I said, he had his own pad but no one ever stayed there with him. So anyway, that's the way it was. And then it was the night that . . . the night the two, you know, the night we're talking about, right?"

"May twenty-first?"

"Yeah, I guess so. The night the two cops got killed. So they're all there in the apartment, see? There's Gabriel and T, that's Francisco, and there's T.B. and Jonas and the Old Man. And it was just getting dark, like I guess eight o'clock, and they went out, so that left Alie and me. The kids were asleep so we just, we did the dishes and like cleaned up and like that. Maybe we watched a show on the TV, we listened to the radio, it was nothing special, just, you know, nothing to do."

Celia took a deep breath, steeling herself to go on. From what she said, and from what he later learned from other witnesses, Keenan was able to reconstruct the scene in the Torres' apartment that night.

Almost exactly at eleven o'clock the door to apartment 2C at 1185 Anderson Avenue flew open. Gabriel

Torres stepped into the room, flushed and breathing heavily. Noah—Albert Washington—walked in behind him, closed the door, and collapsed into a chair. "Man you are out of shape," he panted. "The fact is, you drink too much wine, that's what it is."

He pulled himself up slowly, like an old man, and shambled toward the kitchen.

"Maybe," Gabriel called after him, "but how come you left me? You shouldn't have left me there."

Noah shrugged and walked away. A minute passed slowly, and then the apartment door opened and Francisco Torres stepped in.

"Hey, turn on the news," he shouted excitedly.

Alie Horn clicked on the television and lifted it to the low table in front of the couch. In a few seconds the sound came on. The anchorman was reading a bulletin just handed him about a shooting in Harlem. One police officer was known to have been killed and a second had been wounded, but there was no word yet on the extent of his injuries.

Noah sneered derisively at the last phrase and crossed to the dining table. He took a gun from his waistband and set it down. The announcer promised more information as soon as it became available.

The door opened for a third time. Jonas and T.B. stood in the doorway. Jonas wore an agitated expression, his eyes dark and feverish. Bottom was smiling broadly, his boyish face flushed. He raised both arms above his head and turned a complete circle in the open doorway like a victorious prize fighter glorying in triumph. "We offed two pigs, we offed two pigs!" he chanted as he turned.

Jonas glowered at him, then crossed dramatically to where Noah stood at the table and placed two guns on it. One of them was a long-barreled .38, the other a stubby revolver which everyone in the room recognized as a Colt .38 Police Special. The sight of it touched off an electric spark of excitement that gave a foretaste of the celebration that was to follow. But Jonas wasn't ready yet for rejoicing.

"One of the pigs was black," he said softly, his mouth set tight, his eyes perplexed. He turned slowly, facing each of the men in the room with an unasked question. "One of them was black," he repeated in the same tone. "I didn't know one of them was going to be black."

"So what?" Albert Washington challenged from the other side of the table. His gray eyes bore coldly in on the younger man's anguish the way ice numbs a burn.

Jonas started to reply but couldn't, leaving the last word to Washington. "A pig's a pig," the Old Man hissed. "Fuck 'em all."

Someone laughed, but the tension in the room refused to crack.

"Was it on the news?" Tony Bottom asked.

Alie Horn nodded, but no one said anything.

"Yeah?" Bottom demanded.

"One of the pigs is still alive."

Bottom snorted. "That's Jonas's guy. Man, you ain't much of a shot. You just lucky pigs ain't elephants or you woulda got stomped. My man went down like that"—he snapped his finger three times—"bam bam bam! Like that. He went over like a fucking tree and that's the truth. And there's Jonas pumping away like a machine gun. The pig's just wiggling around and Jonas is shooting and that motherfucker pig's bawling, 'Don't shoot me no more, don't shoot me no more.' "

Jonas smiled with sheepish self-derision, as though it made him comfortable somehow to be the butt of T.B.'s jokes.

Bottom went on, telling how Jonas's gun went empty, how Jonas had trouble freeing the cop's gun from the holster because it was strapped in. As he spoke, he added two guns to the two Jonas had set on the table—another Police Special and his own pearl-handled .45. His story was interrupted by the television anchorman breaking into an ongoing story with an update on the Harlem shooting.

Both police officers were dead.

The apartment on Anderson Avenue erupted in celebration.

The events of the next few hours called up in John Keenan's mind a nauseatingly detailed picture of a savage victory dance that had nothing to do with the elation of successful warriors, the triumphant satisfaction that comes after combat. This was, rather, a simpler and cruder thing, a pure and brutal joy no longer held in check by the uneasy awareness that the white man Jonas had tormented with bullets still clung to life.

Although the men who murdered Jones and Piagentini called themselves soldiers in an army—the Black Liberation Army—the orgy of rejoicing that followed the second bulletin on the eleven o'clock news proved with indelible clarity that they were not soldiers and never could be. In those few minutes their masks fell off and they showed themselves to be simply assassins.

They danced and shouted, slapped palms, cavorted about the living room in manic embraces. Someone went to the kitchen and came back with three bottles of red wine, which passed rapidly from hand to hand. Before long they were drunk and giggling, and every once in a while Tony Bottom rose from where he was seated on the floor to act out another portion of the bloodletting, setting off gales of laughter.

Nine

ALEXANDRA HORN SLOUCHED IN THE CHAIR, legs crossed, arms folded. "You pigs got nothing better to do than hassle me?" she snarled. "Just fuck off, huh? I told you, you're wasting your time."

"I don't think we are," John Keenan said levelly, with no particular tone in his voice.

He had been sparring with her for five minutes, savoring in anticipation the moment he would spring his surprise on her. As he had done every day since the marathon round of interrogations started, he reached for the file of photos on his desk blotter and flipped it open.

"This bullshit again," she said. "How many times do I have to tell you? I don't know these dudes."

Keenan's voice sharpened to matter-of-fact coldness. "You're going into the grand jury this afternoon," he said. "You're going to be under oath and they're going to ask you questions. I want to know what your answers are going to be."

Before she could say anything, before she could tell him that she didn't have any answers, he handed her a photo of Albert Washington. "What time did he get back to the apartment?" he asked. "Who was with him?"

Alexandra's eyes darkened and she sucked in air through her teeth with the quick hissing sound of sharp and sudden pain. She seemed to be calculating something, and for a moment she didn't answer. Those questions had never been asked before and she knew instantly that now the lawyers and the cops knew something. She knew, too, where they had found out: Celia.

"I don't know what you're talking about," she said without conviction. "What apartment?"

Keenan glanced at a slip of paper on his desk. "Eleven eighty-five Anderson Avenue," he said, reading from the paper. "Apartment 2C. We know what happened, Alie. We know you were there. You can't do yourself any good if you don't tell us about it now."

She was no fool. She knew it was all over. She said, "I want to talk to a lawyer."

Keenan smiled paternally and walked around from behind his desk. "You don't need a lawyer," he said. "You understand that if you're a suspect you have a right to counsel. We have to let you talk to a lawyer, that's the law. You know better than I do what your involvement is. Think it over. Do you understand what I'm telling you?"

She smiled ruefully, a wan, weak smile that had in it the first glimmer of human vulnerability he had ever seen in her. What accounted for her, he wondered. She was only twenty-six years old, above average in intelligence. Five months earlier she had celebrated two brutal killings, had rejoiced with the killers. It was inconceivable to him that any amount of social injustice could account for such hostility.

He turned and withdrew behind his desk, knowing she would talk now. Her involvement—that was the word he had so carefully chosen for it—went as deep as the marrow of her being. Even if she had done no more than participate in the orgy of celebration that erupted with the news of the second officer's death, she was so irrevocably "involved" that the coldest and most brutal calculation of self-interest would tell her to seize the opportunity he was offering to be merely a witness.

So he lowered himself into his chair and waited to hear what she would say. He had been in the homicide bureau over a dozen years; murderers were his stock in trade. Yet she chilled him as no killer ever had.

Alie Horn confirmed everything Celia Torres had said. She, too, remembered the night of May 21, remembered the five men leaving the apartment around eight o'clock, remembered them returning at eleven, first Gilbert and Noah, then T, finally T.B. and Herman, who had done the shooting.

Once again she was handed the stack of photographs, but this time she made identifications, leafing through them quickly, almost casually, reciting the names and then handing them back to Keenan. "That's Gilbert, that's Noah, don't know this one, that's T.B., that's T."

Keenan set the stack of pictures on his blotter, baffled, trying to frame a question. He started to ask her something about the fifth man, the one she called Herman, but she cut him off, raising her hand and waving it impatiently to silence him. He was struck by the oddness of the gesture, the familiarity it seemed to take for granted, as though this were a conference, not an interrogation, as though the two of them were trying to solve this thing together.

"Hold it, hold it," she said. "Gimme those pictures again, gimme the colored one."

He handed her the driver's license photo of Samuel Lee Pennegar, and she studied it for a long time. "You know what?" she said quizzically. "That's Herman. It doesn't look like him at all. It's a shit picture, know what I mean. But it's Herman."

Keenan said, "Yes. What can you tell us about him?"

"Nothing."

"What's his name?"

"Herman, that's all I know. Sometimes they called him Jonas. But I never heard him called anything else."

"You lived with him, what, two months, and you never heard his name?" Keenan asked incredulously.

Alie shook her head. "These are heavy dudes, man," she said. "Nobody knows their names except they want them to."

Keenan believed her, for he had run into the same roadblock on other investigations. With the Black Liberation Army the use of pseudonyms was not only a practical expedient but also part of a romantic revolutionary tradition.

"Where is he?" Keenan asked.

"Probably underground," Alie answered matter-of-factly. "Like we were in San Francisco, see, when T.B. and Noah got popped, and then everybody cut out. What happened was after it went down—the shooting, you know—we split for Frisco. We stuck around for a couple weeks because there wasn't any heat but then T and me, that's Francisco, we split for California. And T.B. was there already and so was Herman. I think Noah stayed in New York, in fact I know he did. But the rest of us were in San Francisco. So maybe Herman's still there. Except, you know, like I said, everybody just cut out fast when T.B. and Noah got busted, so I can't say for sure where he is. He's either there or he isn't, right? The only thing I remember was he was living with his old lady."

"His wife?"

Alie laughed. "No, man. Well, like his revolutionary wife, if you can dig it. Not married and all that. Like I met her in June and she had a little baby, a little boy. Her name's Linda Gill, and it's his baby. Herman's."

Keenan grabbed for his phone and called Bill Butler. "Pennegar was living in San Francisco with a woman named Linda Gill," he said. "They have a kid, a little baby. Get on it."

When Celia Torres finished her testimony to the grand jury, the same detectives who had served the subpoena on her that morning offered to drive her home. She shook her head sullenly.

"I've been thinking," she said. "I want to talk to Mr. Keenan."

It was early evening when Keenan concluded his presentation to the grand jury and returned to his office to find Celia waiting for him in the still and gloomy hallway before his door.

"I'm sorry, Mrs. Torres," Keenan said, unlocking his door. "The detectives were supposed to take you home. Didn't they tell you?"

She followed him into the office. "Yes," she said. "What's going to happen?"

Keenan felt a sudden surge of pity for her, as one might

for a lost child. Her home had been headquarters for the party of killers, yet it seemed to him she had been only marginally involved in their deed. It dawned on him for the first time that she had not yet realized her testimony would lead to a murder charge against her husband.

"It's up to the grand jury, Mrs. Torres," he said evasively. "We should know tomorrow."

She seemed unsatisfied with his answer, so he said, "I'm asking for murder indictments against all five men—your husband, his brother, Washington, Bottom, and the one you call Herman."

She seemed neither surprised nor shocked. "Gabriel didn't shoot anyone," she said, not as a protest, but resignedly, simply stating it as a fact.

"I realize that," Keenan said. She didn't seem to want an explanation so he didn't offer one.

For fully a minute no one spoke. Outside Keenan's window the city was dark, glowing coldly.

"I don't want to go home," Celia said, looking out into the night. "I'm afraid."

"Of your husband?" Keenan asked.

She continued to look away from him and didn't answer.

"They're in custody," Keenan said. "Your husband and his brother are in jail here, Bottom and Washington in San Francisco. Do you have any reason to believe that the fifth man, the one you call Herman, is here in New York?"

"He's not here," she said certainly. "He knows what happened to them, he wouldn't come here. But he's not all there is. The BLA is bigger than them."

Keenan nodded. He had already arranged to have

Alexandra Horn released from the prison on Rikers Island and transferred to a safe apartment, where she would live with her children under constant police supervision. Now he asked Celia how she would feel about sharing an apartment with Alie.

The question startled her. According to her own narrative it was Alie's arrival from Denver that precipitated the series of events which culminated with her husband being held on a murder charge. Yet if she had any objections she kept quiet about them. "Anything," she said. "I just can't go home, that's all."

The name Linda Gill meant nothing to either John Keenan or Bill Butler but it clicked instantly with San Francisco Inspector Frank McCoy. "Yeah, we know who she is," McCoy told Butler on the phone. "Strong militant. So's her brother. He's Black Liberation Army and she's not far behind. We have him in custody on a shooting we had here. He turned himself in, pretty badly wounded. It all connects, Bill. Remember that address on the Pennegar license—Pierce Street, a couple by the name of Russell, right? Well, Mrs. Russell is Linda Gill's mother."

Butler was puzzled. "But you showed her the picture, didn't you?" he asked.

"That's right. She said she didn't know who he was."

"Then she was lying?"

"I don't think so. She's a good woman, hard-working woman. Got two rotten kids, that's all. I believe her, but it's worth another check. She says she doesn't know Pennegar, she's probably telling the truth. But she may know where her daughter is."

Grace Russell hadn't heard from her daughter since

September. "It's grief, Inspector, grief every time I see you," she said, the strength and sorrow in her voice reflecting her command of the self-pity that showed through in her words. "But I don't blame you for it," she added thoughtfully. "I understand. It's those children of mine. What have they done this time?"

"It's nothing like that, Mrs. Russell," McCoy said almost apologetically. "We're looking for someone we have reason to believe your daughter knows. Remember, last time I was here I showed you a picture?"

From his breast pocket he removed the Pennegar driver's license photo and handed it to the stolid and heavy-set woman, who took it without looking at it.

"The sins of the fathers are visited on the children," she said absently, as though she were talking to herself. "That's in the Book. It's the law and it's not for us to question. But the sins of the children are visited on the parents, too. That's not the law but it's the way it is. Sometimes I think about those children of mine and the grief I feel, and I ask myself if it's fair. But it's the way of the world, Inspector. I brought them into the world and I raised them up. Lord knows, I didn't raise them to do hurt to people, not in my heart I didn't. And that's my comfort and consolation."

She raised the photograph to her eyes and studied it. "Is this the same picture you showed me before?" she asked, her voice firm again, returning to reality.

"Yes."

She nodded her head slowly, as though she understood now that she was expected to recognize the face. "It is familiar," she said at last. "It is that. I believe what I said is I have seen that man, is that what I said?"

"Yes, ma'am. You said you thought you had seen him in the neighborhood."

She nodded again. "God help me if I'm wrong in what I'm going to say, Inspector. God help me if I'm right. This man could be my grandson's father. It's a terrible thing for a woman to inform against her own. My Linda, you know, she won't have much to do with me. But she brought a man here once when she was expecting. That's maybe a year ago. It could be this is him. A mother not to know her own son-in-law, it's a shame and a pity. He looked different, he didn't smile like this, his eyes was hard eyes, like he was hurting. Mean and hurting. But Lord preserve me, it looks like him."

"We think it is him, ma'am," McCoy said.

She closed her eyes, accepting it.

McCoy asked, "And you don't know where your daughter is?"

"I wish I did."

"Do you know where she had the baby?"

"If that baby's alive and if she's alive," Mrs. Russell said, misunderstanding the question, "he's with her. She's a good mother, Inspector McCoy, there's nothing gonna come between her and her baby."

"I meant do you know where the baby was born?"

"At Mount Zion, Inspector. It's where she was born and it's where she had her baby."

Birth records at Mount Zion Hospital in San Francisco revealed that on October 5, 1970, Linda Gill gave birth to a male child who was named Jonas. According to the birth certificate on file at the San Francisco Department of Health, the child's name was Jonas Bell. The name of the child's father was Herman Bell.

California criminal records on file in Sacramento revealed that a man named Herman Bell had been arrested in Oakland in 1969.

On Thursday, November 11, Frank McCoy flew from San Francisco to New York City, bringing with him a copy of Herman Bell's Oakland arrest card, which he delivered to Bill Butler at the Thirty-second Precinct. In studying the mugshots attached to the Oakland card, Butler and McCoy realized for the first time that the unidentified man in two of the Divisadero Street surveillance photos—the man San Francisco police initially thought was two men—was also Samuel Lee Pennegar. And Pennegar was Bell, who seemed to possess an almost mystical ability to alter his features with each change of clothing or mood. Dozens of police officers in two cities had had the stake-out pictures and the driver's license picture for over a month, and not one of them had caught on to the fact that they were all pictures of the same man.

On Friday, November 12, Detective James Bannon of the latent-fingerprint section of the New York City Police Department, who by his own estimate had made "tens of thousands" of comparisons with the prints found on the fender of the Colonial Park Mustang, positively matched one of the latents with the number-six finger—the left thumb—on the Oakland fingerprint card of Herman Bell.

One hundred and seventy-five days after Joseph Piagentini died, Bill Butler knew who killed him.

• • •

In the back hills of Mississippi, the steam rises from the black soil as though the whole earth were an overheated radiator ready to boil over. Hurmon Bell started working in the cotton fields when he was six years old. He was one of ten children. His parents separated when he was very young, with the father, a man named Jethro Peel, moving to New York while the mother replaced him with another man.

In 1958, when Hurmon was ten, his father sent for him. He was put on a bus by himself for the lonely ride north. In Mississippi the boy had never attended school regularly—because he was needed on the farm, because he had no shoes, because he was ashamed of his clothes, which were poor even by sharecroppers' standards. But he was a clever child who had taught himself to read, a shy, diffident boy who masked his confusion about city life by putting on a face of bright and eager cooperativeness. His teachers invariably took a liking to him, and before long he had made up for lost time, jumping grades until he caught up with his age mates.

Even in his teens, Hurmon seems to have been two people. In a symbolic attempt to free himself from the degradation of his childhood in Mississippi, he normalized the spelling of his name and became Herman Bell. He worked hard and, with the help of a dedicated teacher, became an excellent student, although in his junior and senior years at Brooklyn's Lafayette High he let his grades slip dangerously low. As he matured physically, his skinny little boy's body filled out until he was a sturdy and well-muscled young man, only an inch under six feet, broad-shouldered and handsome, with a slightly withdrawn and enigmatic smile that would have given him an almost dreamy look if it weren't for the startling intensity that shone through his smoldering black eyes.

A report filed by one of Bell's high-school counselors notes laconically that "the transition from living on the farm to life in New York was a relatively difficult one" for him, and apparently he never did feel at home in a world in which he was outwardly succeeding as easily as if he had been born into it. A talented athlete, he played quarterback well enough to win a football scholarship to the University of California at Berkeley. Unfortunately, his poor grades during his last two years of high school kept him out of Berkeley. Bitterly disappointed, he enrolled in Laney Junior College in Oakland, hoping to establish a good enough scholastic record to enable him to transfer to Berkeley after two years.

It didn't work out that way. For reasons that aren't at all clear, Herman never applied himself at Laney. He began cutting classes in his first semester, and before long he had withdrawn from most of the courses in which he was enrolled. Apparently he was having trouble supporting himself, and it may be that at that time he came under the influence of the Black Panther Party. Ever since high school, Herman had had an intense though largely intellectual interest in the question of racial injustice, which he seems to have studied in a curiously detached way, as though it were a sociological problem that did not touch him personally.

In Oakland, though, his perspective began to shift. From the few biographical data that are available about him at this crucial time of his life, it seems almost as though the two contradictory sides of his personality came apart and then recombined with an explosive force. The lonesome, uprooted child who inwardly longed to return to the squalid farm where he was raised now looked back on his childhood in Mississippi with fear and loathing. The brightly promising boy who outwardly tried to make a place for himself in the impersonal city now saw himself as the victim of a cruel hoax. Somewhere in the depths of his mind he mentally reboarded the bus that had carried him, as a ten-year-old, from his mother's world to his father's. Only this time, when he got off that bus he hated both where he was and where he had been.

One afternoon in May 1969, Herman Bell walked into a Jack-in-the-Box restaurant in Oakland and pointed a cap pistol at a teenage girl behind the cash register who was too frightened to see that the gun wasn't real. As far as is known, it was his first crime. It netted him fifty dollars, a criminal record, and three years probation.

Two years later, in May 1971, Herman Bell committed his second crime. He came back to New York to do it, for California meant nothing to him. It was simply where he happened to have been when the dreams he had nurtured through high school fell apart. But New York was his father's city, the cold and lonely stop at the end of the bus line, the heartless, faceless city where he could revenge himself by searching out and killing a faceless victim.

Where would he go now, with the police beginning to close in on him? Perhaps he would go into hiding in San Francisco, with his wife and his year-old son. Perhaps he would retreat to his mother's world in the Mississippi hills, where he had learned about poverty and shame but hadn't yet learned to hate.

Ten

DETECTIVE OLGA FORD WAS ASSIGNED TO supervise the team of male and female detectives who shared a two-bedroom apartment in Brooklyn with Alie Horn, Celia Torres, and their small children. The two women were technically classified as material witnesses.

Celia was quiet and withdrawn, keeping to herself when she wasn't preoccupied with her month-old baby. Alie, though changed subtly as the weeks passed. Her blind hatred of cops gradually eroded from the friction of constant contact with police officers. She was sensitive and intelligent enough to appreciate the fact that the detectives guarding her treated her and her children with a courtesy and consideration that were, under the circumstances, remarkable. Her open hostility imperceptibly gave way to an almost good-natured bantering, although the most she would concede was that the cops with whom she happened to be living weren't "pigs" like the rest of them.

Occasionally, to break the monotony of confinement, the cops on duty at the apartment would take Alie, Celia, and their children to dinner and a movie. By mid-December relations had become so comfortable that the women would go out with only one guard, while the other would remain behind to babysit. The first time this was proposed, Celia seemed hesitant, apprehensive about leaving her baby. "Then sit here," Olga Ford snapped. "Look, nothing's going to happen to your kid. We've got enough hassles without that."

It wasn't exactly reassurance, but Celia had been cooped up a long time. "You'll take care of him?" she asked.

"Sure," Ford said.

But it wasn't Celia Torres's infant son who interested Detective Olga Ford. It was Alie Horn's two oldest children, a six-year-old boy and his four-and-a-half-year-old sister, whom she pumped for information every time their mother left her alone with them. Her questioning was so adroit, so carefully concealed, that the children never even suspected they were being interrogated. She would lead one of them to mention Uncle Francisco, and then get them to talk about what happened when he came home from California. She would drop a reference to Uncle Herman and then test their childish recollections. She would complain about the weather, look forward to the spring, and then subtly shift the topic back to the spring of '71.

It was a shot in the dark, but finally, a few days after New Year's, 1972, it hit the target. On a brutally cold January morning, while Detective Al McPherson escorted Celia and Alie to the supermarket, "Auntie Olga" struck up a conversation with the children about the Christmas presents they had received. The cops had bought the boy a tricycle, and Olga already knew from earlier talks that the little girl's plastic motorcycle had been new around the start of the playground season last year.

"By next Christmas you're going to need a new bike," she joked to the little girl, who was almost as tall as her older brother. "Maybe you ought to start hinting to your mamma now. Did she buy you that one?"

The little girl shook her head, suddenly too shy to speak.

"Who did? Uncle Francisco?"

The little girl nodded.

"She's fibbing, Aunt Olga, she's fibbing," her brother erupted triumphantly from the other side of the room, dancing sideways across the floor to stand directly in front of the detective. "Uncle Francisco didn't give it to her. It was Aunt Christine."

Olga hid her surprise. "Oh, she isn't fibbing," she said gently. "Maybe she just doesn't remember. Aunt Christine was here the same time Uncle Francisco was, wasn't she?"

"Yeah, but he didn't give it to her, she did."

"Well, anyway, it's a nice motorcycle," Olga said. "You know, I don't think I know Aunt Christine. Is she a friend of your mamma's?"

"No-o-o," he drawled mockingly, stretching the syllable out to dramatize how silly her question had been. "She's my aunt."

Later that night Olga managed to get Alie alone in the kitchen. "Who's Christine?"

Alie wheeled to face her as though she had been struck from behind, her small eyes momentarily wide with surprise. Instantly, she composed herself. "I don't know no Christine," she lied.

"Is she your sister?"

"None of your fucking business," Alie snapped. "You been questioning my kids?"

"I wasn't questioning them. They mentioned her."

"Pig bitch!"

"Take it easy, that's not gonna do you any good," Olga said softly. "She is your sister, isn't she?"

"Trust my kids with a pig," Alie muttered to herself in a rage. "I should have known better."

Olga Ford owed Alie Horn nothing and hadn't the slightest qualm about using Alie's children against her. Still, she had expected the rage, knew she had it coming, and let it burn itself out before she spoke. She waited a long time, then said, "They mentioned her, Alie. She was here in May. We've got to talk to her."

"She's not involved," Alie answered categorically.

Olga nodded, accepting that as a possibility. "That's for us to decide," she said. "We've got to talk to her. The easy way is for you to tell us where we can find her. The hard way is we find her ourselves."

On January 6, 1972, Olga Ford and Detective Joe Kiernan flew to Denver to question Christine Rochelle Rowe, who had been picked up by Denver police at the address her sister had given Olga. Nineteen years old, tall and beautiful with the molded features of an African princess, Christine bore not the slightest resemblance to her older sister. Like Celia Torres, she, too, had given birth to a baby in October, and she had brought the child, a sturdy infant named Malcolm, with her to the Denver police headquarters. She paced the floor holding him as she was interrogated, her lean but full-hipped body gliding about the room with a catlike sensuousness. She spoke softly, so as not to wake him. Denver authorities told Olga that Christine had expressed no surprise when they came to her door to tell her they were taking her downtown to be questioned by New York City police.

Christine Rowe's story confirmed everything Celia and Alie had said. She had come to New York from Denver early in April on Black Panther Party business. For a few weeks she stayed with her sister in an apartment on Stebbins Avenue in the Bronx. At the time she was about two months pregnant. Sometime early in May Alie went out in the afternoon with her three children and didn't come back for days. Christine was neither surprised nor alarmed. "We weren't that close," she said. "That's just the way she was."

When Alie finally returned to the Stebbins Avenue apartment, she told Christine they were moving. "And that's when we went over to stay at Celia's," Christine related.

"Did you know Celia or Gabriel Torres at the time?" Olga Ford asked.

"No, but I knew who they were. I knew Francisco in Denver, so I knew this was his brother. See, when Francisco came back from Nam he was, you know, in the Air Force and they stationed him there, at the base there, whatever it's called, I don't know the name. And that's when he met my sister and they were pretty tight. She got him into the Panthers, right? Like I was just a kid then, but I saw what was going on. They had a whole chapter at the base—some Chicanos, you know, and Puerto Ricans, it wasn't all black. What they did was they took over some buildings, like a demonstration. They had a hostage, too, a colonel I think it was, and they held him for a while, like a couple of days. And then I don't remember how it went down, but Francisco and all the others ended up in the stockade. And then he was out of the Air Force and he went to live with Alie. So that's how I knew who he was, okay?"

"Did you know a man named Albert Washington in Denver?" Joe Kiernan asked.

"No."

"They called him Noah or the Old Man."

"Yeah, I heard of him, I heard he was pretty heavy. But I didn't know him, not till we got to New York. Want me to tell you about that now?"

"However you want to tell it," Olga Ford said.

Christine picked up the story in late April, when Albert Washington arrived at the Anderson Avenue apartment. He was joined there a few days later by Francisco Torres, Tony Bottom, and Herman Bell. Christine, of course, knew Washington, Bottom, and Bell only by their "revolutionary names," but she was able to identify all three from photographs.

Washington was unquestionably the ideological leader of the group. He expounded endlessly on the theory of urban guerilla warfare. The others listened raptly, deferred to him at all times, nodded their heads as though he were a sage. Herman Bell even took notes during the indoctrination sessions and studied them as though he were preparing for an exam. For a while it looked like the group was nothing but talk. Christine found them amusing; Alie became mocking and contemptuous.

Then the Greyhound shipping office called to say that a package had arrived for Gabriel Torres. Gilbert—Christine always referred to Gabriel Torres as Gilbert—took the subway to the Port Authority bus terminal and returned a few hours later to say that the package apparently had not arrived yet. "How come they called if it ain't there yet?" Herman asked. A few days later Gilbert tried again and this time returned with a parcel wrapped in brown paper. Under the wrappings was a cigar box containing a single gun—a pearl-handled .45 automatic that Bottom claimed as his own. Herman was upset. "There's supposed to be two pieces," he growled. "Where's my piece?"

After a few minutes he calmed down and turned to Christine, who had been listening to the conversation. "So he asked me, 'Know where I can get a piece?' " Christine told the detectives. "I say, 'Yeah, I think so.' And I go next door, it's like the next building but they connect in the back. Ronnie Carter lives there and he's in the BLA too. So I ask Ronnie if I can borrow a gun and he says, yes, I could. He gives me this gun and I unload it. It's got six rounds in the chamber and he gives me an extra twenty rounds."

"What kind of gun was it?" Joe Kiernan asked.

"It was a thirty-eight. I don't know what kind, but it was a thirty-eight. With a very long barrel."

"Are you familiar with guns?"

Christine smiled broadly, remembering something. "Yeah," she said. "My grandmother taught me about guns, taught me how to shoot." She looked straight at Olga Ford and said, "That was one tough old lady. Maybe you can relate to that."

Olga nodded, returning the girl's smile, and asked her to go on.

"Okay. So I get the piece from Ronnie and I give it to Jonas."

"Herman Bell?" Kiernan asked.

"If that's his name, yeah. I knew him by Jonas. And he had it a couple of days, then he gave it back to me and I gave it back to Ronnie. Then when the thing was gonna go down I borrowed it for him again."

"By 'the thing' you mean? . . ."

"I mean when the cops got killed. That's what we're talking about, isn't it?"

She glared at Kiernan as she said it, as though she didn't like being reminded. Olga cut in quickly. "Yes, that's what we're talking about. Where is this gun now, Christine? Do you know?"

The girl paced the floor in silence for a few moments, rocking the infant she held in her arms. When she had composed herself she said, "I don't know. I guess Ronnie's got it."

"Did you return it to him after the police officers were shot?"

"No. But when we went to California after . . . after it went down, Ronnie drove us to the airport, so Herman could have given it back to him then."

She hesitated as she sought to find the lost thread of her story. "Okay, so I'm not dumb," she said at last. "I know something's going down. But like I don't know what it is, okay? After it happened, you know, I could put it in perspective and see what it was, but then all I know is something's going down. So the day before it happened—only I don't know it's the day before anything because they don't tell me what they're fixing to do—the day before it happened they borrowed this stopwatch I had."

"This what?" Kiernan asked, not sure of what she had said.

"A stopwatch. When I got pregnant a friend of mine gave it to me—you know, timing contractions and like that. It was sort of a joke. But I guess they saw me fooling around with it and they borrowed it and went out in the car."

"They had a car?"

"Yeah."

"Whose car was it?"

"I don't know. I think maybe it was rented, I don't know."

"What did they want the stopwatch for?"

"Well, they didn't say when they went out but there was some conversations when they got back. They were, like, timing lights, timing police responses and like that. They said they were surprised, it took them less time than they thought it would."

"It took them less time or it took the police less time?"

"I don't know. Like I didn't pay too much attention to what they were doing. They had their thing and I had mine."

"All right," Olga said, recognizing the girl's deep moral need to put some distance between herself and the killers. At the same time Olga realized clearly that Christine was clever enough to stake out a safe position for herself in case the police tried to charge her with complicity in the crime. "Go on, this was the day before the shooting."

"Right. So the next day what I remember is we were all in the apartment. I mean me and my sister and Celia, and there was Noah and Jonas and T.B. and T— that's Francisco, Gilbert's brother. And Gilbert, too— he lived there. And then it was getting toward dark, maybe it was dark already, like say eight or nine o'clock. T.B. and Jonas go out. See, they don't all go out together. And Noah's going out, too. He says to give T and Gilbert a message. They're in the bedroom talking. He says, 'Tell 'em I'm going to my pad to get my piece, tell 'em to get it moving.' So there's a little hall back of the living room, if you know the place. That's where the bedroom is. I go back there to give them the message and I hear them talking in the bedroom. They're talking low but they're having an argument. Not loud, though, because the kids are asleep in there. Gilbert's saying he's not ready to do whatever it is they're going to do. And T is telling him he's chickenshit. Then they come out and I tell them Noah said he went to his place to get his piece. So they split."

"Were you worried? Nervous?"

"Well, there was some, you know, tension. Not worried, but tension. Because we knew something was going down, I mean you couldn't help knowing that, right?"

She went on to describe how the five men returned, echoing the account her sister and Celia Torres had given. First Gabriel Torres and Albert Washington, out of breath; then Francisco Torres, who asked the women to turn on the television. Finally Herman Bell and Tony Bottom. In all, Christine Rowe saw five guns that night—Tony Bottom's pearl-handled .45, the long-barreled .38 she herself had borrowed for Herman

Bell, two police service revolvers, and a gun in the possession of Albert Washington. She recalled the drunken celebration that erupted when a bulletin on the eleven o'clock news confirmed the death of the second police officer. She recalled Tony Bottom acting out the murders, clowning about the agony of Joseph Piagentini.

She stopped her metronomic pacing of the tiny room in Denver Police Headquarters and fixed her eyes somewhere on the blank gray wall behind Olga Ford as though with effort she could bring herself back to apartment 2C, 1185 Anderson Avenue, on the night of May 21, 1971. "They were saying," she said, her voice coming from far away, "it was a right-on thing. They related back to some previous shootings and they said theirs was better because, you know, they killed them. Their cops died."

Her voice trailed off.

Olga asked, because she wanted to know, "Did you take part in this celebration?"

"Yes," Christine said, surprising the detective by looking straight at her when she said it.

Kiernan asked, "Did Celia Torres take part?"

Christine blinked, taken off guard by the question, which forced her to call the images back again. She answered hesitantly, as though she hadn't expected what she now saw. Suddenly she was aware of a difference between herself and Celia she had never noticed before. "Not really," she said softly. "As much as she participates in anything, I guess. She was kind of withdrawn."

"How long did the party last?" Kiernan asked.

Christine laughed contemptuously, breaking the spell, bringing herself back to the present. "It'd still be going on today if they hadn't got caught," she said.

• • •

A prosecutor's axiom says that disinterested witnesses in a case, such as innocent bystanders who happen to observe the crime, should be required to make as few formal statements as possible. Conversely, when the witness is an interested party, such as a friend, relative, or associate of the accused, it is wise to get him or her on record as much and as thoroughly as possible. As with every other aspect of trial law, the general rule is based on a balancing of advantages and risks. With a witness like Christine Rowe, the overwhelming reason for requiring her to testify before a grand jury as quickly as possible is the fear that she might rethink her position and come down somewhere else. From everything she told Olga Ford and Joe Kiernan in Denver, it was apparent that she did not sympathize with the murderous aims of the Black Liberation Army. But she was nonetheless a militant radical whose loyalties could shift mercurially.

"She's on our side right now," John Keenan told the detectives he had sent to Denver to question her. "Get her back here on the next plane out. I want to nail her down before she moves."

On January 11, 1972, Keenan reconvened the October grand jury to hear her testimony. Seated alone at the long wooden witness table in the grand jury room on the ninth floor of the Criminal Courts Building, Christine sullenly recounted the facts she had told Ford and Kiernan a few days earlier, this time addressing herself to an audience of twenty-three grand jurors who faced her in three arcing rows of banked chairs.

As Keenan proceeded through the day-long examination, he noticed that Christine's willingness to talk about events immediately surrounding the double murder was matched by a puzzling reticence about her trip to California a week or two after the killings. The topic seemed to pain her and she was at first unwilling to discuss it. Finally she said, "They knew how I felt about them. I didn't agree with their politics—if you call shooting people politics. I don't. So they made me very uncomfortable."

She emphasized the word *uncomfortable* as she said it, and Keenan sensed it was an evasion. "Why did you go with them to California if you didn't agree with their politics?" he asked.

Christine cocked her head and shrugged. "Good sense."

"What does that mean?"

"It means they killed two cops they didn't even know. They could kill me."

"Do you have any fear of that?"

"Not now," the girl answered with a tone of forceful certainty. "But it was different out there. I was making a phone call from the booth out front of the apartment. And all of a sudden Francisco slams open the door and hangs up the phone. He kind of drags me inside. I am asking him, 'What's this all about?' and he's not saying anything. But I knew, I could tell. So anyway, we get inside and they have a meeting. Francisco, Jonas, and T.B. And my sister, she was there too. They're talking about whether they should kill me, whether I'll talk. In the end I guess they figured they scared me good enough and Francisco says if I ever tell anybody about what went down in New York, they'll kill me. And my sister's there the whole time. And she doesn't say a thing, just listens while they're making up their minds to shoot me. So after that I split, went back to Denver, and had my baby."

There was no reason to keep Christine in New York after her testimony, for Keenan hadn't the slightest doubt she could be counted on to appear at the trial. Just to look at her was to know that her grand jury appearance had deeply etched itself into her psyche. She came out of it having committed herself in public, before a jury of stern, judgmental strangers, to a course from which she would not waver.

By the time Christine flew back to Denver on January 13, the case was already beginning to take shape in Keenan's mind. He divided it into three parts, calculating the strengths and weaknesses of the evidence, cataloging what the prosecution already had and what it still lacked.

First, there was the case against Washington and the Torres brothers. Although none of the evidence would show that any of them had played specific roles in the killings, the words they exchanged on returning to the Anderson Avenue apartment that night suggested they all had been at the Colonial Park murder scene on the night of May 21, 1971. For this he had the evidence of the three women, all of whom were essential. Christine was the strongest but it was still a touch-and-go thing. Unless she were convincingly corroborated by Alie Horn and Celia Torres, her credibility with a jury was at best doubtful.

Second was the case against Tony Bottom. One witness would identify him positively. He had been arrested in an attempt to shoot a police officer. In the car he was driving, the San Francisco police found Waverly Jones's service revolver and the .45 automatic that had fired four slugs into Patrolman Jones's head and spine. Stated baldly, the evidence seemed overwhelming, but even here there were problems. The defense would contend that the attempt to machine gun Sergeant Kowalski in San Francisco was irrelevant and prejudicial. They would probably win, and the trial judge would allow no reference to the incident. As for the guns, mere possession of them in California in August proved nothing. So again it came back to the credibility of Christine Rowe, who had seen Bottom take the pearl-handled .45 from a cigar box in the Torres living room. And it came back to Gloria Lapp, the only eyewitness who could identify either of the gunmen. Shy and frightened, would she be able to hold her own on the witness stand? Keenan had seen men and women with far greater inner resources crumble under cross-examination. If the jury disliked or distrusted Christine and Alie, if it was suspicious of their motives, if it had the slightest doubt about Gloria Lapp's clear-headedness on the night of the killings, how much of the case against Bottom would be left?

Finally, there was the case against Herman Bell. In Keenan's mind it was the strongest of the three, because it depended least on human variables. Herman Bell's fingerprint had been found on the fender of the white Mustang exactly where Gloria Lapp and Ruth Jennings said the killer had been sitting. That was the plus side.

Then Keenan added up the minus side. He didn't have the murder weapon—the long-barreled .38 Bell had borrowed from Ronnie Carter and probably returned to him. He didn't have the service revolver Bell had torn from the holster of the writhing cop.

And he didn't have Herman Bell.

• • •

In the early morning hours of January 18, 1972, the two policewomen guarding Celia Torres and Alie Horn were watching their third late movie of the night on the television in the living room when they were suddenly distracted by the crying of Celia's three-month-old son. Hours earlier, around midnight, Celia and Alie had withdrawn to Alie's room to talk, as they often did, late into the night.

A minute, two minutes passed and the infant's cries became more urgent. On the couch in the living room, the two policewomen eyed each other apprehensively between glances toward the door to Alie's room. An attentive, somewhat over-solicitous mother, Celia rarely let her baby cry.

"What, she fall asleep in there?" one of the policewomen grumbled rhetorically, pulling herself to her feet and crossing quickly to the closed bedroom door. She knocked once softly, then louder when there was no response. She opened the door and was hit by a blast of cold winter air from the open window on the far side of the room. Alie Horn and Celia Torres were gone.

While one of the policewomen rushed to the children's room to quiet the now screaming baby, the other phoned Olga Ford. Olga immediately notified the local precinct and all squad cars were alerted to scour the neighborhood for the two fugitive witnesses. A city-wide alarm, quickly extended to an all-points bulletin, was sent out. Finally, when all the machinery for recapturing them was in gear, Olga called John Keenan, waking him at home a few hours before sunrise.

Keenan was livid with rage. Normally a soft-spoken

man who shuns profanity, he unleashed a volley of choice expletives that summed up his spur-of-the-moment opinion of the policewomen Olga had assigned to the apartment. Yet even as he spoke, and even as Olga began her heated defense of the women under her command, the bleary-eyed prosecutor knew that the policewomen hadn't been at fault. The simple fact was that no one, himself included, had ever considered the possibility that Celia and Alie would flee without their children.

At his office in the morning, the rumpled bureau chief had to put his anger aside and plan his next move. He vowed to himself that when Alie and Celia were recaptured they wouldn't get another chance to escape. But that was in the future. The thing to do now was to make sure that he didn't lose Christine Rowe, his one remaining witness against Washington and the Torres brothers.

Before noon that day, a detective boarded a DC-7 at Kennedy Airport for the flight to Denver. He was met at the Denver airport by local police, who drove him to Christine Rowe's tiny third-floor walkup above a bodega in the Chicano section of town. The detective explained the situation to her and told her she would have to come back to New York with him.

"I told him I'd be available," Christine protested. "I ain't gonna run away."

"The others did," the detective countered.

"That's them, I'm me," Christine said. She looked her antagonist straight in the eye, her smooth dark skin flushed with anger, as though her pride were hurt by John Keenan's sudden, undeserved distrust. At such moments she could be incredibly beautiful.

"I know," the detective conceded. "But we can't take that chance. I've got orders to bring you back."

"You're not arresting me, are you?" Christine asked. "What if I won't go? I've got a choice, haven't I?"

"Yeah, you've got two choices," the detective said blandly. "You can go voluntarily or you can go involuntarily. Want me to explain how that works?"

"Don't bother," Christine said, amused by the phrase, smiling in spite of herself. "I'll go voluntarily."

Eleven

GREGORY FOSTER AND ROCCO LAURIE WERE foot patrolmen in the Ninth Precinct. On the night of January 27, 1972, their sector ran along the shabby, litter-strewn sidewalks of Avenue B below 14th Street, one of the worst sectors in one of the most sordid and drug-ridden precincts in Manhattan. Since 4:00 on a raw, damp afternoon Foster and Laurie had been patrolling their beat. The weather promised rain, snow if the temperature dropped low enough. They would have gotten off duty at midnight.

Rocco Laurie was twenty-three years old, just two years in the job and already bucking for detective. Foster was a few years older, a few years more experienced, and a shade less ambitious. They had served together in Vietnam, and much would be made of this later by newsmen bent on exploiting the sentimental angle of their story. Actually, they had known each other in the service only noddingly, for they had little in common beside the fact they were both from New York. Rocco Laurie was Italian, Gregory Foster black—just like Piagentini and Jones.

A few minutes before eleven, the patrolmen spotted

an illegally parked car on the south side of Avenue B just below 11th Street. Foster began to write it up, but his partner stopped him. The car might belong to someone in the restaurant across the street, he suggested. Crossing the avenue with Foster behind him, he stepped into the Shrimp Boat Restaurant and called out to the proprietor behind the counter, "You know who owns the car across the street?"

The owner wiped his hands on the towel at his belt and moved to the window. "Sorry," he said. There was only one customer at the counter, a young man in a navy pea coat who hadn't looked up when the cops walked in. Foster and Laurie returned to the sidewalk, the restaurant owner watching them idly from the window. They had walked north only a few strides when they were passed by three young blacks heading south. Suddenly the black men whirled simultaneously, as though the movement had been rehearsed. As they turned, they drew guns from under their coats and began firing into the backs of the departing patrolmen. They held their revolvers high, sighting down the length of their arms, which were held rigid but which lowered with each shot as their targets crumpled to the pavement. Neither of the cops had time to reach for his weapon.

As Foster and Laurie lay motionless on the sidewalk, the team of assassins moved in closer, firing steadily. The killers apparently were determined to sexually mutilate their enemy, for Patrolman Laurie was shot repeatedly in the groin after he was already down. His partner was shot three times in the eyes after he was dead.

Suddenly the firing stopped. Two of the gunmen stooped over their victims and stripped the service revolvers from their holsters, as Bottom and Bell had done at Colonial Park eight months earlier. Then they took off at a dead run, heading north up Avenue B. The third killer remained behind, dancing a jig of victory on the sidewalk, firing ecstatically into the air. Then he, too, vanished into the East Village night.

In investigating the brutal murders of Foster and Laurie, the police department had more to go on than it had had in the Piagentini-Jones case. It had, first of all, the fruits of eight months of intensive investigation into the doings of the loosely interconnected band of cross-country assassins who called themselves the Black Liberation Army. And it had nine witnesses who claimed to have seen the three killers loitering in the neighborhood as much as four hours before the shooting. Around six o'clock, the suspects had gone into a store to buy groceries, and one of them had left a satchel behind. In it detectives found a number of disassembled guns, a few dozen pamphlets of black extremist literature, and some latent fingerprints which were quickly traced to two well-known militants named Andrew Jackson and Twyman Meyers, both of whom already were wanted for questioning in connection with other terrorist activities.

At police headquarters, Chief of Detectives Albert Seedman's eagerness to break the case in a hurry led him into a serious blunder. When a cab driver came forward claiming that the third gunman had commandeered his cab at gunpoint, Seedman insisted on personally interrogating the cabbie. Breaking all the rules for securing an eyewitness identification, he threw a single photograph in front of the driver and asked if that was the man. The driver thought perhaps it was. The picture was a copy of the Oakland mugshot of Herman Bell.

A few days later, a team of Brooklyn detectives working on an unrelated case stumbled upon a real lead. Their investigation of a two-week-old shooting incident in Brooklyn led them to the apartment of a young black man named Henry "Sha-sha" Brown. Brown was gone and the couple living there, a fourteen-year-old girl called Twiggy and a man who went by the name Akbar, claimed to know nothing of his whereabouts. All they knew was that Brown rushed into the apartment about 11:30 on the night of the 27th, threw his few belongings into a suitcase, and ran out. Twiggy thought he said something about a shooting and a cop.

The Brooklyn detectives immediately forwarded this information to the chief of detectives' office at headquarters. The brass there wasn't impressed. They already had worked out their own scenario of the case and none of them had ever heard of Henry "Sha-sha" Brown. In effect, the Brooklyn detectives were told to mind their own business and leave the big cases to the pros.

The pros, though, were conducting themselves in a manner better suited for generating headlines than for generating clues. With the support of Deputy Commissioner Robert Daley, a professional writer who was then serving as Commissioner Murphy's chief of press relations, the machinery was set in motion for a press conference at which the Black Liberation Army would be painted as a nationwide conspiracy. Seedman prepared a series of poster-sized charts listing known members of the BLA and tagging them with responsibility for specific crimes all across the country. In addition, a supplementary chart gave the names and pictures of all the suspects on the individual charts along with a series of variously colored lines purporting to show that they were all in some way connected with each other. According to Deputy Commissioner Daley, "The purpose of this poster was to show how interlocking all of these crimes and all of these people were, to show without any question that these people did constitute a dreadful conspiracy." In his book *Target Blue*, Daley writes that he not only approved of the press conference but that he considered it a matter of such magnitude that it should be conducted by the commissioner himself rather than by the chief of detectives.

Half a dozen blocks south of the granite headquarters on Centre Street, District Attorney Frank Hogan learned of the planned press conference only a few hours before it was scheduled to take place. The seventy-year-old Hogan, who already had been running Manhattan's criminal justice system for four years when Patrick V. Murphy was just a rookie patrolman, immediately called John Keenan, the chief of his homicide bureau, into his office. "Get it stopped," he ordered. "If they go ahead with this, they are going to make it impossible to try these men if they are ever caught."

Hogan wasn't concerned merely with the issue of prejudicial pretrial publicity. "The Foster-Laurie investigation has been going on less than a week," he told Keenan. "They don't really know who the killers are, they haven't that kind of evidence. If they announce the names of the killers and they're wrong, we'll never be able to convict the real perpetrators when they're caught. Their lawyers are going to be able to turn the police commissioner into a defense witness and those posters are going to be defense exhibits. They'll leave the jury wondering why the men on the charts aren't the ones on trial."

What especially troubled the district attorney and the homicide bureau chief about the proposed press conference was the inclusion of Herman Bell as a suspect in the Foster-Laurie killings. The cab driver hadn't picked his picture from a group of pictures, but had identified him after being shown only a single photo—a slipshod procedure that often leads to false identifications. Hogan and Keenan thus were not convinced that Bell actually was involved in the latest terrorist killings. "When we catch up with him and try him for killing Piagentini and Jones," Hogan argued, "I don't want him coming into court and arguing that the cops were out to frame him, that they were in the habit of putting his name on the list any time a cop got shot."

As soon as Keenan returned to his own office, he placed a call to Chief of Detectives Seedman, informing him that the district attorney urgently requested that the press conference be canceled. Although, as Robert Daley writes, a request from Hogan "had always in the past seemed virtually a command," Seedman was noncommittal, merely assuring Keenan he would inform his own boss about Keenan's boss's feelings on the matter.

At police headquarters, reporters were kept waiting while the commissioner, the chief of detectives, and half a dozen top aides debated whether to go ahead with the briefing or accede to the district attorney's request. Finally, Commissioner Murphy picked up his phone and called Hogan. He told him he intended to go ahead with the conference. On his end of the line, Hogan spelled out all the arguments he had used earlier with John Keenan. Angry words were exchanged. The conversation ended with the venerable D.A., who had never before been defied by the police, slammed down the phone after informing Commissioner Murphy, "This isn't the way things are done around here."

At the press conference, Murphy tolled off the charges lettered on the posters while Deputy Commissioner Daley stood next to the easel, flipping from one chart to the next. Four men and a woman were listed as "wanted for questioning" in connection with the murders of Foster and Laurie. Four men were listed as the murderers. One of them was Ronald Carter—the same Ronnie Carter who had lent Christine Rowe the gun with which Herman Bell killed Joseph Piagentini. The second was a twenty-year-old named Ronald Anderson, also known as Floyd Brown. The third was Andrew Jackson, twenty-five years of age, also known as Harvey Mitchell or Kenneth Haynes. The fourth poster read, "Wanted for Murder, Herman Bell, male Negro 24, six feet tall, 185 pounds. Also known as Samuel Lee Penegard [sic], Herman Jonas, Herman Jethro Peel. Wanted for homicide of Patrolman Piagentini and Patrolman Jones. Wanted for homicide of Patrolman Foster and Patrolman Laurie. Wanted for bank robbery—California."

At the end of the conference, the reporters had a sensational story of a nationwide web of revolutionary antipolice terrorists. But perhaps an even bigger story was the one they didn't get—the behind-the-scenes struggle between the police department and the district attorney's office. Hogan never forgave the commissioner for his reckless and ill-considered use of the press in such a way as to jeopardize an active investigation. The police department, in turn, retaliated by seriously curtailing its normal cooperation with the D.A.'s office. Within a year, both Patrick Murphy and Albert Seedman had retired from the police department. Frank Hogan died in office in 1974, having lived long enough to see his gloomy predictions come true.

On February 14, St. Valentine's Day, a pair of St. Louis cops on routine motor patrol flagged down a maroon sedan bearing cardboard license plates. Not particularly expecting trouble from the four blacks inside the sedan, the cops nevertheless played it by the book, approaching the car cautiously, one officer moving to the driver-side window, the other hanging back on the curb.

Their caution saved their lives. Bullets thick as bees from a hive spewed from the inside of the sedan, cutting down the officer by the door but leaving his partner untouched. The wounded cop managed to squeeze off six return shots as he lay in the street with no possibility of seeking cover. His partner got off only three shots as he ran for shelter out of his attackers' restricted line of fire. The maroon sedan sped off.

From the pavement the wounded cop called to his partner, "I'm okay, call it in!" But even before the partner could reach his radio he heard the comforting sound of sirens. An undercover narcotics team in the neighborhood had heard the gunfire and responded, picking up the fleeing vehicle and giving chase less than a block from the scene of the shootout. Within minutes, four patrol units had joined in the pursuit and others lay ahead, speeding for intersect points with the constantly changing course the narcotics agents kept updating on the radio.

The driver of the maroon sedan tore through St. Louis as though it were a race course, hitting speeds approaching a hundred miles an hour, taking impossible sidewalk-to-sidewalk turns that spun out his pursuers time and time again. But always there was another police car to take up the slack, always the car that had been lost recovered itself in time to swing in at the back end of the crazed caravan. "If that bastard ain't made a deal with the devil, then he surer'n hell's scared of something," one of the cops murmured admiringly.

On and on the maroon sedan sped, its improvised course zigzagging erratically until it found itself hurtling along the Mississippi River waterfront, a long straight-away with nothing but water to its right. The narcs who had begun the chase were once again leading the pack in pursuit. "C'mon, baby, this is our chance," growled the undercover detective behind the wheel, pulling out to overtake. He asked his car to give him more than he really thought it had, but it surged forward, closing space, bringing him in on the tail of the fugitive sedan, then alongside.

The moment the driver of the maroon sedan realized he had been overtaken, his foot dropped off the accelerator and he spun the wheel into a hard left, sending his car skidding around behind the narcs, in front of the next pursuer, who lost control as he fought to avoid a collision.

Like a skater on ice, the maroon sedan slid sideways

across the boulevard, turned completely around, and hopped the sidewalk, coming to rest against a chain-link fence bordering a rubble-strewn vacant lot, all four tires blown, the engine dead. As the police closed in on the crippled vehicle, they were driven to cover by a rain of gunfire from inside the car. Then three men leaped out of the car and scrambled for the fence, one of them returning police fire so effectively that his two companions were able to make it over the fence and into the lot. Left alone on the near side of the fence, the third man dropped his gun and raised his hands to surrender.

Half a dozen cops moved in on him and on the car, while others fanned out to seal off the sides of the empty lot. The man at the fence was handcuffed and thrown into a cruiser. In the back seat of the maroon sedan the police found the body of a young black man, dead of a bullet wound in the chest. He had been shot by accident near the end of the chase when his companions opened fire at the cops from inside the car, one of their own bullets catching him exactly on the left nipple.

Of the two men who made it over the fence, the St. Louis police managed to apprehend only one. He was unarmed when they caught up with him a block and a half away, blood pouring from a wound in his wrist. He had discarded his gun, but a team of patrolmen followed the trail of blood back until they found it in a bush at a corner of the lot.

Miraculously, the fourth man in the car managed to get away. Fingerprints lifted from inside the maroon sedan identified him as Twyman Meyers, who had also left his prints in the satchel abandoned by Foster's and Laurie's killers.

The man arrested at the chain-link fence was Thomas "Blood" McCreary, a name new to the cops working on the Black Liberation Army. The injured man who almost got away was the same Henry Sha-sha Brown whose name Brooklyn detectives had forwarded to Chief Seedman. The gun he threw away in the empty lot turned out to be a .38-caliber Smith & Wesson that only three weeks earlier had belonged to New York City Patrolman Rocco Laurie.

The dead man in the back seat was identified as Ronald Carter. Ballistics tests showed that Carter had been shot by the gun Sha-sha Brown tried to get rid of.

If Ronnie Carter was indeed one of the gunmen in the Foster-Laurie case, his death robbed the criminal justice system of a chance to prove it. But back in New York, when the story came in, not many cops felt cheated. There are times where death seems hardly justice enough, but who could quibble with a Providence that worked things out so that Rocco Laurie's killer was executed by Rocco Laurie's gun?

In the passenger compartment and the trunk of the maroon sedan, St. Louis police found a high-powered Belgian rifle with a telescopic sight, two .30-caliber carbines, a Remington 30.06 carbine, a .44 Magnum carbine, an automatic rifle, and three handguns—a 9-millimeter Browning automatic, a .357 Magnum Colt, and a Colt .38. They also found hundreds of rounds of ammunition for the miscellaneous assortment of weapons.

In New York, Bill Butler was particularly interested in the Colt .38. It was only a long shot, but he hoped it would prove to be the gun Carter had lent to Bell on

May 20, 1971. For a day and a half, Butler waited nervously for the results of the St. Louis tests.

They came back negative. The gun that killed Joe Piagentini had not been in Carter's possession when he died. The news came as a bitter shock, not only because hopes had run so high, but because suddenly the investigation, which had started so slowly and then made so much progress between August and November, now seemed to be running sickeningly backward. First there was the disappearance of two key witnesses, the continuing inability to locate Herman Bell, and now the loss of the last realistic chance of ever finding the second murder weapon.

And thus matters stood as winter mellowed into spring. March and April passed, then May, taking with it the first anniversary of the deaths of Patrolmen Jones and Piagentini. Summer came. In July, Policewoman Gertrude Mitchell, riding in her own car on Harlem's Lenox Avenue, spotted Celia Torres and Alie Horn as they came out of a bodega carrying small bundles of groceries. In December Mitchell had spent a dozen nights guarding the two women in their Brooklyn apartment. She pulled to the curb at a pay phone and called for backup, careful to keep the women in sight as she did. When she had followed them on foot less than two blocks, she was joined on the sidewalk by four uniformed officers.

With her hand on the gun she carried in her shoulder bag, Mitchell quickened her pace, the patrolmen barely a step behind her, two on each side. When she was only a few feet behind the girls, she called their names and they turned to find themselves staring into the barrels of five revolvers. Policewoman Mitchell informed them they were under arrest and snapped on handcuffs just as a carload of detectives spilled onto the scene.

Under questioning, Alie and Celia denied that their escape had been in any way abetted by the Black Liberation Army. They said they had gone to Ohio and had come back only because they were hoping to reestablish contact with their children. Celia's infant son was being raised by his grandmother, Gabriel Torres's mother; Alie's three children had been put in a foster home. Their only reason for fleeing, the girls said, was that they had been going stircrazy cooped up in an apartment with cops all the time.

"Well, that's something you won't have to worry about now," John Keenan snapped in response. Alie and Celia were brought before a judge, who was presented with an application naming both women as material witnesses in the Colonial Park homicides. They were remanded to civil jail, where they were told they would remain until the case came to trial.

Time passed slowly, drawn out torturously by an incredible array of delaying motions filed by the defense. August, September, October. It was fall and winter, then spring again. Now Piagentini and Jones had been dead two years and still their killers had not been brought to trial.

Each month, for thirteen months, Alie Horn and Celia Torres were taken from their cells in civil jail and brought to court, where a judge renewed their status of material witnesses for another month. Angry and bitter about being imprisoned, they refused to talk to Keenan or any other member of the prosecution team.

As the summer of 1973 wound down and the seemingly endless string of defense delays began to play itself out, the prospect of going to trial with a pair of implacably hostile prosecution witnesses began to loom as a nightmare.

Then, suddenly, it wasn't John Keenan's nightmare any more. Earlier in the year the Queens county district attorney had been removed from office under indictment. During the summer Michael W. Armstrong, who had been appointed by Governor Nelson Rockefeller to fill out the unexpired term, asked John Keenan to come over to Queens to help rebuild a demoralized and badly shaken staff. Keenan accepted, and, less than six weeks before the trial was to start, the Piagentini-Jones case needed a new prosecutor.

PART THREE
On Trial

Twelve

I WAS JUST COMING OFF TWO MAJOR TRIALS involving brutal murders. In the first one, one of Joey Gallo's bodyguards had summarily executed the floor manager inside the Broadway Pub, a bar next door to the Peppermint Lounge. The other trial involved the alleged head of the Colombo crime family. I was feeling pretty cocky and had myself convinced that the two cases I had won were about as difficult as trials can get. In short, I felt I was ready for anything.

Then, on August 10, District Attorney Hogan called me into his office and told me I was taking over the Piagentini-Jones case. A few minutes later a young assistant D.A. who had worked with Keenan knocked on my door and asked if I wanted him to bring me the files. Sure, I said, expecting him to hand me something. He stepped out of the office and returned shortly with a large carton filled with documents, which he set on the floor. Then he went back for another. And another. And another. When they were all in place, I had to commandeer two file cabinets to hold them.

I spent the better part of the afternoon just familiarizing myself with the labels on the individual file folders. Inside those folders, I slowly realized, was the written record of literally hundreds of thousands of man-hours of work. Two-and-a-half years' worth of rage and agony and frustration, of fatigue, despair, and elation had been palely copied onto those pages. For a layman unfamiliar with case reports and investigative summaries, they would make dull reading, a seemingly infinite succession of meaningless details, with no connections between them and no apparent direction, the triumphs recorded in the same laconic prose that dutifully logged all the dead-end defeats.

But I had been around long enough to be able to read the story hiding in those thousands upon thousands of pages of official documents. Just as a musician hears violins and cellos in his mind when he reads a score, I became able, gradually at first and then with increasing clarity, to see the faces, to hear the voices, to feel the anguish and passion of the cops, the witnesses, the killers themselves.

I remember one sheet of paper in particular, an official police department form set up in tabular arrangement with columns for Make of Weapon, Serial Number, Test Slug Number, Evidence Slug Identification, and Determination. The top of the page was datelined San Francisco, the bottom signed by Detective George Simmons, his signature followed by his shield number. Noted on the page were a series of comparisons, only the essential facts recorded, no indication of whose guns these were, where they had been found, where the evidence slugs had come from. Yet, if one possessed the key to the code, even the simple identification numbers of the evidence slugs told an agonizing story. Scratched into the casing of one of the slugs used in those tests was the marking JR/4. J for Jones, Waverly Jones, dead at the age of thirty-two; R for Rho, Dr. Young-Myun Rho, who had performed the autopsy on the dead police officer; 4 because it was the fourth bullet Dr. Rho removed from Waverly Jones's body, the one that lodged in his brain.

Reading down the last column, the column that recorded the findings, one saw only a sequence of single-word notations—negative, negative, negative, positive, negative, negative. *Positive*. No more than that. Later, Bill Butler would tell me how he had been standing over George Simmons's shoulder at that moment and how the room had suddenly fallen silent. Tears had come to his eyes and a curse to his lips and a San Francisco lab man he had never met before whispered his congratulations so softly that neither Bill nor Simmons could be quite sure he had heard it. All this was on that form, invisible behind the callous sequence of typewritten words and numbers.

I studied the files until I was familiar enough with them to feel confident of my own evaluation of the material. As moved as I had been by the account of the investigation, I could not help but feel somewhat appalled by what had become of the case. In the first place, the investigation had come to a dead stop, even though one of the killers was at large and a valuable piece of evidence was missing. To be sure, detectives were still putting in their time, and the special phone numbers the police department had set up a few days after the killings were still in service. But ever since January 1972, when Joe Kiernan and Olga Ford first questioned Christine Rowe in Denver, not one new lead had been developed, not one new piece of evidence uncovered. Twenty months of absolutely nothing.

What was more I was shocked to learn that Celia Torres and Alexandra Horn had been locked in civil jail for thirteen months. In some of my previous cases I had had occasion to jail witnesses I was afraid might disappear before trial, but never for more than a week or two. Yet here were two girls well into their second year of imprisonment. Although I could understand why John Keenan wanted to lock them up after they escaped from his police guards, I still felt it was an unconscionable situation that couldn't be justified even on coldly pragmatic grounds. From some of Keenan's assistants I learned that the women had been refusing to talk to anyone about the case for months. By this point, what they would say when they were put on the stand was anybody's guess.

Before I could make another move on the case, I knew I had to get Horn and Torres out of jail and reunited with their children. I sent a pair of police officers to the civil jail to get them and bring them to my office. When they were brought in, I introduced myself and asked them to sit down. Celia moved obediently to the chair I indicated, but Alexandra stood her ground defiantly. "How come we gotta take bullshit from a new guy?" she asked. "We're already used to the bullshit that other turkey was handing out."

"No bull," I said. "Mr. Keenan is not with this office any more. I'm taking over the case. I brought you down here for just one reason. I wanted to meet you and I wanted to tell you I'm going to get you out of jail. We'll arrange something."

Alexandra's eyes went toward the ceiling, a look of

disgust and disbelief. "Forget it, man," she said. "Whatever you want, forget it. We're not falling for any more promises."

I looked straight at her and waited for her to look at me. A physically imposing woman, five-nine or -ten, with a powerful body and an intimidating amount of self-possession, she could be a very difficult person to deal with. It was a comfort to realize I had a good six inches in height on her, because she was used to getting by on the psychological advantage her size gave her. When her eyes met mine I said, "I'm not asking you for anything. I'm not making any promises. I'm just telling you what's going to happen."

There was a long silence, and I could see she was trying to figure me out. She was smart enough to realize she was in jail of her own doing, having forced Keenan's hand by her escape. Still, she couldn't help resenting the treatment she was getting. Imprisoned by the people she had consented to help with her testimony, she felt betrayed and had become mistrustful. She was looking for someone she could trust and I could see in her eyes that she was willing to give me a chance.

"If you want to talk now," I said, "we can talk. If you want to wait till I get you set up somewhere, that's fine with me."

Alie nodded and pursed her lips. "Let's see what happens," she said.

I turned to Celia and made her the same offer. She answered in exactly the words Alie had used, "Let's see what happens." I thanked them, told them I would be in touch with them in a matter of days, and sent for the police officers who would escort them back to jail.

As soon as they were gone, I began to make arrangements for freeing them. Detectives were sent to secure a suitable apartment, lawyers in the office were assigned to draw up the necessary court papers, and police headquarters was asked to draw up a duty roster for teams of around-the-clock guards. I made it clear that I expected results before the end of the week.

The next job on the agenda was to pick the team that would assist me on the case. I already had made up my mind I wanted only one assistant D.A. working with me. Some prosecutors in the office had used as many as half a dozen trial assistants on some big cases, but in my experience too much help is often worse than none at all. Whenever responsibilities get divided, there are bound to be some blanks, some bases left uncovered. If I could get the right man, and if he was willing to work his tail off and learn the case as thoroughly as I intended to learn it, we could handle everything ourselves.

I sent for the dossiers of every lawyer in the office. First I eliminated all those who were tied up with impending cases from which they couldn't be removed. Then I eliminated all those who had worked on this case under Keenan. They had been on it too long, I felt, and couldn't approach it with the freshness I wanted. I was willing to sacrifice their knowledge of the intricacies of the case for the less tangible advantages of a new approach.

In the end, I was left with dozens of names. I was particularly impressed with the file of a young man who had just been moved over to the homicide bureau from the supreme court felony trial bureau only the week before. His name was Kenneth Klein, and although he was twenty-five years old he was only a few months out of

Columbia University Law School, having lost two years to Vietnam when the army drafted him out of law school. He had been wounded in battle, a mortar fragment through the hip, and had returned to the front just two weeks after he was hit. He had won decorations for valor in addition to his Purple Heart and had been promoted to sergeant in the field. I figured that whatever pressure this trial was going to put on him, he would be able to stand up to it. I also liked the way he had been able to come back from the war and pick up the pieces of his life.

I sent for him, and the moment he came into my office I knew I had my man. He had thick curly hair, which he wore in the style we jokingly called a Jewfro. If he seemed a trifle cocky and self-assured, I had his military record in front of me to testify that he could also follow orders and do what was asked of him. We hit it off so perfectly that I didn't bother to tell him I was conducting interviews. After we had talked for half an hour, I simply informed him I was assigning him to assist me on the Piagentini-Jones case. He said he had been hoping that was why I had wanted to see him.

With the legal half of the prosecution team now set, the next step was to do something about the police half. A lot of cops had dedicated themselves to this case for an incredibly long time, and not one of them had worked on it any harder or any better than Bill Butler. He and the dozens of other detectives who worked with him had done a remarkable job, struggling all the way against almost impossible odds. They started with two dead bodies, no clues, and no motive. Now they had four of the five men charged with the murders in custody and the fifth positively identified.

Unfortunately, that wasn't the whole story. For the past twenty months the police had been banging their heads against a solid wall without learning anything new about what was on the other side. To make matters worse, communications between the police department and the district attorney's office had broken down after Frank Hogan's showdown with Commissioner Murphy over the press conference that followed the Foster-Laurie killings in January 1972. Neither side was telling the other what it was doing.

By the late summer of 1973, Murphy was no longer the commissioner and it no longer mattered who had started the quarrel or who had been at fault. What did matter was that there had been a devastating rupture in the system. It was my hope that I could turn the situation around by bringing in some new faces. And I wanted some of those faces to be black. Why? Because the killers were black, because the witnesses with whom they lived were black, because at that very moment Herman Bell was undoubtedly in the company of black radicals who hated white men and white authority as intensely as he did. I knew there was a possibility that the witnesses knew more than they had yet divulged, and that a black detective might stand a better change of winning their confidence. I knew that if some of Bell's associates could be found, a black cop would have an advantage in interrogating them.

The idea of choosing the detective to head up the investigation on the basis of color would have made me uncomfortable under any circumstances. But, given the nature of the crime, the question became all the more agonizing, for it seemed to me as though the killers were forcing me to play their racist game. How could I, in all conscience, pass over one man for another because of his race when every drop of blood that gushed from Waverly Jones and Joseph Piagentini testified to the depraved consequences of such thinking?

In the end, though, the delicate scales on which my decision hung were tipped by two men. The first was Clifford A. Fenton, Jr., a square-built, powerful, seventeen-year veteran detective with a wheezing laugh like a car starting on a cold morning. Over the years I had worked with Cliff on dozens of cases. He was a black man and he was in my opinion beyond any doubt the best detective in the New York City Police Department.

The second was Bill Butler. I didn't know how he'd take having another man put over him on the case. I was afraid he'd resent it, and it bothered me deeply to have to do anything to hurt a man who had poured his heart and life and soul into the case for almost two and a half years now, who had brought the investigation four-fifths of the way home and was just one arrest from ending it. As I searched my mind for ways to explain it to him, I couldn't help wondering whether he was aware that he already had gone as far as he could. I intended to tell him it was the ninth inning, he had pitched a brilliant game and got us there with a slim lead, and it was time now to go to the bullpen.

When I called Bill into my office to talk to him, I realized he wasn't a man for fancy metaphors. There was no need to sugar coat what I had to tell him. Instead of a lot of gibberish about starting pitchers and relief pitchers, I told him straight out what I was thinking. I explained to him that I wanted him to stay on the case but that from here on in I thought a black detective should be calling the shots. I talked for a long time, spelling out my reasons as carefully as I could, feeling sheepish and perhaps even a little ashamed.

Bill sat opposite my desk, listening expressionlessly without interrupting. When I finished talking I asked him what he thought, and for what seemed a long time he didn't answer. In the terrible silence I could hear all the things he might have said. He could have told me a district attorney can't make choices in terms of black and white, and I would have had to agree with him. He could have told me he wouldn't stay on under those terms, and I would have had to back down. He could have told me the case was his and he had earned the right to see it through to the end, and I wouldn't have been able to argue. Or he could have told me to go to hell.

But Bill Butler was a team player, as unselfish as he was dedicated. How many of those things he was thinking I have no way of knowing, but what matters is that he said none of them. He looked at me steadily across the pool of yellow summer sunshine that spilled into my office and asked quietly, "Who are you thinking of?"

"Cliff Fenton," I said.

"Cliff's a good man," Bill said, closing the discussion for good. "You couldn't do better."

The voice at the other end of the line spoke with the pleasant, indolent drawl of the deep South. "Mistuh Tane'baum, this is Detective L. J. Delsa of the N'Awlins Police Department," it said. "We have a pack of bank robbers in custody may be of some interest to you. From all we can tell down here, they look like a bunch of Black Liberation Army types. Figure they're the kind of folks you might want to talk to about your ho-micide."

I took the names of the arrested suspects from Detective Delsa. Of course, Herman Bell wasn't one of them, for if he had been, Delsa would have said so at once. Every police department in the country knew we were looking for him and had known it since May, when John Keenan had finally succeeded in cajoling the FBI into putting him on its Ten Most Wanted List—a small triumph we were all later to regret. I thanked Delsa for calling and told him I would be back in touch as soon as I had made arrangements to send someone to interrogate his prisoners. He seemed surprised. "I don't know how you fellas do things up there," he said cryptically, "but I figured this was something you ought to be on top of."

The New Orleans detective's puzzling remark became clear to me a few minutes later when I called Cliff Fenton and Bill Butler to my office, intending to put them on the next plane to Louisiana. Cliff's eyes lit up when I told the news. Less than two weeks on the case, he was thinking, and already we had something that could turn into a big break. He virtually leaped from his chair, ready to head for the airport. But Bill's reaction wasn't what I had expected at all.

"Uh, look, Bob, we, uh, there's, . . ." he stammered. "We already got a cop down there."

I knew I hadn't misunderstood him, but I could hardly believe what I was hearing. "What!" I shouted.

"Tommie Lyons," he said meekly. "New Orleans called a couple days ago so we sent him right down."

I didn't even ask who sent him. "What the hell's going on here?" I demanded angrily. "Why wasn't I told? Don't you people know we've got a murder trial on the calendar in a couple of weeks?"

"I figured you knew," Bill said. "I figured Cliff'd tell you."

"Me?" Fenton retorted. "This is the first I hear of it."

I could see clearly what had happened. Someone in the upper reaches of the police department was trying to pull a fast one on the district attorney's office. Only a few days after he put me in charge of the Piagentini-Jones case, District Attorney Hogan had been taken ill. He was still in the hospital. Some potentate at headquarters with a petty mind and an appalling lack of perspective probably figured he could take advantage of Hogan's absence to give the police totally unprecedented control over a case that was only a few weeks shy of the trial date. I was willing to give Butler the benefit of the doubt, for he had in fact no reason to assume I had not been notified. And Fenton, I am sure, had been purposefully kept in the dark as a punishment for his special status as the D.A.'s hand-picked cop.

"I don't blame either of you for what happened," I said, in a tone that must have left a considerable doubt in their minds as to whether they were being blamed. "But I'm going to say this once, and I want you to get the word back to every cop working on the case. This shit stops here. Anything happens, I've got to know about it before it happens."

Both detectives mumbled vague assurances that there would be no repetition of the incident. Cliff said, "I guess if Tommie's already got it covered you don't need us to go any more."

I laughed. "It's not covered until *I* send someone to cover it," I said. "You're going."

"Both of us?"

"All three of us," I corrected. "If there's still any question about who's running this show, the commissioner can come down to New Orleans and I'll explain it to him."

L. J. Delsa met us at the New Orleans airport and drove us to police headquarters, a large, streamlined building in a disappointingly modernized section of downtown not far from where the grossly oversized skeleton of the still incomplete Superdome rose above acres of rubble.

"Welcome aboard," Delsa said in his dry, sardonic style. "You folks are just about the last ones up the gangplank. We got a full crew, the ship almost sailed without you."

He was a heavy-set man, strong in the shoulders but soft around the middle, with a benign-looking round face and a droopy mustache. Lawmen, he explained, had been converging on New Orleans in record numbers since the arrests four days earlier. "We got everyone here but the marines," he said, "and I reckon they'll probably be stopping by next week. We got Los Angeles P.D., San Francisco P.D., New York P.D., now you guys, and enough FBI to solve the riddle of creation."

The arrests, he explained, had been the result of a month-and-a-half investigation into a string of vicious bank robberies in the area, a few of them involving wanton shootings of bank personnel. Through bank photos, surveillance, and extremely heavy pressure on informants, the New Orleans Police Department had been able to identify and locate a dozen perpetrators from a coordinated ring that seemed to involve eighteen to twenty young black men. On August 25 they staged a massive roundup that netted twelve suspects, an immense arsenal of weapons, and boxes of extremist black-militant literature, most of it relating to the Black Liberation Army. "That's what set us thinking," Delsa said. "We knew we had ourselves a fair-size chunk of the BLA fund-raising operation. So we just started calling around, letting folks know what we got. Figured there's gotta be a lot of people want to ask these dudes a lot of questions. But I never figured we'd get a turnout like this."

"We've got four dead cops in New York," I said.

"I know," Delsa answered, his voice suddenly hard and deep, as though a different man were speaking. "If they shot a cop in New York, then they shot a cop in New Orleans. Any help you guys need you got."

We rode in silence for a few minutes. Cliff and Bill were clearly moved by Delsa's words. Their silence was their way of expressing their gratitude, an acknowledgment any cop would understand. As we pulled into the parking lot behind headquarters, Bill asked Delsa, "Who's here from San Francisco?"

"Big fella name of McCoy. You know him?"

"I know him," Butler answered warmly. "He put the whole thing together for us."

Inside, introductions alone took almost half an hour. For Bill Butler and Frank McCoy it was like a reunion. A real closeness had developed between them in San Francisco, and they peeled off from the rest of the group to exchange notes on the case and bring each other up to date on their personal lives.

My first priority was to get Tommie Lyons alone in a

room where I could explain to him a few elementary facts of life the police department seemed to have forgotten. I chewed him out pretty thoroughly, mostly for the record, to establish that the district attorney's office would not tolerate being relegated to the status of a poor relation. Tommie, of course, was not personally responsible for the situation that had developed, and I realized I wasn't being fair in treating him as though he were. But there were things I wanted to get off my chest once and for all, and Tommie seemed the most eligible target, even though he was, under normal circumstances, one of the ablest and most cooperative cops I have ever worked with.

While I was getting all that out of my system, Cliff Fenton figured it was time to get down to work. He decided it would be a good idea to start interrogating someone, and he asked a bunch of the New Orleans cops to nominate the most likely candidate. The consensus was that the best place to start was with Lester Bertram May, a saucer-eyed eighteen-year-old who had given everyone who questioned him the impression that he was just one interrogation sessions short of making some important disclosures.

Cliff was especially interested in May because of the prisoner's documented connection with two of the men under indictment for the Piagentini-Jones killings. When Albert Washington was arrested by the Salt Lake City police in January 1971, May had been in the car with him, along with Francisco Torres.

Cliff spent over an hour closeted with May in a small room in the prison adjoining headquarters. He returned convinced that May knew quite a bit about the Colonial

Park killings and could be made to talk if the right kind of pressure were applied. "You can't squeeze him hard," Cliff advised, "because he'll fight you all the way. He'll be as tough as he has to be. We could put his nuts in a wringer and we wouldn't get anything out of him. But if we lay back, I promise you he'll tell us something."

That was exactly what I wanted to hear. From the New Orleans detectives I already had learned that Herman Bell had been in New Orleans as recently as the latest bank robbery, only a few days before the arrests. Somehow he had escaped the roundup, and although it was possible he had fled when his associates were arrested, the chance that he was hiding somewhere in the vicinity was something I felt we had to investigate. I was in no position to authorize New York detectives to engage in a manhunt in Louisiana, but as long as the interrogations of the BLA bank robbers gave us a legitimate pretext for being there, Butler, Fenton, and Lyons could use their "spare time" to take part in the search.

The afternoon had long since worn into evening. A couple of New Orleans detectives took up a collection and sent out for sandwiches. We sat around the spacious squad room, FBI agents and cops from all over the country, pooling information and swapping hunches as we ate. Pictures of Herman Bell were on every desk, and it seemed to me that at any given moment one detective or another was holding a copy of the photo in his hand and staring at it, as though concentrating hard enough on Bell's features would bring the man himself into view. Occasionally, local cops not connected with the case would wander into the room, drawn by a natural curiosity to see what all the commotion was about. One of these, a young, black, uniformed officer, leaned over someone's shoulder to look at the picture of the man who had drawn so much attention.

"Hey," he said casually, "I know that dude."

The silence in the room was suddenly deafening, and I remember noticing there were no street noises coming from outside. It was as though for a moment all of New Orleans had stopped moving.

Then, as abruptly as the silence had come, the room erupted with shouts and movement. Everyone converged on the young patrolman, barraging him with questions. He seemed stunned and confused, unable to answer anyone. Where'd you see him? How do you know him? Who is he? Try to remember, try to remember, try to remember. The poor young man, barely in his twenties, could no more than mumble apologetically, "I don't know, man. I just can't think. But I know I've seen him somewhere."

His confusion only frustrated his questioners, who grew more angry and demanding, driving the situation toward hopelessness. I stood helplessly to the side, not knowing what to do. Then Cliff Fenton shouldered his way through the crowd until he was face to face with the boyish patrolman, who by this point looked like he was ready to cry. "All right, everybody shut up!" Cliff barked in a voice that commanded instant obedience.

He took the young patrolman by the arm and led him through the crowd to an empty corner of the squad room. Delsa and two other detectives followed at a safe distance, hanging back a few desks away.

"Okay," Cliff said, speaking softly and reassuringly. "I know it's confusing when everyone jumps on you like that. I want you to try and relax, don't think about anything. Just close your eyes and try and picture the guy."

"I can't."

"Try. You can."

The patrolman closed his eyes.

"Now just get a picture of him in your mind," Cliff urged, his voice low, like a hypnotist's. "Try and see his face. And his body. Try and see what he was wearing. It'll come to you. You'll start to see his face and then the rest of him and then where he was. Don't rush it."

The young patrolman held his eyes closed. Even from across the room we could all see the muscles under his face working. He opened his eyes and looked at Cliff pathetically. "It's no good," he whined.

Cliff pondered his next move for an instant, then sprang into action. "Now watch me," he said brightly. "Let's try to build up a picture of this dude. How'd he walk? Was it like this?" As he spoke, he started to parade between the desks in an exaggerated bopping stride, springing from the balls of his feet with each step, knees bent, arms swinging loosely. He stopped ten feet from the patrolman and pivoted on his heels to face him, his head bobbing as he turned. "That him, man?" he asked, still in the spirit of his supercool impersonation.

A broad smile creased the patrolman's face. He looked like a fretting child who is being made to laugh in spite of himself, who fights it but laughs anyway. "No," he said lightly. "That's gotta be someone else."

"Well, try this," Cliff said, striding back toward the patrolman in an entirely different gait.

The patrolman stopped him before he had taken two steps. "Hold it, hold it," he said urgently. "I got it now. He wasn't moving. It wasn't him I seen, it was his picture."

From across the room a dozen voices groaned in disappointment. "Of course you seen his picture, turkey," someone shouted cruelly. "He's on the ten most fucking wanted list. His picture's all over the goddamn place."

The patrolman looked in the direction the taunt had come from. "That ain't it," he answered defiantly, his confidence restored. "I never look at those anyway. This was a picture my old lady got, a picture of us. We was at a bar and her girlfriend took our picture. And there's this cat at the next table you can see better'n you can see us. That's him, I swear it is."

Delsa said, "Can you get us that picture?"

"Gee, no, I can't," the young man said. "We split up."

"She's not gonna shoot you if you go see her, is she?" Delsa snapped.

Someone else asked, "Do you want us to send someone for it?"

"No," the patrolman answered quickly. "She wouldn't like that. I'll give it a try, but this ain't gonna be no fun."

He strode across the squad room and out the door, accompanied by a chorus of encouraging shouts. By this time, I think, most of the cops in the room had come to regard the whole incident as a joke. One of the New Orleans detectives waved a ten-dollar bill and offered five-to-one odds the kid wouldn't come back with a picture of Herman Bell. He couldn't get any takers.

Still, no one left, as though we couldn't call it a night until the patrolman returned. "That boy's not wrapped too tight," someone suggested, and everyone laughed.

About an hour and a half later the young patrolman, whose name I never learned, had the last laugh. He pushed through the door to the squad room and let it swing closed behind him, for all the world like Duke Wayne making a big entrance in a tavern full of bad guys. He held the pose a moment, then sashayed across the room to where Delsa was sitting. From the inside pocket of his uniform tunic he drew a Polaroid snapshot, which he slapped down on the desk. "Had to steal it," he said. "She's gonna kill me when she finds out it's gone."

Delsa glanced down at the photograph. "Holy Mother of Jesus!" he gasped.

The picture passed quickly from hand to hand. I grabbed for it and managed to study it a few seconds before surrendering it to the next man. The scene was a simple barroom, nothing fancy. In the left foreground sat the young patrolman, dressed for a night on the town. He had his arm around a pretty, slender girl with a flower in her hair. The other two seats at the couple's table were unoccupied. At the next table, almost in the center of the badly aimed picture—badly aimed! for us, it was a miracle—sat Herman Bell, facing almost directly into the camera, his head tilted slightly upward as he looked into the eyes of the leggy, shortskirted waitress who bent over him serving a mug of beer. His arm was round her waist, his hand resting on her hip. Her large, rounded breasts seemed almost to be brushing his cheek.

"Let's check out that waitress," Cliff Fenton suggested. "She seems to be pretty chummy with him."

Bill Butler volunteered to go with him, but it was out of the question. "There's not a white face in that place," Delsa pointed out. "They'd know you were cops."

Delsa assigned Horace Lukes, a black New Orleans detective, to accompany Fenton. Cliff stood and reached for the picture, which he wanted to take with him to make sure he got the right woman, although she didn't look like she would be easy to forget. He waited with his hand outstretched while the photograph continued to circulate among those who hadn't seen it yet. When it reached Frank McCoy, the San Francisco inspector studied it for a long time.

"I'll tell you why they're so chummy," he said, handing the picture back to Cliff. "That waitress is his wife. That's Linda Gill."

The Round Robin Bar and Grille was a large neighborhood gin mill in a predominantly black section of downtown New Orleans. The patrons seemed to be almost all regulars, but Cliff Fenton and Horace Lukes managed to fit in comfortably, socializing easily with the obese bartender and the well-dressed old man on the stool next to Lukes. Cliff sat at the last stool before the waitress station, where he could flirt amiably with the girls and get to know them without asking any questions that would tip them off that he was looking for Linda Gill. He and Lukes planned to give it a night or two, playing it laid back, just waiting to see what turned up. They didn't want to take the chance someone would call Linda to warn her the cops had been asking around after her.

Shortly after midnight, a waitress they somehow hadn't seen before came to the station to pick up a round of mixed drinks. A light-skinned girl, slender and shapely, with the delicate features of a black fashion model, she bore enough resemblance to Linda Gill to get both detectives staring at her. "Where you been all night?" Cliff bantered. "Pretty girl like you oughta come around here more often."

She smiled warmly, her lips soft and friendly. "Keeping busy, handsome," she said, stretching up one foot to reach a handful of swizzle sticks in a glass on the counter behind the bar, her skirt rising to the tops of her thighs, her breasts caressing the surface of the bar provocatively.

"I'd offer to help," Cliff said, "but you look so good when you do that."

She slid back to the floor and stabbed the swizzle sticks into the drinks on her tray. "Don't get carried away, honey," she teased lightly. "We don't close till three."

She pivoted neatly on her high heels and slid past the first bank of tables, her tray held high, her hips swinging easily as she threaded her way toward a tableful of kids dressed for somewhere else.

Cliff watched her go until she seemed to disappear in the large, smoky room. He turned on the barstool to face Lukes, the joviality gone from his face, which was suddenly all business. "Was that her?" he whispered urgently.

Lukes shook his head uncertainly. "Damn," he muttered. "I don't know, man. Looks like her. What d'ya think?"

"Wait here," Cliff said. He slid from the stool and headed for the men's room behind the elbow of the bar. He stepped into an unoccupied stall, closed the door behind him, and took the Polaroid snapshot from his pocket. His plan if he found Linda Gill was to tail her wherever she led him. But he didn't want to tail the wrong girl.

He closed his eyes to bring back the face and body of the waitress he had just seen, then opened them to examine the photograph. It was the dumbest kind of dumb luck. They looked enough alike to be sisters. It had to be her. Can't be two chicks in the same place look that much alike, he told himself. But it wasn't quite a perfect match. Linda Gill had darker skin and better legs. Maybe the lighting when the picture was taken made her look dark, maybe working on her feet so much hadn't done her legs any good. He couldn't be sure.

He palmed the picture in his big, meaty hand, flushed the toilet, and strolled back to the bar. "See what you think," he said softly to Lukes, slipping the photo into his hand like a pickpocket passing the goods. He climbed onto a barstool and Lukes climbed down.

A few minutes later the New Orleans detective returned. "Damned if I know. Could be her sister," he mumbled angrily, as though someone had arranged this trick deliberately to thwart him. "What d'ya think we oughta do?"

Cliff considered a long time. "What's the number downtown?" he asked.

Lukes gave him the office phone number.

At a pay phone near the lounge area, Fenton got Bill Butler on the line. "Linda Gill got a sister?" he asked.

Butler laughed. "You gotta be kidding," he said.

"Do I sound like I'm kidding?"

"Hold it a minute. Frank, Linda Gill got a sister?"

Inspector McCoy's voice, far from the receiver, answered the shouted question. Butler came back on the line. "No sister," he said. "She's got a brother. You sure it's not him in drag?"

Cliff hung up the phone and started back for the bar but thought better of it. He ducked into the men's room again for another look at the picture, but it didn't answer any of his questions. At the very least, he decided, he would need another look at the waitress before he made up his mind. He went back to the bar and told his partner Linda Gill didn't have a sister.

Fifteen minutes passed, during which the waitress didn't return. Cliff toyed with the idea of going to look for her but figured it would be better to be patient. Suddenly, he was aware that the room had fallen strangely silent. The bartender was staring straight over his shoulder in the direction of the front door. A thin, heavily accented voice filled the silence. "Don' nobody move," it said, "an' nobody gits hurt."

Cliff raised his hands slowly above his head and turned on the stool to face the reedy voice. All along the bar, a dozen men were executing the same move. In front of them stood three young white men brandishing automatic weapons—two handguns and a lean and lethal-looking automatic rifle. The oldest of the stickup men couldn't have passed for twenty.

Just what I needed, Cliff thought. Later, when he told the story, it would come out funny, but it wasn't funny at the time. He kept his gold detective's shield in a shield case, not in his wallet, and prayed that Lukes did the same. Not that it would matter if Lukes had any ideas about taking them down. For himself, he didn't care two shits about a team of teen-age stickup men; it was Linda Gill he wanted. But this was Lukes's territory, and it would be asking a lot to expect him to sit through a stickup for the sake of an out-of-state case. He tried to think what he would do if he were on Lenox Avenue now, assisting a Louisiana cop. Then he realized that was irrelevant, because if Lukes moved on them he would have to move too.

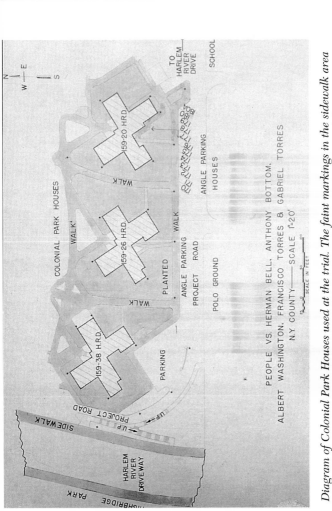

Diagram of Colonial Park Houses used at the trial. The faint markings in the sidewalk area around building 159-20 are notations made by the witnesses in the course of their testimony.

Aerial view of Colonial Park Houses.
The four large buildings to the left are the Polo Grounds Project.
The circle denotes the area around the murder scene.

Patrolman Waverly Jones
(N.Y. Daily News Photo)

Patrolman Joseph Piagentini
(N.Y. Daily News Photo)

The white Mustang on which Herman Bell's fingerprints were found. In this police photo, taken the night of the killings, black smudges on the fender of the car show it had already been dusted for prints.

The murder scene, showing the chalked outlines where the two officers fell. Jones lay across the sidewalk; Piagentini was crawling toward the bushes at the right when Richard Hill found him. Police photo, taken the day after the killings.

(ABOVE AND OPPOSITE PAGE)
The funerals of Patrolmen Waverly Jones and Joseph Piagentini in Harlem, New York, and Deer Park, Long Island.
(N.Y. Daily News Photos)

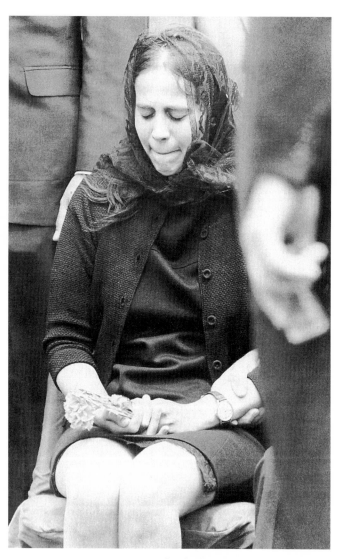

Diane Piagentini at her husband's funeral.
(N.Y. Daily News Photo)

Herman Bell. a. At his arrest in Oakland, May 1969;
b. The driver's license photo in the name Samuel Lee Pennegar;
c. At his arrest in New Orleans, September 1973.

The line-up in San Francisco. Number 2 is Anthony Bottom; number 6 is Albert Washington. Note Bottom's slight facial swelling.

Artist's sketch of Anthony Bottom drawn from the descriptions of the witnesses. A remarkable likeness.

NO. 1

Gabriel Torres.

Francisco Torres. Surveillance photo taken outside Bottom's apartment in San Francisco.

Cliff Fenton, Bob Tanenbaum, and Bill Butler: New Orleans, the night Herman Bell was arrested. (Photo by Patti Tanenbaum)

A farm near Cordelia, Mississippi; the search for Piagentini's gun. The man at the far left, behind the backhoe, is Ken Klein. Digging the dirt in the foreground is New York City Detective Tommy Lyons.
(Photos by Cliff Fenton)

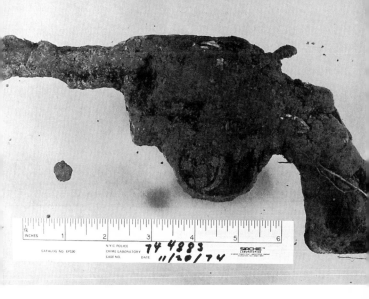

Joseph Piagentini's gun. (TOP) As it looked when it was unearthed in Mississippi (BOTTOM) after cleaning.

(ABOVE) The guns in the case. The submachine with which Albert Washington tried to kill Sergeant George Kowalski in San Francisco; Tony Bottom's pearl-handled .45 automatic; Waverly Jones's service revolver; Joseph Piagentini's service revolver. The leather ammunition pouch was attached to Bottom's belt when he was arrested.

(LEFT) Jones's service revolver. The half inch of space between the letter and six numerals in the serial number led to an almost-tragic mistake.

(RIGHT) Four bullets removed on autopsy from the body of Waverly Jones.

One of the stickup men stayed by the door, his automatic rifle scanning the premises with a steady swaying motion. Another, carrying a small-caliber automatic, was moving along the bar, collecting the money the grim-faced patrons were peeling from their wallets and thrusting toward him. When the kid, who probably weighed a hundred fifty and couldn't have been more than sixteen years old, reached Lukes, the detective opened his wallet as the others had done and pulled out the bills that were in it, handing them over dutifully. The kid stuffed the money into the pocket of his windbreaker and poked at the inside of the billfold with his finger, checking for hidden compartments. Satisfied, he moved on to Cliff. Then he ordered the bartender to bring him the contents of the till. "No tricks," he snarled. "Somebody git hurt."

He pulled a plastic bag from his waistband and shook it open with one hand. He let the bartender fill it, then walked backward to rejoin the lookout by the door. Soon the third stickup man, whom Cliff had lost sight of, returned from fleecing the couples at the tables. Together, the three heavily armed boys backed through the door and disappeared.

For a few seconds the Round Robin remained strangely quiet. Then it began to fill with rumbling, discontented murmurs. "Thanks," Cliff whispered appreciatively.

"We got bigger fish to fry," Lukes said. "I'll call it in. They're not gonna last long in this business anyhow." He walked to the phone booth.

"One round on the house," the bartender shouted. "Nobody got hurt, let's just forget about it."

The offer of a free drink didn't do much to revive sodden spirits. Everyone, it seemed, was still grumbling—everyone, that is, except the well-dressed old man to Cliff's right, one stool past the vacant stool where Lukes had been sitting. He was grinning like a Cheshire cat.

"I foxed 'em," he crowed triumphantly. "Foxed 'em good. Jes' keep a coupla bills in my wallet for show, got the real bread right here."

He reached under his belt and pulled out a small leather pouch, from which he drew a thick wad of folded money. Holding it up for Cliff's inspection, he smiled with idiotic complacency and turned to show it to the man at his right. The smile fell from his face as though it had been dropped as he found himself staring cross-eyed at the glinting point of a switchblade knife.

"Yeah, you foxed 'em good, old man," the man with the knife said. Politely, with thumb and forefinger, he plucked the wad from the old man's hands and backed away from the bar. "Gits me back where I was before them dudes come in," he explained almost apologetically, then turned and ran for the street.

Cliff Fenton turned to the bar and covered his face with his hands. Behind them he was laughing, a silent, gut-shaking laugh that came from deep inside him. "Too much," he murmured to himself. "Too fucking much."

He felt a hand at his elbow. Horace Lukes said, "What's the matter with you? I called in the robbery."

"You did, huh?" Fenton said. "Which one?"

Lukes looked at him uncomprehendingly. "Did I miss something?" he asked.

"Not much. Guess I'm not used to the big city," Fenton deadpanned. "Just answer one question for me, I gotta know. Is this what it's like around here all the time?"

Thirteen

WE ALL TALKED IT OVER IN THE OFFICE LATE that night and decided to send Fenton and Lukes back to the Round Robin the next day. Inasmuch as the bar was open from noon to 3 A.M., the two detectives chose to return in the middle of the afternoon on the chance that Linda Gill worked an early shift. Delsa suggested sending two other men, since Fenton and Lukes hadn't been able to determine whether the waitress they had seen was in fact Herman Bell's wife. But I didn't look at it that way. I thought Cliff had done the right thing in holding back until he was sure. I trusted his judgment and couldn't see replacing him with someone who might go off half-cocked.

Cliff and Horace walked into the almost empty bar a little after three o'clock the next afternoon. The moment they stepped through the door they saw what they had come for. The girl at the waitress station was Linda Gill, no two ways about it. She was standing with one foot on the bar rail, talking to the bartender, a younger man but every bit as fat as the one who had been on duty the night before. Taking the two stools next to her, the detectives ordered beers.

While the bartender waddled to the tap, Fenton turned to Linda Gill and smiled encouragingly. "Beautiful day," he said.

She took her foot from the railing. "Wouldn't know," she said. "Been in here all day."

Fenton held his smile despite the rebuff. "What the hell, beautiful day for being in here," he grinned. "Leastways if you're drinking."

"Sure, mister."

She walked away from the waitress station, cold and insolent. But Fenton had had as good a look at her as he needed, good enough to leave him wondering how he and Lukes could have been so wrong about the girl last night. Linda Gill was an inch or so taller than the other waitress, bigger in the bosom, thinner in the waist. Though not as dark as Fenton himself, her complexion was a closer match than last night's girl's to the rich, polished walnut tones in the Polaroid snapshot. Her face was less conventionally pretty, less delicately modeled, but more memorable. She was intensely beautiful, in a way her coldness only complemented.

"What's eating her?" Fenton asked as the bartender set two almost headless glasses of beer on the bar.

The bartender shrugged, a small gesture with his head that barely rippled the rolls of fat piled around his neck. "She's like that," he said.

"Too bad. She's something to look at, though."

"Don't waste your time."

"Married?"

"Yeah."

Cliff called the office from the pay phone in the bar around three-thirty. He got me on the line. "She's here," he said. "Let's tail her when she leaves. Get everyone you can, let's do it right."

Rounding up enough men for a sophisticated tailing operation was no problem. Even the FBI agents, normally a phlegmatic bunch, seemed enthusiastic and excited. By four o'clock, about twenty men had left police headquarters in nine cars to deploy themselves in the vicinity of the Round Robin Bar and Grille. Not being a cop, I was left behind in the office with nothing to do but wait. The hours passed slowly and I had to keep reminding myself not to be impatient, that nothing could happen until at least six or eight o'clock, whenever it was she got off work.

In the bar, Fenton and Lukes sat nursing beers and talking about football. Whenever Linda Gill came to the waitress station, Fenton tried to strike up a conversation with her. He played it cool, keeping his interest just barely on the lighter side of obviousness, but each time he met with the same chilly reception.

"What time she get off?" he asked the bartender late in the afternoon.

"Eight. But told you, you're wasting your time. That's advice, man, know what I mean?"

"Her old man?"

"Yeah."

"He don't scare me."

"He don't scare me neither. I'm just telling you."

"You know him?"

"Not to talk to. Comes in once in a while."

"Tough guy?"

"Not so tough, maybe. I don't know. I wouldn't fuck with his old lady though. If he comes in, you'd be in a lot of trouble."

Cliff thought, If he comes in, he's the one gonna be in a lot of trouble. But he said, "What is it, he picks her up after work or something?"

The bartender was getting annoyed with the questions. "How the fuck would I know, man? I gave you my advice. You wanna take it, take it." He lumbered down the bar and busied himself rinsing glasses.

Horace Lukes phoned the office to report that Linda Gill got off work at eight. He and Cliff left the bar shortly after six so they could be in on the tail without having to leave with her. Lukes got the radio frequencies that would be used on the surveillance from a black-and-white team of New Orleans detectives parked on the block behind the gin mill. Then they settled in to wait in Lukes's car.

At four minutes after eight, Linda Gill stepped onto the sidewalk and paused, squinting in the bright slanting sun to get her bearings. It was late summer, the Saturday before Labor Day, and there was still a good forty-five minutes of sunlight left. She had changed from her short-skirted uniform to blue jeans and a brown tank top. She took a deep breath and exhaled slowly, breathing out the fatigue of a long eight hours on her feet. Then she turned to the right and walked quickly, with a forceful, almost mannish stride, to a tomato-red Volkswagen Beetle parked at the curb. A block and a half behind her, two New Orleans detectives started their engine. "We got her," they radioed. "Red VW, moving east on St. Charles. Who's gonna catch her at Marengo?"

"Baker here, I'll take it," a transmission came back.

With ten cars full of cops and agents, it was possible to tail her for miles without ever leaving a particular vehicle in her rear-view mirror for more than a block or

two. As she continued along St. Charles, driving easily in
the moderate Saturday-evening traffic, the surveillance
units switched roles almost playfully, one car cutting in
behind her from the left at an intersection, passing her
a few blocks down and leaving her to another unit,
which slid out from the curb, pulled out from another
intersection, or slowed down to let her overtake it.

When she turned right a few blocks past Jackson
Avenue, Delsa guessed she was heading for the bridge
and sent half his units ahead to wait for her along the
expressway. Moving at moderate speeds, they would let
her overtake them, and she would never guess she was
being followed by cars she herself had passed.

She crossed the Mississippi River almost exactly at
eight-thirty, by which point Delsa was thanking his stars
he had had the foresight to bring so many units into the
operation. Wherever she was going, it was pretty far from
where she worked, but with so many cars switching off all
the time, the chance of getting burned was kept to a minimum. As she cruised along the West Bank Expressway,
Delsa ordered all units behind her to overtake and pass,
letting the slower-moving cars already ahead of her pick
up the tail as she passed them. Barely a minute later
Detective Richard Hunter, using the radio code designation Baker, called in that he had her visually. In another
minute Fenton and Lukes had her too.

The red VW raced on, the casual pace of its city driving giving way to a sudden hurry. For five miles the caravan rolled on in the thickening darkness with all units
now in place, a constellation of taillights that couldn't
be seen in the heavy traffic unless one knew which particular dots to connect.

Worried by the speed she was making, Delsa jock-eyed to the lead. Had she made the tail? It didn't seem possible. Then why the rush?

He didn't have long to wait for an answer, which turned out to be comically irrelevant. At five minutes to nine the red Volkswagen signaled a turn at the Avondale shopping mall. Most of the stores in the center closed at nine and Linda had some shopping to do.

She raced through the half-empty parking lot and pulled to a jolting stop in a no-parking zone directly in front of a shoe store. The clerk eyed her malevolently as she pushed through the door, undoubtedly cursing him-self for not having thrown the lock a minute early. But she consoled him with a brilliantly promising smile as she lifted her right foot onto the fitting stool and began to untie the laces of her heavy, rubber-soled waitress shoes.

Delsa by this time had pulled into a parking space from where he could watch her through the plate-glass store window. She was flirting with the clerk, a gawky white boy in his early twenties with bad skin and limp, straw-colored hair. Squatting on the stool in front of her as he slid a shoe onto her foot, he was grinning so broadly it was all he could do to keep from drooling.

As Delsa watched, one of the three FBI cars in the surveillance detachment cruised slowly past the shoe-store window, its long whip antenna rising above its trunk as obvious as a flasher in a playground.

Delsa grabbed for his microphone. "Damn it, get the hell out of there! I got her covered," he barked. He realized at once he had made a mistake. FBI agents didn't take orders from cops, especially when the cops were tactless enough to let them sound like orders.

The dark sedan rolled slowly past the shoe store, the two agents in the front seat staring ostentatiously through the driver-side window at Linda Gill. Delsa waited breathlessly for the car to clear the window so he could get another look at Herman Bell's wife. When it did, he tried to read her face for a sign that she had noticed something suspicious. He didn't think he saw one.

Picking up speed, the agent's car turned left into one of the parking access lanes and sped away from the store, then turned left at the far end of the lot, apparently circling around for another pass.

"Damn fools," Delsa muttered to himself, but he was saved a longer, harsher string of expletives by Linda Gill, who was now standing by the cash register paying the overwrought clerk for the contents of the shoebox she held under her arm. He walked her to the door, locked it behind her, and watched lugubriously as she swung around in front of her car, climbed in, and drove off. He was still in the doorway, looking out with mournful eyes, when Delsa drove by half a minute later, a good hundred yards behind Linda Gill's red Volks.

The tailing operation went as smoothly on the way back as it had gone on the way down, with Delsa choreographing an automotive ballet as his cars bounded past her, then slipped back to let her pass. In a few minutes it was clear she was heading back for the Mississippi River Bridge. When she got back into the city, Delsa planned to use a parallel-type tail, with cars on the streets to her left and right spotting her as she passed each intersection. He would put no one on the street behind her.

"She's signaling a turn, getting off at St. Charles. Give her a little room. Let me know which way she goes."

"I'm with her, I'll take it."

There were a few seconds of silence.

"Got her."

"Which way?"

"West on St. Charles. I have her solid, could use a little help here."

"Roger. Drop back, let her go. Units One to Four, spread out on Carondelet. Rest of you guys take Prytania."

"She just passed Thalia."

"Who's at Melpomene? Someone get Melpomene?"

"Roger. Haven't seen her yet. Hold it, hold it, that's her, made the light. She's still on St. Charles."

"All right. She's goin' home, goin' home, must be gettin' close. Jes' stay loose, no time to get burned now."

"L. J., she just passed Felicity."

"Roger on that. I'm at Jackson and Prytania, let you know when she comes through. Jes' sit tight, sit tight, sit tight. Got half a dozen vehicles coming through right now. Got her! She's turning left. Pick her up at Philip and Coliseum."

"Will do. She's coming this way now. L. J., you better shift everyone over this way."

"Right, right. All units, move south, follow on—"

"Hold it, she's turning right on Magazine. Want me to stay with her?"

"I'm at Phillip and Magazine."

"Christ, no, stay out of her mirror. Horace'll get her when she goes by. Let's cover Camp and Constance all the way down, First, Second, Third, and Fourth. Horace, let her go."

"She passed Philip."

"Passed Philip."

"Roger."

"Left on Second."

"Okay, this has gotta be it. Who's got Second and Constance? Someone get ready at Laurel."

"I'm waitin'."

There was a long silence on the airwaves.

"Anyone got her?"

"Negative."

"Who the fuck's that? What's your position?"

"Second and Constance."

"Right, right. And she's not through yet?"

"Still on the block."

"Well sit tight, keep your eyes open."

Delsa checked his watch to give her one more minute following the second hand as it lock-stepped around the face. "Go take a look," he ordered when the minute was gone.

Detectives Collins and Reid of the New Orleans Police Department rounded the corner onto Second Street. Facing them, halfway down the block, a red Volkswagen stood at the curb, its headlights off, its body jerking with the spasms of post-ignition. As they drove slowly toward it, the tremors stopped, the door opened, and Linda Gill stepped into the street. Not even bothering to look at the unmarked police car rolling toward her, she strolled behind her car with her shoebox under her arm, crossed the sidewalk, and hurried at double time, almost jogging, up the short cement walkway to 820 Second Street, a small two-story bungalow. She turned at the front steps and went around to the side of the house, where an external staircase led to an upstairs apartment. The detectives noted a light burning in the front window. Within a matter of seconds she had climbed the stairs and disappeared through the door. She was home.

"There's lights on," Collins radioed. "She's inside now."

Three blocks away, at the intersection of Constance and First streets, Bill Butler was sitting in the passenger seat of a New Orleans police car when he heard the transmission. After almost two and a half years of looking for him, he had found Herman Bell. Maybe.

Delsa positioned two cars where they could keep the house under observation. He had no intention of making a move until the lights in the second-floor apartment went out, and even then he would clear his plans with the cops from New York. He wanted Bell for bank robbery, they wanted him for murder. As far as Delsa was concerned, Herman Bell was theirs.

At eleven-thirty the front window went dark, but detectives with a view of the side of the house still could see a light coming from what they assumed to be the bedroom in the back. It went out a little after twelve. Delsa asked Butler, Fenton, and Lyons to meet him half a dozen blocks away.

"It's your show, whadyall think?" he asked when all three New York detectives had rendezvoused at his car.

Butler said, "Well, the first thing is, is he in there?"

"Someone is," Tommie Lyons offered. "There were lights on when she got there."

"And she's got a kid, couldn't have left the kid alone," Fenton said.

Butler considered for a long time. "Okay, but say it's not him, say he lammed out a week ago. I don't wanna take that chance, do you?"

Lyons shook his head. Fenton said, "No, let's not. She's all we got. Sooner or later she's gotta lead us to him as long as she doesn't know we're out here." He turned to Delsa. "What d'ya say?" he asked. "Can you give us the troops to stay on her as long as it takes?"

Delsa smiled. "I was hoping you'd say that," he confessed. "Tell you the truth, I don't quite fancy sending anyone in there."

Every Black Liberation Army suspect busted up till then had been armed like a Mexican bandit. Their homes, when searched, proved to be veritable arsenals. In New York, New Orleans, San Francisco, and Los Angeles, police had confiscated sidearms, rifles, shotguns, machine guns, dynamite, plastic explosives, and hand grenades. Even if Delsa's men sneaked up on Herman Bell in the night, the chances of taking him down without a fight were no better than even. And that meant people were going to get killed. Bell for certain wouldn't come out of it alive, and neither would anyone else in the apartment when the shooting started. If Bell had grenades and automatic weapons, he would probably take more than one cop with him.

"So we sit tight till morning," Fenton concluded. "See what shakes."

Back at police headquarters, I had moved downstairs to the communications center, where I kept myself posted on the surveillance by monitoring the transmissions. When Cliff returned to his car after the meeting with Delsa, I raised him on the radio and asked if he thought the situation was on hold for the night. He said he thought it was.

"Then meet me somewhere, you tell me where," I

said. "Bring Butler and Lyons. I want to get some signals straight before anybody moves on him."

Butler conferred with Lukes, who knew the neighborhood, then named an intersection where we could meet. I got a radio patrol car to drive me there. It was about one-thirty when we met in Lukes's car, Lukes and Fenton in the front seat, me in back jammed in between Bill Butler and Tommie Lyons. As I passed out the containers of coffee I had picked up on my way to the meeting, Fenton brought me up to date on the plan. They would keep the house under continuous surveillance and tail Linda Gill whenever she came out.

I approved, then directed my next question to Lukes. "Horace, you know all the men you've got here. What do you think is going to happen?" I asked.

The black detective turned in the seat to face me. "He's gotta come out," he said. "I don't reckon he's a churchgoing man, so it might not be in the morning. But sooner or later he comes out."

"And then what?"

"Then I think we got ourselves one dead nigger."

"What's the chance of taking him alive?"

"We ain't killers, man," Lukes said. "I guess we draw a shade quicker than you Yankees do, if that's what you're thinking. Ain't no way Herman Bell's gonna get off the first shot. He's gonna be lookin' at more cops than he ever thought there was, and if he so much as stops to think he's gone."

I turned to talk to my own men. "All right, you get the picture," I said. "Bell's probably not coming out of this. So my problem is how the hell's it gonna look if Bell gets blown away and there's New York cops fifteen hundred miles from home getting in their shots at him? It's going to look like a goddamned vendetta, and it could even fuck up our case against the other four. I want you guys to lay back, move up when you have to, and if you have to shoot, God knows, shoot. But let the feds and the New Orleans take the front positions."

Butler and Lyons jumped all over me. It sounded to them like I was asking them to let other cops take the heat for them. But Fenton saw my point at once. "He's right," he said. "If one of these tigers down here gets trigger-happy and the whole thing blows up, the FBI's gonna lay it off on New Orleans and New Orleans is gonna lay it off on us. We're gonna be left holding the bag."

"Yeah, and there's another thing," I added, jumping in right behind him. "If Bell is taken alive, I want the FBI to make the arrest. I'll check it with Delsa, but I'm sure it's okay with him."

I went on to explain my thinking. Regardless of who actually put the cuffs on Bell, he could be arrested in three different ways. The New York cops could arrest him on the homicide warrant I had in my pocket; the New Orleans cops could hit him with a bank-robbery warrant for some of the same robberies that had led to the massive BLA roundup the week before; or FBI agents could get him on a federal warrant for the California bank robbery he had committed in September 1971. If either New York or New Orleans made the arrest, we would have to go through extradition proceedings in order to get him back to New York to stand trial for the Piagentini-Jones killings. There would be a hearing, which would mean at the very least that we would have to disclose enough of our case against him to justify extradition. It would also mean a loss of valuable time, for these things, even when they are routine, can drag on for months. If that happened, I might well lose the chance to try Bell along with Bottom, Washington, and the Torres brothers in a single trial.

On the other hand, if the suspect was in federal custody, I could return to New York and draw up the papers for a writ of habeas corpus ad prosequendum, a writ ordering the delivery of the named party for the purpose of prosecution. Because a federal prisoner can be brought before any federal court in the country with no right to an extradition hearing if he is carried across a state line, federal authorities—in this case, U.S. marshals—would then bring Bell to the United States Courthouse in Manhattan. At the conclusion of the proceedings there, he would be released from federal custody and arrested on a New York murder warrant while he was still in the courtroom.

"If we do it this way," I said, "we can have him in New York so damn fast we'll kill any shot they've got at separate trials. They'd like nothing better than to be tried without him, because it's got to confuse the jury if one of the trigger men isn't there. I want to cut their legs from under them in that one, even if it means letting the FBI take the collar. What d'ya say?"

They were all proud men, and I knew it meant a great deal to them to be in on the arrest of Herman Bell.

Bill Butler spoke for all of them. "Any way you want it," he said. "I don't care who grabs him, just so you make sure that bastard gets what's his."

Fourteen

CLIFF FENTON PROBABLY KNOWS MORE TRICKS than any other cop in the world. Unlike most detectives, who get bored and listless on stake-outs unless they can relieve the numbing monotony with conversation, diversions, and horseplay, Cliff tends to grow more tensely expectant with each uneventful moment that passes. A stake-out for Cliff is never dead time; it is the landing operation before a beachhead assault.

And so it was on that Saturday night in New Orleans. His mind raced ahead, juggling contingencies, until the electricity in his nerves reached sparking intensity. By four o'clock in the morning he was as tense as he would have been if he had been under fire, and the coffee I had given him a few hours earlier wasn't doing anything to help calm him down.

That was when it dawned on him that Herman Bell wouldn't be coming out. Not in the morning, not in the afternoon, not for days. He was on the lam, hiding out, underground. Either he wasn't in that apartment at all or he was staying in there until the heat died down. If he was running true to form, he would pull another robbery to bankroll his escape, as he had done in San Francisco when he had to get out of town. But that wouldn't be until Tuesday at the earliest, since the banks were all going to be closed on Monday. And it might not be for another week or two. Bell had all the time in the world, and until he was ready to move he wouldn't show his face.

What were the chances, Cliff wondered, that the stakeout wouldn't be burned by Tuesday? Next to none. This wasn't New York, with large apartment buildings and busy sidewalks, where a cop could always set up a plant in a vacant apartment or even pretend to be nodding on a stoop if he had to. This was a black residential neighborhood where strangers on the street would be noticed, where groups of men, mostly white men, sitting in parked cars would draw a great deal of attention and everyone would know they were cops. It was easy enough to keep out of the sight lines from Linda Gill's upstairs apartment, but there was no way to hide the stakeout from the neighbors. In some of these houses Bell must have had friends. Perhaps some of these shabby bungalows housed sympathizers and supporters of the Black Liberation Army.

The conclusion Cliff Fenton was coming to was that the stake-out would be lucky to make it through the daylight hours. If Bell was in fact inside and learned that the police were laying siege for him out on the streets, he would unpack the artillery and wait it out. And if he weren't in there, Linda Gill certainly would go nowhere near him once she learned the cops were counting on her to lead them to her husband. Besides, the whole thing was academic. Delsa may have had the best intentions in the world, but there wasn't a police department anywhere that would let a detective tie up over a dozen men indefinitely on the mere suspicion that a fugitive, however dangerous, would walk into their trap. Sooner or later his superiors were going to order him either to go in or to back off. And if that's what it was coming to, now was as good a time as any.

Every way Cliff turned it, the arguments all reinforced his most basic instinct as a cop. If he had ever bothered to reduce his philosophy to an axiom, it would have been this: The choice between riding it out and forcing the issue is no choice at all. A cop who would rather react than act ends up no better than a close second in a game in which the winners get promotions and the losers get inspectors' funerals.

"Hey, Horace, you carry a knife, man?" Cliff asked abruptly, remembering a trick that had worked for him once in East Harlem. Coming at the end of a long silence, his voice boomed brilliantly, like sudden bright colors in the darkness.

Horace Lukes was somewhere else and it took him a minute to get back. "What d'you need a knife for?" he asked thickly, like a man just waking.

"Teach you rebels a couple things," Cliff said. "Mind if I do some shopping around?"

He reached for the radio and broadcast his question to all units. In a few seconds he got a sheepish affirmative. Knives weren't an item of standard weapons issue in the New Orleans Police Department.

"Great, man," Cliff said into the microphone. "Meet me at the corner of Second and Constance."

"On foot?"

"Yeah, on foot. With the shiv, right."

L. J. Delsa's voice cut into the transmission. "Cliff, what y'all fixin' to do?"

"I'm fixing to save you folks some overtime."

"Not gonna do anything crazy, are you?"

" 'S not my style."

While Delsa pondered Fenton's ambiguous answer, a few blocks away Bill Butler picked up his microphone. "Cliff. Bill. Don't cut him up too bad, huh," he joked.

"Which one-a you slickers is pullin' my leg?" Delsa demanded. "I don't want you doing nothing you oughtn't, Fenton. Hear?"

Cliff Fenton looked across the car seat at Lukes and laughed his short, gaspy laugh. "He'll be all right," he said, indicating the receiver that was still spluttering with unanswered questions from L. J. Delsa.

He climbed from the car, heading for his rendezvous at Second and Constance. Puzzled and amused, Lukes watched him go, shrugged to himself, and picked up the microphone.

"You ain't askin' anybody that's here, L. J.," he said. "He's gone and I ain't got a clue."

For twenty minutes the airwaves were silent. Then one of the units reported two men approaching Bell's residence from the east. "Just keep me posted," Delsa responded.

"Hold it, hold it. I think one of them's Wilson. It is Wilson. The other's that dude from New York."

"Fenton?"

"Yeah, him."

"What they doin'?"

"Ain't doin' nothin.' Just walkin'."

"Where?"

"Comin' up on the house. . . . They're slowin' down."

"What're they up to?"

"Not up to nothin' far as I can tell, just moseyin' down the sidewalk. Wait a minute, they stopped. . . . Wilson's bending over. . . . They're walkin' again. They're walkin' right past the place. Just right on past. Pretty good clip, too. Comin' up on the corner. . . . I lost 'em, went around the corner."

Ten minutes later Cliff Fenton was sitting beside Horace Lukes again.

"What was that all about?" Lukes demanded.

Fenton smiled smugly. "Just a little psychology, a little sociology," he said. "When you figure it out, let me know."

Through the night, no further mention was made of Cliff's little walking tour. Morning came early. Sunday papers had blossomed on a few of the porches, delivered just before dawn by a shriveled old man in a station wagon who probably wouldn't have noticed if J. Edgar Hoover himself had been directing traffic on the corner. Around seven-thirty a door opened in the house next to Bell's, then closed behind a beige short-haired mutt that paused to sniff the air. For a full minute the dog weighed the situation, his head turning slowly, a few degrees at a time, as though it were on ratchets. Satisfied, he lowered his nose to the ground and followed it in a crazy zigging course around the house to the backyard.

Down the block another dog emerged to relieve himself. A middle-aged couple dressed for church drove off in a tan Pinto and a heavy-set woman in a navy-blue dress and white shoes walked to the corner, passing the police car four doors up from Bell's house. She studied the occupants with a mixture of curiosity and indifference, the set of her mouth and her round hounddog eyes saying almost in words that it was none of her lookout but it did beat anything what a couple of strangers would be doing sitting in a car on Second Street come a Sunday morning.

Three more cars drove off to church; two more dogs came out. From the house next to Bell's, a man in a sleeveless undershirt whistled the mutt back in. Then a half hour passed without a sign of life. Across the street from number

820 a little boy, three, maybe four years old, his face scrubbed to a polish, climbed down the porch steps in his Sunday suit. He kicked at the grass fretfully and dug a divot or two with the back of his heel, then looked over his shoulder into the house to see if he had been seen. He was wearing a red clip-on polka-dot tie and new brown shoes with buckles.

"C'mon, mamma, c'mon, papa," the detective four doors down urged under his breath. Through the night the thought that there were kids in the neighborhood had crossed the minds of every cop on the stake-out. If Bell went down the hard way, God help anyone on the street.

A door opened behind the little boy, and the detective, who heard it at the same time the kid did, heaved a sigh of relief. The boy ran for the car at the curb and waited at the back door for his mommy and daddy to open it. They were a handsome couple, the man almost six feet tall, the woman only an inch or two shorter. They didn't speak to each other, didn't say a word to the child when they joined him at the car. While the mother walked around to the passenger side, the father opened the back door for his son, slammed it after him, and climbed in behind the wheel. They drove off, leaving a tired, bleary-eyed detective to speculate sadly about a tense and alienated family he had never met.

Someone must have checked a watch at that point, because a report filed later said that at exactly 8:27 Linda Gill stepped onto the upstairs landing and started down the steps. She was wearing blue jeans and a man's-style cotton shirt. Her sleeves were rolled up just over her wrists.

"She's in the car, she's pulling out. I'm sittin' on the house, someone catch her at Magazine."

Cliff Fenton came on the air. "Sit tight, she ain't going nowhere," he said.

"She's takin' a right on Magazine. Wait a minute, hold it, hold it, she stopped. What the fuck's going on? She's getting outta the car."

"All right, back off. Don't approach her till we see what she's fixin' to do. What's she doing now?"

"She's walking around the car. Aw, shit! She's got a fucking flat tire."

Fenton said, "Like hell. She's got two flat tires."

A light came on somewhere behind Horace Luke's eyes. "Hell, man, is that what you done?" he laughed. "You are a male chauvinist pig, you know that?"

"Guess so, but I didn't write the rules," Fenton answered. "Did you ever know a lady that'd change a tire while her husband's sitting on his ass?" He put his mouth to the microphone. "When she goes back to the house, let's start moving in," he ordered.

"That right, L. J.?" someone asked, wanting verification.

"You heard the man."

"In that case you clowns better get your hands off your dongs and get ready to move, 'cause that's just where she's going."

"Awright, everybody, hold your positions till she's inside."

"She's goin' up the steps, she's goin' up. Okay, she's in the house. Let's roll."

Two FBI agents in a car at the corner of Constance and First, one block east of Second Street, scrambled to the sidewalk and headed for the back yards between the two rows of houses. One of them carried an automatic rifle, the other a .38. Two blocks to the north and west of them, at the corner of Camp and Third, Bill Butler took the shotgun his partner offered him. Walking quickly, the two cops, one New York P.D., the other New Orleans, cut in through a hedge and ran for the side of a newly painted cottage. They hugged the building wall, then dashed through the back yard into the back yard of 823 Second, inching forward until they were just shy of the front of the house. Butler was in the lead. He stuck his head out just far enough to catch a glimpse of Bell's bungalow across the street, then pulled it back in. He pumped the action on the shotgun and took a deep breath. His partner held a walkie-talkie to his ear.

Another team of federal agents cut across the tidy back yards between Second and First, coming up on Bell's house from the back. They rendezvoused with the first pair of agents in the yard on the far side of the house next to Bell's. Bell would be walking away from them toward Magazine Street, which meant that when it went down they would have him dead from the back.

Tommie Lyons was teamed up with a New Orleans cop three blocks away. They drove to Camp and Second and turned left onto Second, then pulled to the curb about thirty yards shy of the intersection with Magazine. Ahead of them, just beyond the intersection, they could see Linda Gill's red Volkswagen where she had left it a couple of feet out from the curb. Another car with two New Orleans detectives pulled in behind them. Lyons and his partner waited in their vehicle, hunched low behind the dash, their weapons drawn. The pair from the second car hid behind the corner house.

L. J. Delsa and his partner crouched behind their car, which was parked on Second Street just a few yards north of the intersection. As Bell walked from his house, he would be heading straight toward them. It was Delsa's plan to let him get all the way to the corner so he would be covered from all four sides at once. Directly across the street from Delsa, to his right, an FBI team waited behind a thick hedge. The feds carried heavy-caliber automatics; Delsa and his partner had shotguns.

Ahead of Delsa, slightly to his left, four men pressed their backs against the side of the house on the southeast corner of Second and Magazine. At the right moment they would come around to the front of the house, cutting off any possible escape to the south. Three of them were New Orleans cops, the fourth Cliff Fenton, who had declined the shotgun Horace Lukes offered him, electing to go with his .38. The new Orleans cops all had shotguns. In the unnatural stillness of the morning, the hish-whoosh of the actions tinkled in the air like twigs crackling in a deep forest.

That was when it struck Delsa that he had put his men in a full three-hundred-sixty-degree circle. If there was going to be a shootout, Bell would be in the middle of it but the cops would be shooting at each other right over him. It was too late to change the deployments, and all he could do was pray that the men behind Bell knew enough to stay covered.

"Jackpot! He's coming down. Oh Jesus Christ no! He's got his kid with him!"

Jonas Bell was just a month or two short of three years old. His father held his hand, practically lifting him by it as he lowered him from step to step. When they reached the ground, the boy pulled free and skipped ahead. Linda Gill came down the steps quickly and joined Bell. She said something to him and laughed, but his face was set, unresponsive. It was a look of annoyance, not anger, the annoyance of any husband dragged from a somnolent Sunday morning to fix a flat tire on his wife's car. The two New

Orleans cops who had been watching the house all night saw the look and understood it. One way or another the career of Herman Bell was going to be over in less than five minutes. He had emptied two guns into a cop in New York, he was wanted for bank robbery, and he was a prime suspect in at least one other police murder. And in the end he would turn out to be just a poor jerk with car trouble. If he had ever pictured what it would be like when they finally caught up with him, it wouldn't have been like this.

"He's coming down the walkway. Okay, they're turning. Tighten up in back of him."

Bill Butler leaned out from behind the corner of 823 for the first look he had ever had at Herman Bell. He saw him from the back, a tall, broad-shouldered black man who carried himself straight, his arms swinging easily as he walked. He was wearing a white T-shirt and old bleach-stained jeans, pale blue, streaked with white. Christine Rowe said he had been wearing jeans like that the night he left the Anderson Avenue apartment to kill Waverly Jones and Joseph Piagentini.

Butler's eyes ran the length of Bell's body, following the lines of it the way a man looks at a woman, except that Butler was looking for a gun. He didn't think he saw one and realized he didn't care. Whichever way it went down was fine with him. After so many months, he sometimes worried that Bell had become almost an abstraction to him, so that now he was almost surprised to recognize that what he was feeling was not merely rage, not merely anger, but a pure and clear hatred. He had to force himself to pull back and let Bell out of his sight. Then he sprinted for the back of the house, turned the corner, and crossed the back yard at a run, his partner just a step behind. He let Bell get safely ahead, then ran for the next house.

In the back yards on the other side of Second Street the four FBI agents were doing the same thing, drawing the net tighter. Bell walked into it slowly, at a sulky pace. When he was still three houses from the corner, he called out to his son, "Hey, Jonas, where you runnin' off to?"

He had a deep voice, strong and forceful, startling in its suddenness. For an instant it snapped the tension in the air, like a clap of thunder one has been waiting for. Then the nerves of twenty cops screwed tighter. Little Jonas, who had been scampering ahead on the lawn, cut back to the sidewalk and waited for his father to catch up.

Then suddenly a dog barked, not once, but five or six times. Bell turned in the direction of the sound. Now no one could be sure if he had seen anything, heard anything, suspected anything. It was time.

As Bell turned to continue toward his car, he noticed out of the corner of his eye a man running straight toward him. For an instant he didn't relate it to himself, and when he did it was too late. There were other men running with the first. He heard their shouts and recognized their guns. His upper body wheeled around to the right, but his legs, like those of an animal at bay, were rooted to the ground. Wherever he looked, guns stared back at him like cats' eyes in the night, and in that moment of surreal panic it almost seemed as though he had looked straight up the barrel of each of them in turn. With a violent wrench, out of control of his movements, he turned to the left and saw more cops closing in on him. They seemed to be walking slowly, stalking him. He looked away, his eyes glazed with absolute terror. Now his whole body was trembling violently. Slowly, as though pulled by winches, his arms raised to his shoulders, then above his head as a dark stain spread at his crotch.

The circle of armed men around him tightened from all sides. One of the new Orleans cops stepped forward to pat him down for weapons, then turned him around, jerked his arms down behind him, and snapped on the cuffs. Automatically the gauntlet of guns trained on Bell's back and chest lowered to the ground as an FBI agent with a warrant in his hand informed the prisoner he was under arrest. A few feet to the side, separated from Bell by a solid wall of cops, Linda Gill held her little boy in her arms, her hand stroking the back of his head as his face lay cradled against her shoulder. In the crowd of cops she recognized Cliff Fenton. Her face was expressionless, whatever she was feeling then of anger and fear lost for the moment in what must have been the bitter realization that it was she who had led the police to her husband.

As the FBI agents started to push Bell in the direction of the car, L. J. Delsa stepped in front of them. "We'll take him," he said.

"He's our prisoner."

"You'll get him, nobody's stealing your collar. But we're taking him in," Delsa said, his voice hard and uncompromising.

The agents exchanged glances but did as they were told, backing off to let Delsa and a New Orleans detective assume custody. Delsa, though, had no intention of taking Bell in himself. His eyes scanned the scattered ranks of cops until he found the three New Yorkers huddled together at the curb. "Butler," he called loudly. "This here's your prisoner. Stick him in the car, le's git goin'."

Sitting in the back seat of a New Orleans police car a

few minutes later, Bill Butler couldn't even begin to sort out his feelings. Triumph was a part of it, but only a small part. Like a fighter at the bell ending the last round, he was too drained by the long struggle to have a sense of victory. That would come later. For the time being he had enough to do just convincing himself it was finally over. He slumped against the back cushion and reached into his pocket for a cigarette, lit it, and took a long drag. He turned his head to face Bell.

"Want a smoke?" he asked, surprising even himself with the question.

Bell cocked his head and studied Butler quizzically, as though there was something in the question he couldn't understand. His dark eyes still glinted with fear, for the terror that had gripped him on the sidewalk hadn't yet let loose. For a few seconds the corners of his mouth worked convulsively, sending tiny ripples across the taut skin of his cheeks. Then his tightened brows relaxed and he nodded his head, accepting the offer for what it was. A simple human gesture, it hinted at no forgiveness and promised no abatement of the soul-consuming hatred the two men felt for each other. Both knew that if either of them had been unconstrained for even a fleeting moment, the other would have been dead at his feet.

Butler lit a second cigarette and held it to Bell's lips, gripping it backhanded in his left hand. Bell took a short, tentative drag, exhaled the smoke, and leaned forward for more.

"I figured . . . I figured . . ." he stammered, but his voice came out high and uncertain, so he stopped himself and made a visible effort to regain control. Then he took a deep breath and said, "It was good the way you did it. Thanks for not killing my kid."

Fifteen

NEW YORK CITY COPS HAD BEEN WORKING
on the Piagentini-Jones case for two and a half years. It
was New York City cops who found and arrested the
Torres brothers, two of those accused of the killings. It
was New York City cops who produced the first leads
that ultimately led them to identify the gunman who
shot Joseph Piagentini. And it was a New York City cop
who found Linda Gill in New Orleans, setting off the
string of events that led to the capture of Herman Bell.
Yet even before Bell could be transported from Second
Street to police headquarters, FBI agents, communicating with the base by radio, sent out the word that led
to a lightning-fast press release crediting the Federal
Bureau of Investigation with the capture of a long-
sought fugitive on its Ten Most Wanted List. The story
went out instantaneously over the wire services.

Publicity, though, wasn't what was on our minds just
then. The essential thing was to question Bell the
moment he was brought in. Even a hardened militant
like Bell could go soft for a while after all he had been
through. For those first few moments when Bell found
himself suddenly surrounded, he must have known he

was a dead man, the only question in his mind whether they would kill him cleanly, as Bottom had killed Waverly Jones, or whether they would skewer him to the sidewalk with bullets, the way he himself had killed Joseph Piagentini. I already knew from detectives who had made it back to headquarters ahead of the car bearing the prisoner that Bell was badly shaken. "That fucker fancies himself some tough kind of item," one of them told me. "But he pissed in his pants when he saw us coming down on him." Given time—and it wouldn't take long—he would pull himself together. I wanted to question him before that happened.

It was then that I learned the price we were going to have to pay for cajoling the FBI into putting Bell on its Ten Most Wanted List and for letting the feds make the arrest. Throughout the law-enforcement community, it is widely believed that the FBI is reluctant to put a fugitive on the list until it has a reasonably good idea of where he can be found, for the bureau has no desire to embarrass itself by calling attention to its failures. Yet District Attorney Frank Hogan and Assistant D.A. John Keenan, who was in charge of the Piagentini-Jones case at the time, wanted Bell's name on the list and pressured the bureau until it complied. They knew that all around the country, especially in smaller communities, cops and deputy sheriffs study the list assiduously, for an assist in the capture of a most-wanted suspect is the capstone of their fantasies.

Unfortunately, there is another side to the coin, and that was the side I was getting to see in the hours after the arrest. When the FBI puts a man on its list, it takes a proprietary interest in him. As far as the bureau was concerned, Herman Bell was their prisoner—a position I had unwittingly strengthened by arranging to have him arrested on a federal warrant.

The moment Bill Butler brought Bell into headquarters, FBI agents descended on him, insisting that he be handed over to their custody. I tried to intervene but met with a quick rebuff. "All we need is a few minutes," one of the agents told me. "Then he's yours until we gotta bring him in for the arraignment."

I reminded the agents that their questions concerned a bank stickup while I wanted to question him about the murder of two police officers, but that argument cut no ice with them. A couple of high-ranking New Orleans police officials overheard the exchange and came forward to support me, but they had no more authority over the FBI than I did. I watched impotently as half a dozen federal agents escorted Bell down the corridor to a small interrogation room they had commandeered. The door snapped closed behind them. I checked my watch. It was nine-thirty.

The morning passed with maddening slowness. Ten o'clock came and went, eleven, eleven-thirty. Along the way I notified a desk officer that I would be needing a stenographer when I questioned Bell—if I ever got to question him, a contingency that was coming to seem more remote with each passing minute. "On a Sunday?" he asked, his tone incredulous, as though shocked that I had the presumption to ask his assistance in breaking the Commandments. "Besides," he added, modulating to a less pious but more pragmatic approach, "it's a holiday weekend. Even if I could find one of them at home, which I doubt, there's no way I could get him to come in."

"Try," I said.

He shrugged but went obediently to the phone. In half an hour he reported that he had called all the stenographers on the department's list with no results. Settling for second best, I sent Butler and Lyons off with a couple of New Orleans cops to track down a tape recorder. In the end they came up with two recorders but no microphones. When they finally located a mike, it didn't fit either of the machines, which turned out to be broken in any event. I gave up. The four of us—Butler, Fenton, Lyons, and myself—held an impromptu election at which Cliff was unanimously voted our recording secretary.

All the while, agents were going in and out of the room where Bell was being questioned. Every time I could, I buttonholed one of them to remind him we were still waiting, and each time I was told it would be just a couple of minutes. Around noon, one of them called the courthouse from a phone not far from where I was pacing. I could hear him making the arrangements for Bell's court appearance, explaining to a clerk why a federal magistrate would have to be located and dragged into court on a Sunday. I heard the agent say he expected to have the prisoner at the courthouse by twelve-thirty.

"What the hell are you talking about!" I shouted at him.

He covered the mouthpiece with his hand. "Take it easy," he said. "I'll be with you in a minute."

"The hell you will!" I yelled even louder. "It's twelve o'clock now and we haven't even had a chance to see him!"

Ignoring me, the agent buried his face in the phone,

speaking into his cupped hand. "I don't care who you get, any federal magistrate," he said. "Just so he's in the courthouse by twelve-thirty." Then he hung up and turned to me.

He was in his early thirties, with short blond hair, almost colorless eyes, and an impudent way of speaking he must have gone to school to learn. "Don't get all lathered up," he said, making a feint at walking past me.

I stepped sideways to block his way and his tone changed slightly, bringing it a small step closer to reasonableness. "Look," he said, "the guy's entitled to a speedy arraignment no matter what he's done. That's the law. It's not gonna take us but a half hour. When we bring him back, he's all yours. You c'n question him all you want."

"After the court assigns him a lawyer!" I shouted. "No fucking way."

"What can I tell you?" he answered with a shrug. "You'll get your chance."

He took one step past me, but I grabbed him by the shoulder and turned him around. "I got my chance right now," I said, looking straight down into his eyes.

Apparently that did the trick, because he nodded his head and scurried off for the interrogation room. Two minutes later an agent I hadn't seen before came out and asked me where I wanted them to deliver Bell. I indicated another interrogation room a few doors down.

Bell was brought in wearing handcuffs, two agents pushing him ahead of them through the door. If either of them said anything at all, it was no more than a perfunctory acknowledgment of our presence. Then they disappeared, closing the door behind them, leaving

Herman Bell standing in the middle of the room, his hands manacled behind him.

"Take the cuffs off him," I said.

Cliff found the right key and unlocked the handcuffs. Bell grunted his thanks and massaged his wrists for a moment as he looked straight at me. There was no hostility in his eyes, no anger, no fear. They said only that he had been brought in to talk business and that he was ready for it.

"Sit down," I said, indicating a chair in the center of the tiny square room. I leaned back against the desk behind me, five feet of space separating me from Bell. Fenton and Butler stood to either side of him, a few feet off, Cliff resting easily, almost casually, against the wall, a notebook in his hand, Butler at parade rest facing me.

"We've got some talking to do, but before we get started, is there anything you want?" I said. "You want a cigarette, cup of coffee, something to eat?"

"Uh, yeah. A cigarette, okay?" he said.

Butler handed him a pack and lit one for him.

"What about coffee?"

"Yeah, fine."

"Want some food?"

"No, just the coffee."

"Can you get him a cup of coffee, Bill?" I said. "Get one for me too. How do you take it?"

"Light," Bell said. "With sugar."

Butler left the room. I passed Bell a tin ashtray from the desk and he rested it on his knees, then looked up at me, waiting to hear what I had to say.

"All right," I began. "I'm Bob Tanenbaum, from the

district attorney's office in New York. This is Detective Fenton and the man who just left is Detective Butler. I assume you have been informed of your rights, but I'm going to repeat them anyway so there is no misunderstanding." I then recited the standard *Miranda* warning, and he indicated his comprehension at each of the appropriate places. I had an arrest warrant in my pocket, and I took it out and showed it to him. I explained that he had been indicted by a grand jury on two counts of murder, the intentional murder of Police Officer Jones and the intentional murder of Police Officer Piagentini.

"You understand the seriousness of the charges," I said. "If you don't want to talk to us, you're aware that you don't have to. If you want a lawyer before you talk to us, just say so."

"That's all right, go ahead," he said, stubbing his cigarette in the ashtray, which he then set on the floor between his feet. The utter absence of emotion in the room was shocking, as though we were merely two professionals at the preliminary stage of a business negotiation. Just then Butler returned with four paper cups of coffee. Bell took a sip from his, the steam curling at his eyes. He raised his head and waited impassively for me to go on.

"I'll level with you," I said, "because I think you're smart enough to realize we're holding all the cards. I don't have any reason to bluff. I'm not offering you any deal and I don't want you to get the impression it will go easier on you if you talk to us, because it won't. But I want you to understand we have a very strong case against you. We had a number of witnesses in the grand jury, including a lot of people you know. They did a lot of talking. So if you want to give us your side of it, this is your chance."

He shifted in his chair, the first sign of discomfort I had seen in him, so I said, "Before you tell us anything, I think you should know that we don't have capital punishment in New York. Even if that changes in the future, it won't apply to you. There is no death penalty in this case."

His eyes tightened and his head bobbed slightly, nodding his comprehension. I knew I had reached him with my last statement, but his response caught me completely off guard. "How can I prove to you that I haven't been in New York since 'sixty-seven?" he asked.

It was an uncanny choice of words, so perfectly delivered that I wondered if he had rehearsed it. I had heard scores of guilty men protest their innocence before, insisting they were somewhere else at the time of the crime, but I had never run into one with the cool gambler's nerves to merely insinuate his alibi in a rhetorical question. For an instant I didn't know what to say. I took a few steps away from the desk and then walked back to it and sat on the desk, my feet hanging a few inches off the floor, my hands tucked under my thighs. I could see in Bell's face he thought he had me confused, so I let him enjoy it a few seconds.

Then I leaned forward and said, "It won't work, Herman. Because when you sat on the car while you were waiting for the cops to come out, you left your fingerprints there. We have a fingerprint and a palm print and witnesses who saw you sitting there. Your hands were under you, you were sitting just the way I'm sitting right now, remember? So, Herman, unless someone else was using your hands that night no New York jury will buy your story."

His eyes went down to my hands and then came back again. He did remember. His face darkened with confusion as he studied me fixedly, seeing in my posture on the desk an exact duplicate of himself on the fender of the white Mustang a few minutes before the killings. In that instant he knew I could prove everything I had just said. I thought at the time, and still think today, that he was on the verge of confession, and would have confessed before we let him out of the interrogation room if we hadn't been interrupted by a sudden pounding on the door.

As Fenton crossed to the door, Bell turned in his seat to watch him go, breaking the spell.

"Okay, let's wrap it up, we gotta take him now," an FBI agent said.

I could see Cliff stiffen with rage. "You'll get him when we're done," he said, swinging the door closed.

The agent caught it against the palm of his hand, like a first baseman casually swiping at infield throws. "The arraignment's scheduled for twelve-thirty, it's twelve-thirty now," he said coolly. "We told you guys you could talk to him and you talked to him. C'mon, party's over."

He tried to step past Cliff into the room but Fenton shoved him back and slammed the door. Bell turned to face me again, but now I could see in his eyes I had lost him. "I don't know anything about that," he said. "I told you, I haven't been in New York since 'sixty-seven."

For the next five minutes I tried to get at him from half a dozen different directions. But his new awareness that I was the one under pressure took the pres-

sure off him and he was able to block or counter everything I threw at him. A number of Black Liberation
Army pamphlets offer advice for the "soldier" who
finds himself a "prisoner of war." He should buy time
and keep his captors off balance by pretending to cooperate. He should make an active attempt to confuse his
interrogators by feeding them useless information and
answering as many questions as possible, telling them
only what they cannot use or already know. Herman
Bell gave me a crash course in how it worked.

He readily identified pictures of Bottom, Washington,
and the Torres brothers, giving me both their real names
and their "revolutionary" nicknames. He even identified a
picture of Tony Bottom's pearl-handled .45 and admitted,
almost smirking when he said it, that he had seen it in
Bottom's possession in California a few months before the
killings. Bell was no fool. As I would learn in the course of
the months to come, he had a fairly substantial knowledge
of the law. He knew perfectly well there was nothing I
could do with what he told me because the statements of
one defendant are inadmissible as evidence against any
codefendants. I suspect he was deliberately taunting me
with his statements, knowing how badly I needed corrob-
orative evidence tying Bottom to that gun before he was
picked up with it in San Francisco.

All the while we talked, we could hear the voices of
what now sounded like half a dozen FBI agents in a
heated shouting match just outside the door, debating
whether to try coming in again. The interrogation was
becoming a complete farce and nothing I did could get
it back on the track again.

A few minutes passed, there was a knock on the

door, and two agents stepped through. Enraged as I had never seen him before, Cliff wheeled and charged them, his forearms in front of him like a pass-rushing lineman. But the only satisfaction any of us got out of the whole situation was that Cliff managed to get in a couple of good shots at them. They staggered backward a few steps before crashing heavily into the wall and Cliff was on them in an instant, his elbows in their chests screaming into their faces.

I had to shout his name three or four times before he heard me. "Give it up, give it up, Cliff!" I yelled. Butler was trying to pull him off the agents from the back, but Cliff didn't seem to notice at first. Then he stepped clear, realizing the futility of his rage. He bolted through the door, the pounding of his footsteps in the corridor quickly fading as he hurried away. The agents peeled themselves from the wall and tried to compose themselves, shaking their suits into place the way a dog shakes water from his back. As I passed Herman Bell on my way out of the room, he chuckled under his breath, the only man there who had enjoyed the show we all put on for him.

At the federal courthouse a few blocks from police headquarters, I saw two more faces of the chameleon personality whose photographs had baffled the San Francisco police two years earlier. The prisoner brought into the court to face the federal magistrate bore no resemblance at all to the wily and self-possessed young man who had confronted me in the interrogation room. His shoulders sagged and he moved slowly with an exaggerated shuffle, his eyes glued to the floor. When he spoke, it was in the low tones and the self-effacing, ungrammatical English of a southern black deliberately playing the humble and obedient "good nigger" before white authorities.

The purpose of the hearing was to set bail and determine Bell's eligibility for court-appointed counsel. "Yessuh," "No suh," "Yessuh," "Nosuh," he answered the questions, his voice so soft that half a dozen times he had to be asked to repeat his answers. He testified that he was unemployed and that his wife worked as a part-time barmaid. When he was asked how much money he had, he truthfully told the court he had seven thousand dollars.

"How does an unemployed man whose wife has a part-time job happen to have seven thousand dollars?" the magistrate demanded.

"Ah saves mah money," Bell muttered. There was laughter all around the courtroom and Bell smiled sheepishly, glancing from face to face as though it gratified him to have been found amusing.

I couldn't help wondering whether anyone was taken in by the act. In a sense I think they were, although I'm sure no one there imagined for a moment that this was the real Herman Bell on display. My reading of southern mores may be all wrong, but it seemed to me I was watching an age-old ritual in which what mattered was not the sincerity of the black man's performance but simply his willingness to give it. As far as Bell himself was concerned, I have no doubt that his ironic and mawkish overacting was motivated by very real and perhaps not groundless fears about what might happen to him in a southern jail if he didn't act right.

In the course of the hearing, I made a brief statement

in which I explained that although the prisoner was being held only on a bank-robbery charge, he had been indicted in New York for the murder of two police officers. I informed the court I soon would be filing papers for his transfer to New York for the purpose of answering those charges. I requested that he be held without bail. Earlier that morning I would have considered a satisfactory response by the magistrate to be a foregone conclusion, but the way things had been going for the past couple of hours, I had some very uneasy moments as the hearing went on. It was a great relief when the magistrate ordered Bell remanded without bail, pending a hearing scheduled for the middle of September.

At the conclusion of the proceeding, the court asked the prisoner if he had anything to say.

Bell raised his head slowly, his back straightening but his voice still low when he spoke. "It's already been written," he said, speaking so softly that only those within a few feet of him could make out his words.

"I'm sorry, Mr. Bell, could you please keep your voice up," the magistrate said.

My eyes had gone from one speaker to the other, and when I looked back to Bell I was shocked by the transformation. He stood tall, his shoulders squared defiantly. For the first time I was seeing the arrogant, self-righteous revolutionary who was the driving force behind the Black Liberation Army cell that planned and carried out the murders of Patrolmen Jones and Piagentini.

"Everything I have to say," he announced in a voice that echoed in the high-ceilinged, half-empty courtroom, "has already been written in the history of black people in America."

• • •

Our work in New Orleans was just about concluded, our mission far more successful than any of us had dared dream when we left New York barely two and a half days earlier. On Friday morning we had flown down to question some bank robbers; by Sunday afternoon Herman Bell had been arrested, arraigned, and remanded to a federal house of detention. Bill, Cliff, Tommie Lyons, and I booked seats on a Sunday-evening flight back to New York. Then we hung around headquarters, waiting for the New Orleans detectives to return with the fruits of the search warrant they had obtained for Bell's apartment.

Late in the afternoon, Lieutenant Eugene Fields of the New Orleans Police Department called us to his office to show us the materials removed from the living room and bedroom of 820A Second Street. In all, the police found five weapons—a 9-millimeter pistol, a .38-caliber revolver, a high-powered rifle, and two 12-gauge shotguns, one with a sawed-off barrel. The only one of these that had any particular interest for us was the .38, although I didn't have much hope it would turn out to be the weapon with which Bell murdered Piagentini. Christine Rowe had been quite positive in describing the gun she borrowed for Bell as a long-barreled revolver, and the gun found in New Orleans had a snub-nosed two-inch barrel. So far, everything Christine told us had checked out, but on the off chance she had been mistaken, I asked Fields to send me a copy of the ballistics test his men would be running on the weapon.

In addition to the guns and the seven thousand dollars Bell had referred to at the arraignment, New

Orleans police also found a small green overnight case at the back of the bedroom closet. In it was an impressive collection of false identification documents, including matched sets of birth certificates, driver's licenses, and social security cards in a variety of names. There was also a collection of New York newspaper clippings relating to the January 1972 murders of Foster and Laurie in the East Village. At the bottom of the case were half a dozen loose snapshots, one of which interested us considerably. In the center of the picture was Tony Bottom, seated in a blank-walled room, his body facing directly at the camera, his head turned to the left. Behind him and slightly to his left, seated with his arms folded across his chest, sat Francisco Torres in a black turtleneck and black leather jacket. At Bottom's right, almost out of the picture, his face partially obscured by an unrecognizably out-of-focus head in the foreground, sat Lester Bertram May, the eighteen-year-old bank robber Cliff Fenton had already questioned in New Orleans.

Obviously, the picture dated back at least two years, for Bottom had been in prison since August 1971.

"What time's our plane leave?" Cliff asked. "I want another crack at May. He knows these guys a lot better and a lot longer than he's letting on."

"Take as much time as you want," I told him. "They've got flights to New York every day."

Cliff met with May in a jailhouse conference room. Everything about Lester moved slowly, even his eyes, which wandered languidly along the bare walls without ever lighting anywhere. He was a shy and quiet young man, who spoke as slowly as he moved and had a habit of repeating anything said to him before responding. As a result, he came across as slow-witted, but Cliff Fenton had no difficulty seeing through the protective mask of stupidity Lester wore to keep a hostile world from guessing how much he knew.

Lester didn't deny that his association with Bell went back to San Francisco—either early 1971 or late 1970—in any case, prior to the murders in New York. Shown pictures of the five accused killers, he identified all of them. Bottom, Washington, and the Torres brothers, he said, had all been members of the same BLA cell as Herman Bell. Cliff asked him about a statement Bottom had made to the press shortly after his arrest, in which he boasted he was a general in the Black Liberation Army.

May laughed impishly and said, "T. B.? Shit, that turkey ain't no general. He's a private, man, a shit-assed little private. Wanted to be a general, though. Better believe it. Wanted to be a general real bad."

Cliff played him skillfully, talking to him about black radicalism in general, drawing him out, then narrowing the discussion from time to time in order to lead him into specifics. "The trick is just to get him rapping to you," the detective explained later. "I made out I agreed with a lot of the things he was saying, for example, about the plight of black people and the need for change. I even agreed with him about terrorism. If anyone from Internal Affairs had been listening to us, they would have figured I was a subversive. And then when we get all the way to cop-killing, I tell him that's where I draw the line. So the next thing I know he's defending cop-killing to me. He's explaining to me how they look at it and why it's neces-sary. I couldn't get him to the point where he would actually tell me about things they had done, but I learned a lot about how this particular bunch of them worked, the dynamics of the group. Bell was their real leader, the action guy. Washington was the big talker, the ideologist. Bottom apparently was unstable and flighty, a big bragger, but he worshiped Bell, and especially Bell's violence."

For all Fenton's expertise in prying information out of hostile sources, it was nevertheless May who set the limits on the interrogation session. He was willing to let the burly black detective, whom he genuinely seemed to like, get more out of him than he might otherwise have cared to divulge, but he shied like a spooked horse every time Cliff brought him to the edges of areas he didn't want to go into. When Cliff realized he had gotten as far as he could with cajolery, he shifted to a new tactic and put on some pressure. He added up the bank-robbery charges against May. "You're facing at least twenty years, man," he said. "You'll be lucky to be out in twenty. These cats'll put you away and forget where they put you. Why don't you smarten up, huh? I can put in a word for you, y'know. It might do you some good."

May threw the suggestion aside with a toss of his hands. "No way I'll do twenty," he said.

"That right? You got a way to add I never heard of?"

May's eyes steadied on Fenton for the first time in an hour and a half they had been together. For a long time he said nothing, the faintest traces of a smile curling the edges of his mouth. "Let's wait an' see," he said. "Don't make sense talkin' to you if I beat this thing, now, does it? But say they hit me with heavy time, then I'll give a holler for you, my man. 'Cause I got an ace in the hole, an' if I gotta play it, I'll play it."

Sixteen

THE PEOPLE OF THE STATE OF NEW YORK *against Anthony Bottom, Albert Washington, Francisco Torres, Gabriel Torres, and Herman Bell* opened in the New York Supreme Court at 100 Centre Street on Monday, January 7, 1974. The Torres brothers were represented by young radical lawyers with varying degrees of commitment to left-wing causes. Bottom had assigned counsel and Bell was defended by a venerable black civil-rights lawyer whose record as an advocate of racial equality was perhaps unequaled in America but who by no stretch of the imagination could be categorized as a radical. Albert Washington, who once had served as his own lawyer in an insanity hearing he won, elected to represent himself.

My assistant Ken Klein and I had been giving our complete attention to the prosecution of this case since I returned from New Orleans early in September. We marshaled the evidence, arranged it, sorted it in our minds until we were completely familiar with all of it and had worked out a detailed battle plan for our presentation to the jury. Ken and I carefully studied every scrap of grand jury testimony, every report filed by the police, in order to familiarize ourselves with what the witnesses would say. It has always been my policy to keep interviews with witnesses to a minimum, because defense attorneys often try to suggest to the jury that the witnesses have been coached. In this trial, where the defense might well rest on its contention that the three women in the Anderson Avenue apartment had been told what to say by the police and the prosecutor, it was especially important that I leave Celia Torres, Alie Horn, and Christine Rowe in a position to testify that there hadn't been an excessive number of visits to the district attorney's office.

I talked to Alie, Celia, and Christine just enough to assure myself they wouldn't spring any surprises on me in the courtroom. I knew there were a number of small contradictions in their recollections of the incidents of May 21, 1971, but that was something I would have to live with. As Christine remembered the evening, for example, Bell and Bottom left the apartment first, followed a few minutes later by Washington. The Torres brothers then came out of the bedroom and left together. Celia, though, was under the impression that all five defendants left together and would so testify. I knew that if I returned to this question often enough, she might begin to remember forgotten details, but I didn't want to do that. And I especially didn't want to tell her what Christine had said. If there were small discrepancies between her testimony and Christine's, I was confident a good jury would be able to put them in perspective. In any case, that was a chance I had to take, for I wasn't willing to put my witnesses in a position where they would have to admit on cross-examination that I had made efforts to coordinate their stories.

My biggest worry as the trial date approached was Gloria Lapp. Her identification of Bottom was positive, but her ability to convince a jury that her observations were accurate was, to put it gently, highly doubtful. I would have felt much more comfortable if I could have bolstered her testimony with Ruth Jennings's, even though Ruth had declined to identify Bottom at the San Francisco line-up. Ruth was a meticulously scrupulous witness who had been unwilling to give a positive identification of Bottom because the puffiness of his face had altered his appearance. If handled correctly in the courtroom, this scrupulousness could actually be turned to our advantage, far outweighing the disadvantage of her failure to pick out the defendant on a prior occasion. I was confident that if she were given a chance to see Bottom again, she would identify him unhesitatingly. Unfortunately, that was out of the question. Married the year before, she was in her fifth month of pregnancy at the start of the trial, had almost lost the baby, and in all likelihood would not be able to undergo the rigors of testimony and cross-examination. I could have asked for a delay but had no inclination to do so because the trial of these men had already been delayed long enough. Besides, I doubted very much that the judge would grant a continuance in order to allow the prosecutor to produce an eyewitness who had never publicly identified any of the defendants.

Gloria, then, would be on her own. If she managed to find some inner reserve of strength that would enable her to sit upright in the witness box, to answer questions forthrightly, to keep her mind clear when the defense started badgering her, we would be in good shape. If she hung her head, clamped her hands between her knees, and mumbled her answers hesitantly, as she did in my office when I questioned her, we were going to be in a lot of trouble. No juror would imagine for even a minute that this shy and frightened child would deliberately lie, but I could easily imagine a jury refusing to have confidence in her powers of observation and recollection.

As for other witnesses at the crime scene, we had very little to work with. Duncan Grant, the young man under the bench, had nothing to say and I had no intention of putting him on the stand. The defense might want to put him on, as a kind of negative witness, but as far as I was concerned they could have him if they wanted him.

Hector Grace, the gypsy-cab driver who first reported the shooting, identified Francisco Torres at a line-up held the day after Torres's arrest. Nevertheless, I decided not to call him as a witness, for I had grave doubts about the reliability of his testimony. In San Francisco, after all, he had picked two stand-ins.

That left Jack Franklin, the self-employed upholsterer who claimed to have seen three men, each around five feet in height. Jack generally had been discounted as a witness from the very first time he spoke to the police, in part because of his wild statements about height and in part because he alone saw three men when all the other witnesses saw two. But in January 1972 he picked out pictures of Francisco Torres and Tony Bottom from a photo display shown to him in the district attorney's office. If Ruth Jennings had been available to corroborate Gloria Lapp, I probably wouldn't have put Jack Franklin on the stand. Since I didn't have her, I decided to take a chance with him.

Except for Franklin's identification of Francisco Torres, therefore, we had virtually no evidence to locate any of the defendants other than Bell and Bottom at the crime scene. I was counting on the testimony of the three women in the Anderson Avenue apartment to establish that all five men had left the apartment with a common purpose and had returned in a manner that indicated that they had been together. I hoped the jury would be able to draw what I regarded as the entirely reasonable inference that all five men had been at Colonial Park. Jack Franklin's testimony, I felt, would put Francisco Torres there, but Gabriel Torres and Albert Washington were another matter.

I thought I knew exactly where Gabriel Torres had been, for his wife Celia had told a detective that Gabriel explained his role to her in bed one night shortly after the murders. According to the detective, Gabriel told Celia he was posted at the top of the staircase leading up to Coogan's Bluff. I assumed he was acting as a lookout and speculated that perhaps he was the driver of the getaway car, if indeed the killers had one—something we were never able to determine. Unfortunately, Celia's statement could not be introduced at the trial. Even though she would be taking the stand as a witness against her husband and would be free to testify about his words and actions in the presence of the other defendants, I would not be allowed to let her tell the jury anything she learned from him in the privacy of their bedroom, for this was a privileged communication between husband and wife and therefore inadmissible in court.

With regard to Albert Washington, I didn't have a clue as to his exact location. My own personal figuring was that Washington and Francisco Torres were in the project parking lot, perhaps near Piagentini's and Jones's patrol car, where it would be logical for the killers to have stationed a backup assassination team. Ken, Cliff, Bill, and I spent a lot of hours working out different scenarios to account for the ragtag assortment of facts and quasi-facts we had gleaned from the various witnesses. The one I liked best had Washington and Francisco Torres near the patrol car, which was parked on the south side of the lot. Moments after the shooting, when Bell and Bottom fled to the west in the direction of Coogan's Bluff, Washington and Francisco Torres would have run in the same direction, parallel to them but on the opposite side of the lot. Somewhere along the way, after passing Hector Grace's gypsy cab but before reaching Jack Franklin's station wagon, Francisco Torres would have cut across the lot to join Bell and Bottom. This could explain why Grace saw only two men while Franklin saw three, one of whom he had identified as Francisco Torres.

According to this hypothesis, Albert Washington, alone now on the south side of the parking lot, would have headed straight for the top of the bluff, where he would have passed Gabriel Torres without stopping. Unable to determine if he should wait for the others as planned or if it was now every man for himself, Gabriel would have hesitated before making his decision to go

with Washington. This could explain why Gabriel
Torres and Albert Washington were the first ones back
to the Anderson Avenue apartment and why Gabriel
accused Washington of having "left" him.

Meanwhile, if Jack Franklin's claim that he saw
three men was correct, it would have been Bell,
Bottom, and Francisco Torres who turned in to the
project instead of going straight for the stairway at the
west end. Continuing with this scenario, somewhere
along the way they must have split up, for Duncan
Grant, in front of building 159-26, saw only two men—
presumably Bell and Bottom, in view of the testimony
that Francisco Torres arrived at his brother's apartment
alone a few minutes ahead of the two gunmen.

Obviously, I could prove none of this. Francisco
Torres's and Albert Washington's specific roles in the
killings could not be substantiated by a single witness
or a single shred of physical evidence, and the only evidence I had that Gabriel Torres may have been located
at the top of Coogan's Bluff was the totally inadmissible
word of his wife. However, I hoped that even without
any specific showing as to the activities of the three
nonshooters, the testimony of the three women in the
apartment would be enough to convince the jury that I
had proved my case.

Making up the slate of witnesses was only the first step
in preparing the case for trial. A prosecutor must know
not only what his witnesses will say on direct examination
but also what the defense will try to get them to say on
cross. By guesswork, intuition, and knowledge derived
from his previous experience, he must try to get as familiar with the defense case as the defendants' own lawyers.

John Keenan's axiom, drummed into me through the years I spent working under him, was my guiding principle: Any time a prosecutor is surprised by something that happens in the courtroom, it means he hasn't been doing his homework.

Ken Klein and I spent countless hours analyzing the defense, calculating the moves open to them, role-playing the opposition attorneys until we had learned their parts by heart. We made an interesting discovery which, to the layman, might seem encouraging, but which is little comfort at all to a trained trial lawyer. We discovered that the defense had no case at all. By that I mean they had no *affirmative* defense, no way to prove themselves innocent. Under our system of law, of course, accused persons are not required to prove their innocence. Yet they often attempt to do so, by establishing an alibi or introducing some other evidence to show that they lacked the opportunity, the capability, or the motive to commit the crime with which they are charged.

We had a number of reasons for discounting the possibility of an affirmative defense in this case. To establish an alibi, for instance, they would need a witness to swear either that they were not in New York at the time of the killings, as Herman Bell claimed immediately after his arrest, or that they went somewhere other than Colonial Park when they went out on the night of May 21, 1971. Yet what sort of witness could they get? A good percentage of their associates were wanted by the law and hardly could walk into court to testify for them. Many of the rest were revolutionary gangsters who would have had insuperable credibility problems with the jury.

The only other possibility for an affirmative defense was a defense which attempted to prove that Bottom and Washington did not come into possession of the pearl-handled .45 and Waverly Jones's service revolver until some time after the killings. And how could that be proven unless someone was willing to testify that he gave, loaned, or sold one or both of them a .45 used to murder a police officer and a .38 taken from the officer's dead body? That was a lot to ask of a friend, since anyone who so testified might end up taking the rap for them.

To say that the defendants did not have an affirmative defense, however, is not to say that the outcome of the trial was a foregone conclusion. On the contrary, it meant simply that we had to be prepared for an all-out attack on our witnesses, for the defense lawyers would attempt to knock them over like a row of dominoes. Basically, there were two directions our opponents could take, and I fully expected them to try both.

First, they would try to turn the case into a political trial. It would be the persecution of black radicals by white authority figures bent on punishing them for their revolutionary views. Second, they would bolster their ideological position with a contention that the five men on trial had been deliberately framed by the police because of their known membership in the Black Panther Party and the Black Liberation Army.

At first glance, a defense predicated on a political frameup struck me as hopeless and puny, for there was absolutely no evidence to back up such a claim. But the more I thought about it, the more I came to recognize the insidious cleverness of such a ploy. For when a lawyer argues that his client has been framed, he does not have to refute the evidence, for it is the essence of a frame that there will be evidence. Instead, he has to convince the jury that the evidence is not authentic because the prosecution is not impartial. I was forced to acknowledge that certain aspects of the way this case had been played into the hands of the defense, particularly the imprisonment of two key witnesses for thirteen months.

In my mind's eye, I could see clearly every detail of the scenario the defendants would lay before the jury:

Two cops were brutally murdered, and for three months the police were utterly stymied, their rage and frustration mounting with each passing day. Then, by chance, two black militants were arrested in San Francisco with one of the murder weapons and a gun taken from one of the slain officers. Never mind how they came by these weapons. The police thought they knew. They flew four eyewitnesses to California. To make sure there would be no mistakes, they told the newspapers that two suspects in the killings were under arrest. The story ran on the front page of the Daily News, where the witnesses were sure to see it and would know that this time they were expected to identify someone.

Even so, only one of the witnesses fell for the trick. A gullible teen-age girl, trying very hard to please the detectives who had been so nice to her, picked out Tony Bottom. Some of the others also tried to accommodate but guessed wrong. One of them fingered a stand-in, another picked two stand-ins. Only the fourth witness stood her ground and identified no one.

Now the police had a serious problem. They had induced this foolish child to identify Bottom, but no one had been lucky enough to finger Washington for them. Yet they weren't about to release a dedicated revolutionary like Albert Washington, especially when they needed two murderers. So they began investigating and learned that their two prisoners had indeed been in New York in 1971. They even learned where they had lived. Their next step was perfectly in character. They rounded up the women these defendants lived with. They jailed them, took their children away from them, and told them they could earn their freedom by going before a jury and implicating their men. After over a year in prison, the women finally agreed to do as they were told. They were spoon-fed a story about five men going out in the evening and returning with guns.

Ladies and gentlemen of the jury, the five men on trial here are indeed radicals. But that is not a crime. They carried guns. But that does not make them killers. We freely concede that the weapons found in their possession are tied to these two brutal murders. Do you think for a moment these men would have had these guns with them if they had known the guns were hot; that is why the killers got rid of them. Yet the State contends that because these men had the murder weapons, they are the murderers. For proof it offers you the testimony of three women of doubtful character, two of whom had to be locked in jail for over a year in order to secure the testimony you have heard. And it offers you the statements of a weak-willed girl who, alone among the witnesses to this crime, was willing to identify one of these men as one of the killers she had seen four months earlier. Can you believe beyond a reasonable doubt that Gloria Lapp is right in her identification while all the others who were flown to the lineup in San Francisco are wrong? Can you believe beyond a reasonable doubt that Christine Rowe, Alexandra Horn, and Celia Torres are not deliberately perjuring themselves in order to secure their freedom and be reunited with their children?

That was the defense I would have to answer. It wasn't the sort of defense I could refute with facts, for it wasn't based on facts. Ultimately, whether the jury found for the People or for the defendants would depend upon only one elusive and unpredictable factor—the credibility of four young black women.

The trial began with a preliminary hearing before Judge Aloysius J. Melia for the purpose of examining the circumstances surrounding the arrest of Bottom and Washington in San Francisco. Sergeant George Kowalski, who would have been killed in his car if the submachine gun Albert Washington aimed directly at him hadn't jammed, testified about the attempted murder, the chase, the arrests, and the seizure of the guns. At one point I asked him if he was familiar with the operation of a weapon such as the one that had been aimed at him. He said he was. I then asked him to show the court the manner in which Washington held it.

A court officer handed the machine gun to Kowalski. For a moment he balanced it in his hands, getting the feel of it, his lean, handsome face working to keep back the emotions it must have stirred in him. He raised it to his shoulder, bending his head to sight down the long barrel, the heavy metal seemingly as light in his hands as a child's wooden rifle. Slowly, he panned across the nearly empty courtroom, sweeping past the prosecution table, past the center aisle, until he came to a stop at the defense table, the muzzle of the gun aimed straight at Albert Washington.

All five defendants and their lawyers leaped to their feet, the defendants screaming obscenities, the lawyers shouting protests. They had all known, of course, that the gun was unloaded and had been rendered inoperable before it was brought into the courtroom. Yet their momentary terror was as real as the involuntary flinching of a driver ducking from a snowball thrown against his windshield. They had seen Kowalski's face, as I had. For an instant, the murderous intensity in his eyes was a more palpable reality than the known condition of the weapon in his hands.

While the judge tried to quiet the courtroom, George Kowalski calmly lowered the machine gun, a pleasant, satisfied smile on his face. "That was the manner in which the defendant held the gun," he said softly.

Kowalski was followed to the stand by San Francisco police officers Robert Rames, Peter Gurnari, and Robert Quinn, all of whom had played key roles in the arrest of Bottom and Washington. After listening to their testimony and the legal arguments on both sides, Judge Melia ruled that the weapons had been seized legally and therefore were admissible in this trial. He also ruled that any allusion to the attempt to murder Sergeant Kowalski would be highly prejudicial to the rights of the defendants. In effect, he was saying that the fact that these two defendants were in the cop-killing business should not be allowed to influence the jury when it came to decide whether or not they had killed two cops.

As a matter of law I knew that Justice Melia was on solid ground, for the previous or subsequent commission of a similar crime is rarely admissible unless some unique and distinctive feature is common to the M.O.'s in both instances. Yet from my point of view, the judge's decision had very disturbing consequences. Because Kowalski and the other San Francisco cops would not be allowed to say a word about the attempted shooting, the chase, and the gun battle, the jury would be left to wonder whether there had been a reason for stopping the car or whether the police were merely harassing a pair of black motorists by stopping them and searching their vehicle. One small piece would be missing from the puzzle, and the defense would be free to insinuate that the missing pieces fit in perfectly with its picture of police countermilitancy. The judge's first ruling in the case thus added a modicum of credibility to the charge of a police frame-up. It was an ominous way to start.

Indeed, one of the most troublesome features of this trial was the general atmosphere in which it was conducted. Frank Serpico and the Knapp Commission, with their revelations of widespread police corruption, melded with the sordid revelations of Watergate to produce a climate in which any public official, and especially any police officer, took the witness stand with a built-in credibility problem. What is more, most intelligent New Yorkers were familiar with stories, emanating from elsewhere in the country, of unprovoked police raids on Black Panther Party facilities. A few years earlier, the notion that a big-city police department and a big-city district attorney's office could join forces with police from the opposite end of the country to frame five innocent men would have been laughed out of court. In 1974, any jury we were likely to be able to impanel would have to admit that such things certainly could happen, and perhaps even went on all the time.

Nothing brought home to me more clearly this diametric shift in the cycle of public opinion than the examination of prospective jurors. In my early years of trying cases, defense counsel invariably asked each prospective juror whether he or she was more likely to believe a police officer than a civilian, whether the testimony of a cop was worth more than the testimony of a private citizen. Over the years I had heard this question less and less frequently, until in the Piagentini-Jones trial I found myself repeatedly asking jurors whether they assumed all cops were naturally biased, whether they could receive a cop's testimony with the same open mind they gave to the testimony of anyone else.

The process of jury selection lasted over a month. We sifted through more than six hundred men and women before finally settling on twelve jurors and four alternates acceptable to both sides—all six sides, I should say, for each juror was questioned not only by me but also by the four defense counsel plus Albert Washington, who was appearing pro se—that is, as his own lawyer.

The procedure for selecting jurors is an exhausting one, both for the attorneys and for the jurors. We start off with about seventy-five prospective jurors seated in the spectator section of the courtroom. They are first addressed by the judge, who questions the group as a whole, asking them to raise their hands if they have problems in certain areas. He reads the names of the defendants, the victims, the defense counsel, the prosecution team, and all scheduled witnesses to determine if any of them are personally known to any members of the panel. Twelve individuals are then selected by lot and sent to the jury box, where the judge questions each of them more specifically, ascertaining their names, their occupations, and any previous experiences with the police, with the courts, or as victims of crime. Then each lawyer gets his turn.

The lawyers are given a wide latitude to ask questions about the attitudes and beliefs of the prospective jurors in order to expose any biases. In a trial such as this, which promised to go on for months and in which the defendants might be assumed to have armed and dangerous supporters on the outside, a good number of citizens are reluctant to serve as jurors and therefore disqualify themselves by giving answers indicative of prejudice. Most prospective jurors, however, give truthful and conscientious answers, which the lawyers on both sides must then evaluate. If a panelist says, for example, that he thinks it unlikely an innocent person would be indicted, the defense can challenge for cause. Since one of my key witnesses was going to be Celia Torres, I asked all the prospective jurors how they felt about a wife who testified against her husband. Many of them said they would be dubious about her testimony, which might be the product of a grudge or some other marital problem. In such cases I would challenge for cause.

The judge must rule on each challenge for cause. If, in his mind, the prospective juror's answers give evidence of bias, of less than an open mind in any relevant area, the challenge will be sustained. Often, however, a challenge for cause may be denied or a prospective juror may answer all the questions satisfactorily and still be unacceptable to the defense, the prosecution, or both, perhaps because of something in his or her demeanor or attitude. In these cases, the lawyers may exercise their right to peremptorily challenge. Unlike challenges for cause, peremptory challenges are strictly limited in number. At most murder trials in New York, each side is allowed twenty peremptory challenges. At this trial, because there were multiple defendants, each side—the prosecution and the defense as a whole—was allotted thirty peremptories.

In many ways, the process of jury selection is like a table-stakes poker game where the bets are laid in peremptory challenges instead of chips. If you run out of challenges you lose. Spend them too freely at the beginning and you may be forced to accept a juror you do not want at the end. But once a juror has been accepted, the decision is final and he or she cannot be challenged later. So if you husband your challenges too carefully you may wind up with half a dozen unused peremptory challenges and some marginal jurors you would rather not have.

In selecting a jury, incidentally, the defense has two built-in advantages. The first is the requirement that a verdict be unanimous. This means the prosecutor must find twelve jurors who will see the issue his way. The defense needs to find only one. Their second advantage, far less important than the first but still of considerable significance, derives from the fact that they always get to challenge last. As a result, whenever a prospective juror is mutually unacceptable, it is the prosecutor who must spend one of his precious challenges, for he cannot afford to assume that the defense will challenge if he doesn't. In effect, this gives the defense perhaps ten or twelve extra challenges over the course of jury selection.

Any prospective jurors not challenged after they are examined become permanent members of the jury at that point. They remain in the jury box while new prospective jurors are promoted to the seats vacated by the challenged candidates. The round of questioning then begins again. When the entire seventy-five-member panel in the spectator section has been depleted, the judge sends down to the central jury room for a new batch and we must start again from the very beginning with the judge's preliminary questions.

Only those who have observed a number of trials from beginning to end can fully appreciate the extent to which the voir dire examination of prospective jurors is an integral part of the trial process, not a detached preliminary. In a sense, it is a comprehensive opportunity for a lawyer to influence the thinking of the jurors without being bound by the rules of evidence. By asking whether all sorts of irrelevant factors will affect their verdict, he can help to assure that they will. At least six hundred times I heard variants of the same question. "Considering all that you have heard and read in recent years about police corruption and lying by government officials, would you be able to keep your mind open to the possibility that the police would fabricate evidence to close a case they were unable to solve?" "Being familiar with the known animosity that goes both ways between the police and black radicals, would you be able to give a fair hearing to the possibility that the police would want so badly to take some radicals they considered dangerous off the streets that they would frame them for a crime they hadn't committed?"

Some of the jurors impaneled early in the process got to hear the defense's statements about police corruption, lying, frame-ups, and intimidation of witnesses as often as I did, for once a juror is selected, he or she must sit and listen, free to neither knit nor read, while the lawyers hypnotically repeat the same questions endlessly. No one knows to what extent jurors are influenced by the questions they hear in the voir dire, but it is inconceivable to me that anyone could completely put out of his or her mind something he or she has heard for six hours a day every day for five weeks.

A few times as the jury selection went on, I tried my hand at counterprogramming. Every time the defense asked, "Could you accept the possibility that a police officer would lie?" I would ask, "You're going to demand evidence, aren't you? Just because the defense says *frame, frame, frame* a thousand times, you're not going to let that influence your thinking, are you?"

For the most part, though, I elected not to fight fire with fire in this area, calculating that the defense was losing more friends by the way it was drawing out the process than it was gaining with its long-winded and unsubtle attempts at indoctrination. I kept my questions simple and to the point, for there wasn't anything special I was looking for in this jury. I wanted what I always wanted—a group of people without any discernible biases, intelligent enough to follow a long trial without getting lost behind the smokescreens the defense would be throwing up in front of them. I didn't want any headstrong types who would make it a matter of ego to go against the majority and a matter of pride to hold out forever. I didn't want any weaklings who would let the name of the Black Liberation Army intimidate them into a pusillanimous vote for acquittal. I didn't want any eccentrics who would fasten on this or that petty inconsistency until they lost all perspective. I looked for a jury of strong, reasonable, and honest individuals.

And every night I prayed that none of the local television stations would put *Twelve Angry Men* on the late show until after we had a verdict.

During lunch recess one day while jury selection was still going on, I got a phone call from Diane Piagentini. She said she wanted to see me. From John Keenan and some of the assistants who had worked under him on the case, I knew she had been following the investigation closely, often coming to the office to be brought up to date. Since September, though, I had been so busy with my preparation that I hadn't had time to be surprised at not hearing from her. I asked her to come to my office at a quarter past four.

When the court adjourned for the day, I returned to

my office to find her already waiting for me. Except for the newspaper picture of Diane and Commissioner Murphy taken at Harlem Hospital the night her husband died, I had never seen her before. Yet she looked exactly as I imagined she would. In the course of a few agonizing hours on a spring night in 1971 a young wife, the mother of two small children, suddenly had plummeted past youth to widowhood. Yet it hardly seemed she had aged a day in the three years that had passed since then. It was as though time had stopped for her, as though the cares and worries of raising her fatherless children could in no way add to what had already been done to her life by men neither she nor her husband ever met. She was pale and tense with the strain of meeting me, yet there was a strength without bitterness in her clear dark eyes.

I offered her the upholstered chair by the window and pulled up another to face it, so that I wouldn't have to sit with my desk between us. She declined coffee.

"I've been wondering what you'd be like," she said, laughing lightly with embarrassment. For about twenty minutes we talked pleasantly, like any two strangers meeting for the first time. After her phone call, I had wondered why she wanted to see me, but I soon began to feel she simply wanted to get to know the man now responsible for seeing that justice was done to her husband's murderers. We talked mostly about me, for she had a lot of questions. She asked if I was married and I told her I was. It seemed to bother her that Patti and I had no children, but I was able to reassure her that we planned on a family. I told her I had been born in Brooklyn, went to college and law school in Berkeley, met Patti while I was in school, along with a hundred other details that fill up the shady corners of small talk. I felt awkward monopolizing the conversation and would have asked her questions about herself except that I didn't know what to ask.

At one point her eyes darkened and she looked at me searchingly. "I hope you don't think I'm prying, only I have to know who you are," she said. "It's all so terribly important to me. Sometimes I feel like my life has stopped and it won't start again until this trial is over. Do you know what I mean?"

I told her I thought I did. I wanted to reassure her about my own commitment to the case, for I had never been involved in anything that meant so much to me. But I couldn't bring myself to say it, for what was my commitment compared with hers?

"I want to go to the trial," she said. "I want to be there. When will it start?"

I told her I thought jury selection would go on at least another week. Then I told her I didn't want her to come. She asked why.

"Please don't misunderstand me, Mrs. Piagentini," I said. "I don't think it's a good idea. There are a lot of reasons. There's going to be a lot of very specific testimony I don't think you should hear."

"About Joe?"

"Yes."

She nodded her head but looked at me hard, and I couldn't help but feel she was remembering the way the commissioner and his staff had treated her at the hospital. Yet it wasn't only her feelings I was concerned about. I could tell she was a strong, self-controlled woman, but I wondered if anyone could be expected to hear what she would hear in that courtroom without breaking down. Sooner or later either her rage or her sorrow would overmaster her, and the repercussions of any outburst might ricochet back to hurt us.

"I can handle that," she said.

"I think you can," I agreed. "But there are other considerations, too. The defense is going to try to make something out of your presence. They'll say that we're playing for the sympathy of the jury."

"That's nonsense," she objected. "The jury won't even know who I am."

"They will after the defense tells them."

I could see in her eyes that I had given her something she would have to think over. She stood up and crossed to the door. "Will that make it harder for you?" she asked.

I opened the door for her. "I don't want to tell you it will make the difference, Mrs. Piagentini," I said. "I don't think it will. But we have a very strong case. They're desperate. They'll try anything. I don't want to give them anything they can turn against us."

She lowered her eyes, signaling her acquiescence. "All right," she said. "I believe you. I hope I can trust you. I think I can, but it's so hard to know who to trust." Then she looked up at me and said, "You will convict them, won't you, Mr. Tanenbaum?"

"I'll do everything I can."

"But you will convict them?"

"Yes."

"Please," she said. "I want to start my life again."

Seventeen

AFTER OPENING STATEMENTS BY THE PROSE-
cution and the defense, the People's case began with a few
technical witnesses who were necessary for introducing
charts and photographs of the crime scene we would be
using throughout the trial. Richard Hill then testified
about finding the bodies of Piagentini and Jones. He was
followed to the stand by Patrolman Michael Warnecke,
one of the first cops to respond to the scene. Although the
testimony of neither Hill or Warnecke had any substantial
bearing upon the guilt or innocence of the defendants,
there were good reasons for putting them on the stand. A
courtroom is like a theater, and every prosecutor must
always think like a dramatist. Hill and Warnecke took the
jury out of the courtroom and brought them to Colonial
Park on the night of May 21, 1971. Through their eyes, the
jury saw the rain-slicked, bloodstained sidewalks, the
fallen bodies of two uniformed men, the hideous brutality
of these murders. The testimony of Richard Hill, a sincere
and personable young black man, was especially moving:

Q: Mr. Hill, are you familiar with the Colonial Park
   Housing Project here in New York County?

A: Yes, I am.

Q: Now sir, directing your attention to the evening of May 21, 1971, do you recall that night, the night that the two police officers were shot at the Colonial Park Housing Project?

A: Yes, I do.

Q: At approximately ten-thirty in the evening, Mr. Hill, can you tell us where you were and what you were doing?

A: About ten-thirty that evening, I was just getting out of a cab on Eighth Avenue. I was, I'd say, maybe thirty or forty feet from the entrance of the project.

Q: Now, when you got out of the cab, where were you going?

A: I was heading inside the project, toward the project.

Q Could you tell us what, if anything, you heard and what you did?

A: Well, I heard what appeared to be gunshots, but I thought they were firecrackers.

Q: Where did you go after you heard the gunshots?

A: I continued walking toward the project. There's a pathway that leads between Building Fourteen and Building Twenty.

Q: You were walking then in a westerly direction, is that correct?

A: Right.

Q: Would you tell us what if anything you observed at that point?

A: Okay. I was walking toward the center of the project and at that time I seen what seemed to be a clump of clothing that was lying on the ground. I turned and started walking toward it because it appeared to be moving. And as I got closer, I ran up on one of the police officers trying to make it toward the underbrush. There was a clump of bushes there in back of a group of benches and he was trying to make it underneath the clump of bushes there.

Q: Was this officer white or black?

A: He was white.

Q: Can you tell us his condition as you observed it?

A: I would say semi-conscious, you know. I couldn't make out really what he was saying, but he was trying to make it underneath the bushes. And at that time I seen another patrolman who was lying face down, no movement whatsoever. He was black. The first thing I noticed was a bullet hole in the back of his head and he wasn't moving at all. He was lying still.

Q: What else did you observe at that time?

A: At that time I bent down to look over him, and I saw there weren't any weapons on him. And the other patrolman, he didn't have his weapon on him either. There was a walkie-talkie lying between them and I picked up the walkie-talkie and called in a Mayday.

Q: How much time elapsed, as best you can estimate, from the time you picked up the walkie-talkie to the time that patrol cars arrived?

A: I'd say no more than a minute, minute-and-a-half.

Q: Did you aid in placing any of the officers in a patrol car?

A: Yes, I did. I aided and placed Piagentini—no, Jones—in the car. They took Piagentini first.

Q: When you say Jones and Piagentini, Jones is the black officer?

A: Right.

Q: Piagentini, the white officer?

A: Right.

Hill and Warnecke were followed to the stand by Gloria Lapp. She and I had gone over her testimony often enough that I felt confident she would handle herself well on direct examination. She didn't let me down. Despite an obvious case of stage fright, which actually may have helped us by winning the sympathy of the jurors, she told her story with an impressive recall of circumstantial detail. She told of seeing two police officers entering the building as she and Ruth Jennings left, of going to the back parking lot to wait for Ruth's father, of seeing two men in the vicinity of the car parked in space number 178. Stepping down from the witness stand, she went to the large diagram of the Colonial Park grounds and marked exactly where she and Ruth had waited and exactly where the two men had waited scarcely a dozen feet away, one pacing the sidewalk, sucking on leaves he tore from the shrubbery, the other seated on the left front fender of a white Mustang.

I asked her if she had gotten a good look at the shorter of the two men, the one seated on the car. She said she hadn't. "Was there any particular reason for that?" I asked.

"Yes. He had his head turned away from me."

At the jury box railing she demonstrated how he had been seated, his body facing toward her, his head turned over his right shoulder, looking fixedly in the direction of the project building. I asked her if she had gotten a good look at the taller man, the one who paced the sidewalk.

A: Yes.

Q: Now, Miss Lapp, do you see in court the taller man you saw picking the leaves by the bushes, and who you saw shoot the officers?

A: Yes.

Q: Will you please stand up and point to that individual.

A: It's him, the one in the blue shirt. [Indicating the defendant Bottom.]

She then went on to explain to the jury how she and Ruth Jennings had grown impatient after ten or fifteen minutes of waiting, how they had walked to the side of the building, passing the two men, to call up to Ruth's apartment.

> So we got off the car and we walked down the walkway past these two guys, and we walked further until we got to where we could call straight up, directly up to Ruth's window. And I turned around and I saw the two officers that were in the building, and the two guys that were seated on the car were walking behind them, and I didn't pay too much attention to it. So we turned back around, and then the two men shot the two officers, and one of them, one of the officers, was laying on the ground, and the taller one shot the officer.

Q: Now, which one, which officer, was on the ground closer to you?

A: The white officer.

Q: Could you tell us what, if anything, you recall the white police officer doing while the two men were shooting?

A: He was moaning and he was begging for his life.

Q: Where was he at that time? Was he standing, kneeling, lying?

A: He was lying.

Q: He was lying on the sidewalk?

A: Yes. And he tried to get up.

Q: And what did the tall man and the other man do as he tried to get up?

A: They shot him again.

She then told the jury that she fled into the building to Ruth Jennings's apartment and returned downstairs about ten minutes later, at which point she was picked up by two uniformed police officers who drove her to the Thirty-second Precinct for questioning. I purposely avoided any questions about her conduct inside the Jennings apartment, where she and Ruth had brushed out their hair and changed clothing in an attempt to alter their appearances. The jury might have found the story touching, but on cross-examination the defense would badger her about whether she was afraid of the killers, who by her own testimony had fled, or of involvement with the police. I knew I could count on their raising the issue of intimidation of witnesses when Christine Rowe, Alie Horn, and Celia Torres took the stand. I had no intention of giving them an opening to start airing that theme with Gloria.

After testifying about seeing Bottom at the 168th Street subway station a few days after the shooting, she told of attending five line-ups and of identifying Bottom in San Francisco. In all, I kept her on the stand less than two hours, a good twenty minutes of which was consumed with legal arguments at the side bar concerning defense objections to some of my questions. Although she had some difficulty keeping her voice up and often had to be asked to speak louder, she came across on the whole as a sincere albeit nervous young woman conscientiously trying to tell what she knew. I had every reason to be pleased with her performance but could take little comfort in that. Not only weren't we out of the woods yet, we hadn't even gone into them.

The defense went after her from the opening bell, trying to throw her off balance with questions she hadn't expected, jumping from one area to another, confusing her, then returning to a topic seemingly abandoned a few moments earlier. Within five minutes, her delicately balanced composure began to erode, then crumble.

Q: Miss Lapp, let's go back to the date this incident happened. You were sitting on a car, is that correct, with your friend Ruth Jennings?

A: Yes.

Q: And you saw two men sitting on another car, is that correct?

A: Yes.

Q: Now did you get a good look at the two men?

A: One.

Q: Were they facing your direction when they were sitting on the car?

A: One.

Q: One was facing your direction?

A: Yes.

Q: Which one, the taller or the shorter?

A: The taller.

Q: What was the shorter one doing?

A: Sitting on the same fender.

Q: Looking the same way, looking toward the west, toward you, right?

A: No, looking straight across.

Q: Did he ever in those fifteen minutes look in your direction?

A: I didn't see him.

Q: You two girls were sixteen years of age, is that correct?

A: Yes.

Q: And is it your testimony that you don't remember the shorter of the two people looking at you. Just in a general way, you do have an interest in boys—in men—don't you?

> MR. TANENBAUM: Objection.
> THE COURT: Sustained.

Q: Well, there did come a time when you got up, you walked past them. Did you look at the shorter of the two men as you walked past them?

A: Not really.

Q: You didn't look at them to see whether they were good looking or not? Anything like that?

A: Yes.

Q: Was he good looking, the shorter one?

A: I didn't see him. I told you, I didn't look at him.

Q: Is that what you told me, Miss Lapp? Well, let's move on. Where did the police first question you that night?

A: At the precinct.

Q: How did you get to the precinct?

A: They took us in a police car.

Q: Did you have any conversations with anybody on the way to the police station?

A: Yes. With the police who was in the car with us.

Q: How many police officers were in that car?

A: I don't know.

Q: Was it a regular police car or an unmarked car?

A: It was a . . . I don't know.

Q: You don't remember, is that correct?

A: Yes.

Q: Had you ever been in a police car before that date?

A: No.

Q: Now, do you remember speaking to Detective Butler at the Thirty-second Precinct about this case that night?

A: Yes.

Q: Do you remember telling Detective Butler that when you were sitting on the car, the two men who were sitting on the other car got up and shot the police officers?

A: Will you say that again?

Q: Did you tell Detective Butler that you and Ruth were sitting on the car when you saw the two men shoot the police officers?

[The witness shakes her head in the negative.]

Q: You are sure of that?

[The witness shakes her head in the affirmative.]

THE COURT: Don't shake your head, Miss Lapp. This gentleman here has to take down what you say.

Q: Now I want to show you this piece of paper,

Detective Butler's notes. It's only one paragraph, right?

A: Yes.

Q: Looking at that, do you want to change your answer in any way?

A: No.

Q: Miss Lapp, could you look at me instead of Mr. Tanenbaum? You don't have to look at me if that's unpleasant, but please try and answer the questions without any help from Mr. Tanenbaum.

> MR. TANENBAUM: Your honor, I object to that.
> THE COURT: Sustained.
> DEFENSE COUNSEL: Your Honor, she was looking directly at him.
> THE WITNESS: I wasn't looking at Mr. Tanenbaum.
> THE COURT: That's enough. Now let's continue.

Q: Miss Lapp, I was asking you, did you tell Detective Butler that at the time of this occurrence you were sitting on a car?

A: Yes.

Q: You did tell those things to Detective Butler, is that correct?

A: I must have. He wrote it down here.

Q: But do you remember? I'm asking you to search back in your memory, not what's down here. Do you remember?

A: No.

Q: So it is fair to say that your memory was better on May 22, 1971, when you talked to Detective Butler, as to what happened on May 21, than it is now?

A: Yes.

With each negative answer, with each "I don't remember," Gloria's confidence shriveled perceptibly. She couldn't help but be aware of my apprehensions about her, and she wanted desperately to prove them wrong. Her nervousness was to a large extent proportioned to her intense desire to impress the jury as a keen and forthright witness. The defense lawyers sensed this in her and tried to undermine her self-image before approaching her recollection of the murders.

The first series of questions succeeded perfectly in forcing her to begin worrying about how she looked to the jury. She said she did glance over at the two men as she passed them, and then she said she didn't look at him, the shorter man. She knew what she meant, but would the jury? It was so simple, and yet it came out so confused. She began to be distracted by doubts.

Without giving her a chance to recover, they threw some papers at her and asked her about what she told Detective Butler. And she had to admit she didn't remember, admitting to herself in the process that she wasn't nearly as sure of herself as she had hoped she would be. She knew she wasn't on the car when the shooting started, but the notes said she was. Had she really told him that? How could she have? That wasn't the way it was. But maybe she had said it; the notes couldn't be wrong.

After less than half an hour of cross-examination, she was slumped in her chair, her fingers knotted in her lap. She studied them intently as she seemed to be withdrawing from the proceedings. More and more often, as the questioning went on, she made no response at all, so that questions had to be repeated to her by the judge.

They kept her on the stand for three hours in the after-

noon. The next morning she was back on the stand at ten
o'clock. After a brooding, sleepless night of torturing herself for her inadequacies, she was weaker at the very start
of the second day's session than she had been when she
left the courtroom at the end of the first day. Now the
attorneys kept hammering away at her relationship with
Detective Butler. How often had she seen him. What
questions had he asked? What had he told her to say?

Slowly at first, and then with thicker, bolder strokes,
they were painting a portrait of Gloria Lapp as Bill
Butler's puppet, whose every word was called into question by her eagerness to please the ubiquitous detective
who had held her hand through the long ordeal that followed the terrible shock of witnessing two brutal murders.
Never did she waver in her positive identification of Tony
Bottom as the man she had seen shoot Waverly Jones. Yet
by the time she concluded her testimony at the end of her
second day on the witness stand, the jury couldn't help but
wonder if such a girl could be positive of anything.

That evening Cliff Fenton and I drove to Harlem
Hospital to see Ruth Jennings. She had been brought
there in an ambulance the day before, bleeding and in
pain. Now the bleeding had been stopped and her doc-
tors no longer felt there was an immediate danger she
would lose her baby, but it was obvious she was still
feeling considerable discomfort.

The moment we walked into her room, I knew there
was no point in asking whether she would be able to testify at the trial. Despite the obvious signs of pregnancy
bulging hopefully under the thin hospital blanket, she
looked drawn and weak, actually thinner than the last time
I had seen her. She smiled wanly, but could do nothing to

conceal the pain that showed in her eyes continuously and a tightening of the muscles of her neck and shoulders every time she tried to move. Cliff unwrapped the flowers we had brought and set them by her bed while she asked us about the trial. I told her it was going well.

"Did Gloria testify yet?" she asked.

"Yes. She's finished now, finished this afternoon."

"It went bad, didn't it?"

"Not particularly. What makes you say that?"

"She didn't come to see me. I knew she wouldn't if they gave her a tough time."

"Well," I answered evasively, "they always give everyone a tough time. That's their job. Gloria did just fine."

I could tell she didn't believe me. There was a brief, awkward silence and then she said, "The doctor says I'll be going home soon. I want to help, you know that. I saw those men kill the policemen, same as she did. If it'll help to have me testify, I can. I'm sure I'll be able to."

This time I didn't believe her. She was brave, but in no condition to endure the ordeal her friend Gloria had just been put through. "We'll see," I said. "The first thing is for you to take it easy and get your strength back. You're going to need it to take care of your baby."

She closed her eyes tightly, then opened them. She had round, innocent eyes, as soft as a deer's. "Okay," she agreed solemnly, convinced more by her weakness and pain than by anything I had said. She talked to Cliff for a few minutes, and then we excused ourselves to let her get some rest. I knew as I left her room that if anyone were going to save Gloria Lapp's testimony, it would have to be Jack Franklin, who also had seen Tony Bottom at Colonial Park. No matter what happened, I was not going to let

Ruth Jennings take the stand. Two men had died and I wanted to see justice done, but I couldn't risk the life of Ruth's unborn baby.

I have seen good defense lawyers demolish solid witnesses with their cross-examinations. I have seen truthful witnesses undermine their own testimony with statements they oughtn't to have made. But in all my years of practicing law, I have never seen a witness blow himself out of the water as quickly, as thoroughly, and as irrevocably as Jack Franklin did. He went so fast that the defense never had a shot at him. He was gone before I was ten minutes into his direct examination.

It started innocently enough. He told the jury he had been by his station wagon unloading furniture when he heard shots. He went to the chart and showed exactly where he was parked at the time. With his finger, he traced the path taken by the men he saw running. Then he returned to the witness stand, and I asked him to look around the courtroom and tell me if he recognized any of the men he had seen that night.

"Yes," he answered in a clear voice that rang with assurance.

I asked him to point them out.

He rose in his seat until he was almost standing. His eyes scanned the defense table for an uncomfortably long time, long enough for me to ask myself what the hell he was waiting for. And then I knew. He raised his arm and pointed his finger. "Right there the first one on the left, with the sunglasses," he said. "That's one of them."

I wheeled to see for myself, scarcely able to believe what I had heard. For a crazy second I thought the defendants must have switched places while my back was to them. But the first man on the left was still Herman Bell, who grinned at me like a mischievous child. My witness had just identified the wrong man. Stunned, I turned back to the stand, hoping there was still something I could salvage. "Is there anyone else you recognize?" I asked.

He pointed again, this time indicating Francisco Torres, whose picture he had selected from a photo line-up at the same time he identified a picture of Tony Bottom. I asked a few more perfunctory questions and then turned the witness over to the defense, my guts churning so violently I didn't know whether I would be able to sit through what I knew was coming.

Mercifully, it took them less than fifteen minutes to pick the bones clean. As soon as they established that Jack Franklin had identified pictures of Torres and Bottom at the photo line-up but was now switching to Torres and Bell, they invited him to step down. When he left the courtroom, he took with him not only the remaining shreds of Gloria Lapp's credibility but also my own. At this point, the jury couldn't help wondering whether the People had any case at all. So far I had produced two eyewitnesses, an unconvincing girl and a man who obviously hadn't yet made up his mind about whom he had seen.

The worst part of Franklin's blunder was that it tainted everything that followed. A jury trial is very much like a prize fight. Damage is cumulative; each solid punch that rocks a fighter and slows him down makes it that much easier for his opponent to score again. If the jury had believed Gloria Lapp, if I hadn't made the mistake of putting Jack Franklin on the stand, my next three major witnesses, the three women from the Anderson Avenue apartment, would have gone in with the momentum going their way. Instead, they took the stand to testify at a point when many of the jurors were already shaking their heads with skepticism and disbelief.

On the whole, the three women did an admirable job of presenting their story. Christine and Alie, being the more forceful personalities, were naturally the more dynamic witnesses, but even Celia, who seemed at times uncommonly vague about what was going on in her own apartment, was solid and unvacillating both on direct examination and on cross. At no point did the defense manage to shake any of them or wring from them an admission that their testimony had been in any way influenced by the pressure brought to bear upon them by the police and the district attorney's office.

Yet nothing they could say, neither the words of their answers nor the staunchness of their demeanor, could make the fact of that pressure go away. Here, too, we were seriously hurt by an incident that occurred during Alie Horn's grand jury testimony in November 1971. When John Keenan showed her a picture of Tony Bottom's pearl-handled .45 he mistakenly asked her if it was Albert Washington's gun. She said it was. A few minutes later, after Alie left the grand jury room, one of Keenan's assistants pointed out the error to him. Keenan, who admitted to some difficulties in keeping the welter of names and nicknames in this case straight—Gabriel Torres, whom some of the witnesses called Gilbert, Francisco Torres, Noah, T. B., T, Cisco, Jonas, the Old Man, Washington, Bottom, Bell—immediately dragged Alie back before the grand jury. "Excuse me, Miss Horn, I'm sorry about this, but I have an additional two questions. A few minutes ago

I erroneously asked you if it was the Old Man who had the white-handled gun. Was it not Anthony Bottom who had the white-handled gun?"

"Yes, it was Anthony Bottom," Alie answered.

"And I was in error when I asked it the other way around, isn't that right?" Keenan asked.

Alie said, "Yes."

Later, when I questioned her about this incident, Alie explained that she knew perfectly well whose gun it was. She hadn't been confused but she had felt no inclination to correct a mistake made by John Keenan, a man she intensely disliked. When I pointed out to her that, error or nor error, he had asked a question, not made a statement, she waved her hand disdainfully. "Look," she said, her eyes flashing with unfaded recollections of her intense feelings for Keenan, "it was his mistake, don't tell me it was mine. He was the one asking the questions, and he asked the wrong question." There was no point in arguing with her; the damage had already been done.

It would have been naïve of me to expect that Alie's sworn correction in the grand jury room would have closed the episode, for in a jury trial nothing is ever closed when the other side wants it to remain open. The defense leaned hard on this incident, the firmest peg they had on which to hang their thesis that Alie, Christine, and Celia were clay in the hands of the prosecution, willingly allowing themselves to be molded by the district attorney.

Q: Miss Horn, when you were arrested, October 14, 1971, along with two of the defendants in this case, did anybody touch you, put their hands on you?

A: I was told not to move or else I would get shot.

Q: Did they say anything else to you?

A: It was mass confusion. I don't really remember.

Q: You just don't remember?

A: It was confusion, because the children were in the house, too.

Q: And you were very frightened about the welfare of the children, is that right?

A: Of course.

Q: Did any of the police officers say anything about the children?

A: They removed the children.

Q: Did they tell you where they were taking them?

A: No, not at that time.

Q: And they brought you to a precinct, is that right?

A: Uh-huh.

Q: And what happened when they brought you to the precinct?

A: We sat around a lot.

Q: Did they question you that night?

A: No.

Q: Did they ask you who you were?

A: Yes.

Q: Did they ask you anything else?

A: They asked me about—did I know Francisco and Gabriel.

Q: And what did you say?

A: No.

Q: What did they say when you said no?

A: They took me to jail.

Q: And the next day, I believe you testified you were brought downtown. Where did they take you?

A: To the Manhattan . . . 100 Centre Street.

Q: This building?

A: Yes.

Q: Did you go up to the district attorney's office?

A: Yes.

Q: And who questioned you there?

A: There were a lot of people up there, different detectives. I don't know.

Q: Did they tell you were entitled to a lawyer?

A: No.

Q: Did they threaten you at all?

A: Yes, one did.

Q: What did he say?

A: He said he would lock me up for fifty years if I didn't cooperate.

Q: And you knew that was a real threat, they could in fact lock you up?

A: They had already locked me up.

Q: So it wasn't an idle threat. Miss Horn, do you know the names of any of the detectives who questioned you?

A: Olga Ford was one.

Q: You hadn't met Olga Ford before that time, had you?

A: I think I had seen her the night of the arrest.

Q: And who else questioned you, Miss Horn?

A: John Keenan, of course. The D.A.

Q: The assistant district attorney, right. And when they questioned you, they asked you about May 21, is that right?

A: No.

Q: What is it that they asked you?

A: They asked me a lot of questions, but I didn't talk to them.

Q: Did you say anything at all?

A: No.

Q: When you refused to answer, what did Mr. Keenan say to you?

A: That I would be locked up, that I'd be locked up. He knew I knew.

Q: Did he raise his voice?

A: Everybody raised their voice that was in there.

Q: They were shouting at you, is that right?

A: Right.

Q: How long were you in that room on October 15?

A: I don't know, because I was very confused.

Q: Several hours, is that right?

A: Yes.

Q: And then they took you back to the Women's House of Detention, is that right?

A: Yes.

Q: It's a very unpleasant place, the Women's House of Detention?

A: Yes.

Q: Now, on October 16, did they come and get you again?

A: They came and got me every day.

Q: Every day?

A: Yes.

Q: And they brought you down to the office?

A: Yes.

Q: And Mr. Keenan shouted at you some more?

A: I got shouted at from the time I was down there until they got through questioning me.

Q: And they were telling you, "We're going to lock you up forever," is that right?

A: It was said.

Q: And each of those days, up until October 28, you refused to answer any questions, is that right?

A: Yes.

Q: And then, on October 28, did they tell you, "We know these five men did it," is that right? Did they tell you that? Isn't that right?

A: Yes.

Q: And they told you the only person you're hurting by not telling us these things is yourself; isn't that right?

A: I don't remember all those words. But they kept telling me to talk to them.

Q: Did they tell you you had the keys to your own freedom?

A: No.

Q: But didn't you think that when you started talking to them, there was a good likelihood that you would get out of jail?

A: Of course.

Q: So finally, on October 18, 1971, after coming back every single day, you decided to yourself, that's it, that's enough, isn't that right?

A: No.

Q: Didn't you reach a decision then that you can't go through with much more of this every single day, being brought down—

A: No. I reached the decision that some other people had appeared in the grand jury before me and they had told everything. And I said, what was the use of me continuing on?

Q: So you went into the grand jury and you told them your story, is that right?

A: I told them what happened.

Q: You told them what happened. Didn't you tell John Keenan what he wanted to hear? Didn't you follow him and let him tell you what he wanted to know and then give him answers?

A: I told John Keenan what happened.

Defense counsel then read into the record the minutes of the grand jury session at which Alie Horn first testified that the pearl-handled .45 belonged to Albert Washington and then corrected it to Tony Bottom.

Q: Do you remember being asked those questions and giving those answers in the grand jury, Miss Horn?

A: Yes.

Q: Am I correct that anything that Mr. Keenan would say, you'd say yes because you thought that's the way he wanted it and you were going to get your behind out of jail by saying what he wanted?

A: No.

Q: Three times you said it was Albert Washington, right?

A: Yes.

Q: And when he changed it, then you changed it, right?

A: No.

Q: Did the stenographer get it wrong?

A: No.

Q: Anything he wanted, you'd tell him, right?

A: No.

Q: But after you told them your story, you came out of the grand jury room, is that right?

A: Yes.

Q: And they took you back to Rikers Island, is that right?

A: Yes.

Q: Only this time they checked you out of Rikers Island, is that right?

A: Yes.

Q: And they put you in a hotel?

A: Yes.

Q: And the hotel was much nicer than Rikers Island, wasn't it?

I could feel the jury slipping farther and farther away with each round of questioning, and I had never in my life felt more powerless. I knew the witnesses were telling the truth, but somehow we were missing the one ingredient that would make the truth ring with conviction. To make matters worse, everyone in the office was demoralized by the results of the trial going on just down the hall from Judge Melia's court. Henry "Sha-sha" Brown was being tried for the murder of Patrolmen Gregory Foster and Rocco Laurie. His defense, based in large part on the fact that the police department already had named other men as the killers, sufficiently confused the jury, which acquitted him in March. When polled by the court after delivering their verdict, seven of the twelve jurors answered, "not proven" instead of "not guilty." For me, it was an ominous warning.

• • •

Shaken, I bolstered my confidence by reminding myself that my strongest card was still in my hand. The defense was tearing my witnesses to pieces, but there was no way Herman Bell's lawyer was going to make the fingerprint and palm print found on the white Mustang go away. Against all five defendants we had the testimony of the three women in the Anderson Avenue apartment. Against the Torres brothers we had little else. By discrediting the women, the defense knocked the bottom out of our case against them. Against Albert Washington we also had the fact that he had been arrested in San Francisco with one of the weapons in the case, a fact which in and of itself proved nothing unless the jury believed Christine's, Celia's, and Alie's testimony. Against Tony Bottom we had two eyewitnesses to the murder, one of whom proved to be unconvincing while the other failed to identify him at the trial.

But against Herman Bell we had absolutely solid and incontrovertible evidence placing him at the scene of the crime. We even entered into evidence weather reports indicating it had rained until seven o'clock on the evening of May 21, 1971. We also lined up the testimony of the owner of the white Mustang, who was prepared to swear that her car had been in the parking lot at Colonial Park all day. There was thus no way for Bell to contend that he left his fingerprints on the car either at some time prior to the evening of May 21 or at some other place than Colonial Park.

Bell's strategy, when it finally came time for him to reveal it, turned out to be shockingly simple. He did not contest the prosecutions' contention that the police found two latent prints on the left front fender of the Mustang. Nor did he contend that the fingerprint pictures shown to the jury were not his. He simply maintained that the police had switched prints, substituting a set of Bell's latent prints lifted from Tony Bottoms' Divisadero Street apartment for the prints found at the murder scene. What is more, he put this argument before the jury without offering a single shred of evidence to substantiate it. Every word spoken on the subject by every witness who had any connection at all with the fingerprints flatly repudiated Bell's thesis.

When Detective Carl Lacho of the latent-fingerprint section testified about lifting the print from the Mustang, he was asked on cross-examination if he was positive the print introduced in evidence at the trial was the same print he found at the crime scene. He swore it was. When Detective James Bannon testified that he had made "tens of thousands" of comparisons between the latents lifted from the car and inked prints on file in the police department's fingerprint collection, he was asked if the print now identified as Bell's was the same one he started with on the morning after the killings. He swore it was.

And when Detective Bill Butler testified that he had remained in San Francisco to continue his investigation a few days after the line-up in September 1971, he was asked if he had gone into Bottom's apartment, dusted it for fingerprints, and then substituted a pair of Bell's prints found there for the latents taken from the Colonial Park Mustang. He swore he had done no such thing.

Not once did a single witness answer a single question in a manner that could give even the slightest color of veracity to Bell's wild accusation. But such was the shambles the trial had become that the questions themselves were damaging, regardless of the answers. Now I could begin to understand why the defense had been at such pains to question Gloria Lapp about her relation with Butler. They even asked Jack Franklin about him, they asked Christine Rowe, Alie Horn, and Celia Torres about him. Naturally, as the detective primarily in charge of the investigation, he had interrogated all of them. Naturally, they said so.

Subtly, Bill Butler was being transformed into the villain of the piece. No matter where one turned in the case, Butler was there. He was the master architect of the vast conspiracy aimed at framing five innocent men because they were black militants, and because two of them had the misfortune to have come into possession of two guns tied into the murders Butler had been unable to solve.

On that note, the defense rested its case. In their summations, they reiterated the charge that all five defendants were being framed. When it came my turn to respond, I attempted to show the utter absurdity of such an argument.

Of Gloria Lapp, I said: "She was nervous, as who wouldn't be under such circumstances? She was frightened, as she had every right to be. She is not a self-confident person, she is shy and unsure of herself. But of one thing she is absolutely sure. She is positive beyond any doubt that she saw Anthony Bottom shoot two police officers on the night of May 21, 1971. The defense wants you to believe she identified Bottom in order to please Detective Butler. She said to herself, Detective Butler wants me to pick out someone and so I will. But remember, this was not the only line-up she saw. In all, she went to five line-ups and identified no one as the killer until she saw Anthony Bottom in San Francisco. Why didn't she want to please Detective Butler at the line-up on May twenty-fourth, or at the line-up on June eleventh, or at the line-up on August sixth, or at the line-up on October fifteenth? No, on all those dates she only wanted to tell the truth. But on September twenty-third she wanted to please Detective Butler.

"Oh, the defense says, September twenty-third was different, because the newspapers reported that suspects had been arrested. Now is that reasonable? There are suspects in every line-up. There is no reason to hold a line-up unless there are suspects. Detectives don't suddenly decide to brighten a slow day by holding a line-up. 'C'mon, you guys, what do you say we get in a line-up, I'll bring Gloria down here, see which of us she picks out?' Of course not. You know that, I know that, Gloria Lapp knows that. The line-up on September twenty-third was no different than any of the others. Except that she saw the killer there. She saw Anthony Bottom and pointed him out, just as she pointed him out here in court."

Of the three women in the Anderson Avenue apartment, I said, "First, let us consider Alie Horn. She is arrested on October fourteenth, nineteen seventy-one. She is questioned by the police day after day, so the defense tries to make a big thing of that—improper police procedures, they badgered her into saying what they wanted to hear. If they weren't trying to coerce her, why did they keep questioning her when she told them she didn't know anything? That's what the defense asks. Why, indeed. The answer is obvious. She was arrested with Francisco Torres and Gabriel Torres, and she was brought down to the district attorney's office. And what happens? She was in the same apartment with them and she won't even say she knows who the Torreses are. Is there any reason why the police question her? If the police don't question Alie Horn, who is arrested with the Torres brothers and says she doesn't know who they are, then the police in this town should be removed and we should get new police who know how to conduct an investigation.

"Or think now about Christine Rowe, who told you she borrowed the gun Herman Bell used on the night of May twenty-first, nineteen seventy-one. If she didn't get that gun for Bell, if she didn't get that gun, which she knew ultimately was one of the murder weapons, if she didn't do it, is there any way on this earth that she would involve herself like that, as someone giving a gun to a killer? Would anyone say that unless they actually did it? Even if they are willing to lie, to help us out, they are not going to put themselves into it. Christine Rowe is telling you she bears her own moral responsibility for this. She partied. She celebrated. She got the murder weapon. Is she going to tell you all that unless it is true?

"And finally, consider Celia Torres. The defense tells you she told this story about five men in order to get out of jail, to be reunited with her children. Yet in October nineteen seventy-one, she went into the grand jury and gave the same testimony. Was she in jail in October nineteen seventy-one? Indeed not. She hadn't even been brought down for questioning before that day. Obviously, she was not pressured. And then what did she do after she testified in the grand jury? She went to Mr. Keenan and told him she did not want to go home, she was afraid someone might come to her house and do something to her. Now if she had been forced and told what to say in the district attorney's office, doesn't common sense say that the one place she would want to go would be home, away from the police? So she can get with her friends, her relatives, and say they are forcing me to lie, help me? But she did just the opposite. Because she is telling the truth. And because she has fear. She knows well, as you know well, from the evidence in this case, that the character of these defendants is stamped forever on the bloody sidewalk outside 159-20 Harlem River Drive. That is why she is afraid, and it is not the police she is afraid of."

Of Herman Bell's fingerprints, I said: "The defense wants you to believe that Detective Butler was so obsessed with solving this case that he substituted Herman Bell's fingerprints for the fingerprints found at the scene of the crime, on the white Mustang where Gloria Lapp told you one of the killers sat. They want you to believe that Detective Butler was so obsessed with solving this crime, the murder of two brother officers, that he gave up after less than four months and decided to frame five innocent men. He decided to let the real killers go free. Because if Detective Butler puts Herman Bell's fingerprints into the case file, then obviously he must throw out the fingerprints of the real killer. He said, I'm sorry, but four months is all we allow ourselves to capture the killers of police officers. I'm sorry, Mrs. Piagentini, but we no longer can take the trouble to find the men who murdered your husband. The statute of limitations has run out on them. We have to close the case.

"The defense asks you to believe that Detective Butler was motivated to do this by his hatred of black radicals. They remind you that these five defendants are indeed radicals. They admit it, indeed, they proclaim it in the courtroom. They make a great show of not standing for the judge and wearing their hats in court. This shows you that they are the type of people Detective Butler would want to frame. Because when Detective Butler decides that someone must be framed so he can close the case, obviously he is going to pick a black militant. Unfortunately for Detective Butler, there are no black militants here in New York for him to frame. He has to go all the way to California, three thousand miles away, to find his victims. The defense asks you to believe that Detective Butler is a vigilante who will stop at nothing in his crusade to clear the streets of militants. But for some reason the defense does not explain, this veteran New York detective decides to solve San Francisco's radical problem by framing a bunch of Californians. That is what the defense contends in this case. It is your choice. Is that what happened? Or were Herman Bell's fingerprints found at Colonial Park because he left them there a few minutes before he murdered Patrolman Piagentini and Patrolman Jones by shooting them in the back?"

Justice Melia charged the jury on Thursday, May 9, exactly one hundred twenty-three days after the trial opened. The jury's deliberations began after the lunch recess. I know of nothing in any other walk of life to compare with the waiting period while a jury is out. For Butler and Fenton and the other cops who worked on the case and testified for us, for Ken and me, for the defendants and their lawyers, time came to a complete stop, frozen until twelve strangers elected to put it back in motion with their verdict. Except for the defendants, who were returned to their cells in the Tombs, the decayed and overcrowded prison adjoining the courthouse, everyone connected with the case haunted the halls of the Criminal Courts Building like ghosts patrolling the attics of an old mansion. We had to be on call at all times, ready to return the moment the jury came in. I remembered what Diane Piagentini had said. She felt like her life had stopped and wouldn't start again until the trial was over. I wondered whether it was possible to live that way for three years. Four days of it wore me to an aching numbness.

Late Monday afternoon we were summoned to the courtroom. We knew it wasn't a verdict because the clerk who notifies the attorneys always informs them if the jury has concluded its deliberations. Ken and I were already in the courtroom when the defense attorneys began filing in. Then the defendants arrived, brought in wearing handcuffs, which were removed when they reached the defense table. Two police officers stood behind them at parade rest, the same officers who had been stationed behind them throughout the trial. Except for the defendants, we all rose as the judge entered the courtroom through the door behind the bench. He asked a court officer to bring in the jury.

They filed in slowly, eleven men and one woman, their faces grim and haggard, counterparts of our own. At Justice Melia's request, the foreman rose and informed the court that they were hopelessly deadlocked. The judge refused to accept their decision. Four days of deliberation after a four-month trial scarcely entitled them to return without a verdict. He lectured them for about ten minutes on their responsibilities as jurors, then sent them back to the jury room.

The handwriting, though, was on the wall. After long, complicated trials, juries have stayed out for weeks, inching glacially toward a verdict, driven toward their goal by stubbornness, determination, and an intense pride that will not let them become the link that breaks the chain forged out of so much effort on all sides. But a jury that reported itself deadlocked after only four days had no pride in itself as a unit. Somehow, in selecting them, I hadn't gotten the right mix to produce the chemistry we needed. I knew then that they would return to the courtroom again and again, as often as they had to, until the judge consented to accept a hung jury.

Justice Melia knew it, too. On Wednesday, May 15, after only five and a half days of deliberation, he declared a mistrial and sent the jury home. As much as I had expected it, his decision came as a profound shock to me, just as death is always a shock, even when it is the death of someone long dying. I felt Ken Klein's hand on my arm and I turned to face him, but neither of us could speak. Behind me, I was told later, the defendants were laughing and shouting with glee, embracing each other and their attorneys. I wasn't aware of them. I pushed myself from the table and walked from the courtroom, past Bill and Cliff, who waited for me in the nearly empty spectator section. They stretched out their hands toward me as I walked on. I heard Bill Butler tell me not to worry, that we would get them next time. I wished there were something I could say to him.

Reporters outside the courtroom rushed at me from all sides, bleating their tasteless questions. I pushed through them toward the fire stairs at the end of the hallway. When one of the reporters asked if there would be a second trial I said, "Of course there will." Otherwise, I answered none of their questions.

I walked down to my office. Alone in the empty stairwell, I thought about Bill and Cliff, about all they had put into this case. They had done everything asked of them, everything their jobs and their consciences told them to do. I thought especially about Bill, who had borne incalculable frustrations without ever admitting the possibility of defeat. In the end, he had accomplished everything he set out to do. I hadn't. I had let all of them down.

I closed my office door behind me and sank into the chair in front of my desk. I wanted to be alone but knew I couldn't. Too pained for tears, I reached for the telephone and dialed Diane Piagentini's number. She would have to be told, and I owed it to her to tell her myself before somebody else did.

PART FOUR

Resurrection in Steel

Eighteen

FOR THE FIRST WEEK I WAS WORTH NOTHING. I went over and over the trial in my mind, brooding about it. But brooding is no more like constructive thinking than wishing is like planning. Then, one morning about ten days after the hung jury, my mood had played itself out and I knew it was time to begin preparing for the second trial, which, with delays and motions, was probably still six months away. Putting the whole process in perspective, it now looked to me something like building a boat. You labor at it to the best of your abilities; you make it as tight and as seaworthy as you can. Then you put it in the water and watch it begin to sink. That was the first trial, from Gloria Lapp's cross-examination to the dismissal of the jury. Once you get over your disappointment, you realize that you don't have to start from scratch and build a brand-new boat. Instead, you have to find the leaks and seal them.

Normally, a second trial is more difficult for the prosecution than a first. Simply in psychological terms, the defense has gained in confidence, the prosecution lost. On a more practical level, the defense also has the advantage of having a written record of all the sworn testimony against it. If a witness alters his or her testimony in the slightest degree, as inevitably happens over the course of a year with memories of distant events—for some details become clearer with the passage of time while others recede out of focus—the defense can use the first trial testimony to impeach the credibility of the witness. Especially in a trial like this, where we were being charged with the manipulation of witnesses, the defense would seize on the tiniest inconsistency and worry it unmercifully, the way a dog shakes the life out of a rat. In my imagination I could already hear defense counsel sneering, "Did anything happen between the first trial and today that refreshed your recollection? Did Mr. Tanenbaum tell you it would be better if you remembered it this way?"

Finally, there is the intangible but often overwhelming obstacle that grows out of the jury's awareness that this is a second trial. Although there are in law a number of reasons for retrial, ranging from a reversal on appeal to technical errors by the judge or the district attorney, most laymen assume that if there is a second trial, the first must have ended in a hung jury. The law strictly forbids any allusion to the outcome of the first trial within the hearing of the jurors, and the judge carefully instructs them to draw no conclusions whatever from the fact of an earlier trial. But no system has ever been devised to stop people from thinking about matters of great interest to them. When twelve people are required to give their entire attention to an issue for four or five months, how can they not wonder about twelve others, much like themselves, who went through the same thing? And how can they fail to be influenced by the fact that those other twelve were unable to find the defendants guilty beyond a reasonable doubt?

Balanced against the ominous prognosis of a second trial even more difficult than the first was one idea I clung to desperately, wringing from it all the hope it would yield. Generally speaking, a defense based on a charge of a frameup is more vulnerable on a second trial than most other defenses, for in the course of the first trial the district attorney learns the defense theory. He knows how the alleged frame works and can amass the evidence to refute it. In other words, I now knew where my boat leaked and had six months in which to plug up the holes.

In the middle of October I sent Cliff Fenton down to New Orleans to have another crack at Lester Bertram May, the baffling young BLA bank robber who seemed to have so much to talk about but always managed to say so little. The last time any of us had spoken to May was when Cliff interviewed him on the day of Bell's arraignment. At that time May boasted he was holding an "ace in the hole." Since then, May and two of the other bank robbers rounded up in New Orleans had given the San Francisco police tape-recorded statements admitting their own involvement in the raid on the Ingleside police station that resulted in the death of Sergeant John Young. According to all three statements, Francisco Torres and Herman Bell also had been involved. It was Bell, they said, who fired the fatal shotgun—an accusation that gained added credibility from the fact that one of the two shotguns taken from Bell's apartment after his arrest matched ballistically with the murder weapon used to kill

Sergeant Young.* We were hoping that May, who had been willing to talk to San Francisco police, would now consent to play his ace and give us information to help us with our case.

Our timing, though, turned out to be wrong. Although May already had been indicted for the California murder, he still hadn't been sentenced on his New Orleans bank-robbery conviction. He told Cliff he was still standing pat.

A few weeks later, around the beginning of November, Cliff got a call from L. J. Delsa in New Orleans. "Got someone here wants to talk to you," Delsa said. Then Lester May came on the line.

"I'm ready to play that ace, my man," May said. "I just gotta know one thing. Are you cats missing a gun in your case up there?"

We certainly were. Joseph Piagentini's service revolver had never been found.

From the very start of the investigation, the disappearance of Piagentini's and Jones's guns was one of the few comprehensible facts Detective Bill Butler had to work with. In a crime so brutal, savage, and unintelligible, it explained everything. For the theft of the slain patrolmen's weapons was as much an expression of the demented rage of the killers as the killings themselves. As soon as Butler learned that the guns of the two dead officers were missing, he knew he would not find the murderers until he found the weapons they ripped from the holsters of their victims.

---

*All three statements were later ruled inadmissible by a California court.

And Butler had been proven right, for it was Waverly Jones's gun that broke the case in San Francisco. After Jones's gun implicated Tony Bottom and Albert Washington, the investigation had been able to move forward, gathering evidence as a snowball gathers snow, until finally Herman Bell stood accused. Yet the chain of logic and evidence tying the killers to the crime was still incomplete.

Objectively, the evidence against Bell—the testimony of the three women in the apartment as well as his fingerprint and palm print on the white Mustang—should have been enough to convict him. But the hard fact was it hadn't been. Like a spot of bare, unpainted canvas in an almost completed painting, the lack of this last crucial piece of evidence—Piagentini's gun—distracted the jurors and drew their eyes away from what was there.

Cliff Fenton and Ken Klein flew to New Orleans on November 12. Arriving too late to conduct any business that day, they checked into a motel and waited until morning to call on Lester Bertram May in his cell in the New Orleans parish prison. The usually languid May, for once solemn and businesslike, wasted no time in getting to the point. Not only had he been hit with a fifteen-year sentence on his federal bank-robbery conviction in New Orleans, he was also facing a murder charge in California, and he wanted help.

Fenton asked him what kind of help he wanted. "You know, we can't give you a plea on a thing like that. It's not our case. We can put in a word for you, but that's about all. And I'll level with you, Lester, that's heavy stuff. If you're thinking about copping to a lower charge, I'd forget about it."

May seemed neither surprised nor disappointed. He had a thoroughly realistic understanding of his situation and a fairly clear sense of what he could ask. "No, man, I can relate to that," he said. "But I wanna get out of here, see. I can't take it no more. So what I'm figuring is I take a plea on that California thing."

Fenton and Klein looked at each other, baffled, totally at a loss to know what May wanted of them. "Plead guilty to a murder count?" Fenton asked.

May flashed a broad, self-mocking grin. "Hey, man," he said, "like if they'd reduce it to criminal negligence, y'know, I'd take it. But they ain't about to. All I want, see, is to get my ass outta here. Now can you do that or can't you?"

"Do what?"

"Just what I'm telling you, man. Fix it so I do that murder time first."

"That's it? That's what you want?"

"Well, no, man, it ain't real exactly what I want. But I figure it's maybe something I can get, huh?"

Cliff and Ken both agreed that the request sounded reasonable, which indeed it was. In fact, what he was asking was so minimal that Cliff began to have an uneasy feeling he and Ken had come to New Orleans for nothing. There were a lot of reasons why a prisoner with information to sell might set the price low, but right up near the top of the list would be his own awareness that his information wasn't worth much.

"I just want you to understand we can't promise you anything," Cliff said. "All we do is we put in a word. We tell them you helped us out. If they want to do the right thing by you, it's up to them. If they don't, there's not a whole hell of a lot we can do about it."

Lester nodded, but Ken, who knew he might be called to testify about a deal with May, wanted a more explicit answer. Lester gave it to him. "Sure," he said. "No promises is fine with me. Don't put much stock in them anyway."

With the purchase price thus settled, it was time to inspect the goods May was selling. Cliff did the questioning. "Okay," let's get down to business," he began. "What's this about a gun? What kind of gun?"

"I don't know, man."

"Whose is it?"

"Herman's."

"Herman Bell's?"

"That's the cat, man."

"Where is it?"

"Mississippi."

"Where in Mississippi?"

"I don't know, man."

"What d'ya mean you don't know?"

"Like he buried it, see. He got this post-hole digger and he buried it."

"Where'd he bury it?"

"About five feet down."

"Yeah, fine, five feet down. Five feet under what?"

"A farm."

"Whose farm?"

"I don't know, man. Maybe I just better tell you how it come to happen."

Lester's story began in San Francisco in the fall of

1971. Herman Bell disappeared from view a few days after the Ingleside attack. A few weeks later—May put the date some time in October—Bell called May from Jackson, Mississippi, and invited him to join him there. "Like there was nothing shaking where I was, see. Everyone split. So I went," May said, while Cliff and Ken silently tried to fit his words in with their own chronology of BLA activities. October was when the Torres brothers were arrested in New York.

Bell met May at the Jackson train station. Bell and his wife and son had a tiny apartment just a block or two from Bell's mother's house, where he seemed to spend most of his time. He had a job as a checker and stockboy in a small grocery store but talked constantly about getting back into revolutionary activities. For the time being, though, he was biding his time, keeping a low profile. He seemed to Lester a very different young man from the fiery activist Lester knew in California. Two of his younger brothers lived with his mother, and Herman lectured them constantly on radical ideology. But his talk seemed bookish and remote, as though he were teaching a course in the literature of protest. For almost a month, life went on that way, a kind of stationary drift, the days unmarked by events, with no prospect of change unless a force from outside snapped the moorings.

Then it was November, and suddenly everything was different. Lester May didn't know what happened but Cliff and Ken did. November was when Frank McCoy in San Francisco learned Herman Bell's name. November was when Detective James Bannon in New York positively matched the Colonial Park latents with the inked prints on Herman Bell's Oakland arrest card.

What Lester did know was that he was sitting in the bedroom of Herman Bell's mother's house in Jackson waiting for Bell to get off work at the supermarket when two FBI agents knocked at the kitchen door.

Mrs. Mitchell—she had remarried since Bell's childhood—opened the door for the agents, who identified themselves and asked her if she had a son named Herman Bell. She said she did. The agents asked if he were there. She said he wasn't. They asked if she knew where they could find him. She said she didn't. They went away.

The agents returned to their office, where they completed their investigation by forwarding a report to New York stating that Bell was not in Mississippi. Lester May, though, figured the heat was on. He watched from the bedroom window as the agents climbed into their car and disappeared down the street. Then he raced from the house, heading around the block in the opposite direction, taking the long way to the market where Bell was just hanging up his gray stockboy's apron. He told Bell some cops had been at his mother's house asking about him. Together, Bell and May hurried to Bell's apartment, where Herman packed a few guns and some clothing in a suitcase and left a note for his wife. Then he headed out of Jackson for the surrounding countryside. It was dark when they got to their destination, and Lester, who had little sense of the local geography, neither knew nor cared where they were.

They spent the evening on a farm, which Lester recalled vividly although he had seen it only at night. He drew a sketch of the farmhouse and yard, the pump and a well to the side, a board fence, and a pigpen out back. A woman Herman called Nana gave them supper in the kitchen. Then a man whose name Lester either never heard or had forgotten sat with the two young men on the front porch. It was a clear half-moon night, and the embers of the old man's pipe glowed warmly in the still darkness. No one spoke.

Some time after ten o'clock a pair of headlights slipped over the low hill a mile or two away and drifted toward them, its path as erratic as a firefly's on the twisting two-lane country road. Herman tensed, watching. The farmhouse was set back about eighty yards from the county road, down a rutted dirt path. The headlights slowed at the mouth of the path, stopped, turned onto it. Herman Bell's eyes glinted like a cat's. He hurried into the house for a gun, followed closely by May. They were both armed when they returned to the porch.

The car stopped. With his gun in his hand, Bell scrambled from the porch and cut across the long yard, crouching behind a row of scraggly bushes. Before they could get to the car, it backed onto the county road and drove off in the direction from which it had come. Herman stared after the retreating taillights until they slid down the far side of the hill. Then he hurried back to the porch.

"Reckon them folks's lost," the old man said mellowly.

"No one gets lost around here," Herman said. "C'mon."

In the house again, Bell went straight for his suitcase, Lester a step behind him, standing over his shoulder as he pulled a second gun from under the jumbled clothing and shoved it into the pocket of his windbreaker.

Lester followed Bell down the three steps to the front yard, then around to the shed at the side of the house, where Herman got a heavy black shovel. In the darkness, he paced the yard, surveying it as though he were looking for something, the shovel held in two hands, ready to dig. A foot or two from a fencepost, he probed it into the dirt and pried free a shovelful of dense earth, then stopped to consider. Two or three times more the shovel bit into dirt. Herman stood up, resting on the handle, and shook his head. "This piece is hot," he said. As Lester remembered it, or least as he told it, that was all the explanation Herman Bell gave.

With the shovel on his shoulder, he double-timed back to the front porch. "You got something I can dig a hole with?" he asked the old man.

"You got it right there, boy," the old man drawled. "Tha's what a shovel for. What kinda hole you thinkin' of?"

"Just a hole. C'mon you must have something."

"Post-hole digger in the shed, if'n you mean like that." Herman turned for the shed.

"You know what it look like, boy?" the old man called after him. "Mebbe I oughta come show you."

"I know what a post-hole digger looks like," Herman called back over his shoulder.

Lester followed like a spaniel. Clicking on the flashlight kept by the shed door, Bell scanned the clutter of tools until he found it. Back outside, after the bright stab of the flashlight, it was darker than it had been before, as though the moon had gone out. Lester stumbled after Bell as they made their way to the fence. They walked counterclockwise along it, the fence at Lester's left elbow. At what seemed to him a corner they stopped and Herman commenced to dig. In no more than a few minutes he had made a hole at least five feet deep, about the circumference of a man's leg.

He took the gun from his windbreaker pocket, studied it distractedly for a long time in the waxy moonlight, and then stooped to lower it into the hole as far as his arm would reach. When he dropped it, Lester heard it hit bottom with a soft plop, like the back of a spade patting the earth. Bell pushed himself to his feet and stood over the open hole as though someone he had known a long time was being buried in it. With his shoe, he kicked at the mounded earth, showering dirt onto the buried gun. Then he went back to the shed for the shovel, which he used to fill in the hole. When he was finished, a small swelling of earth rose to mark the spot until the weather would get around to leveling it.

They didn't stay at the old man's house that night as they had planned to. Instead, they drove about fifteen minutes to another house, where they stayed two weeks, with Bell barely venturing out of doors. The house belonged to a woman in her fifties, who apparently lived alone. May didn't know her name. Every morning she rose early, put on a white dress and white shoes, and went to work. He remembered she said she had a son in the army.

When the two weeks were up, Herman Bell packed his belongings and called a friend with a car. Half an hour later, a very skinny black man in an old Dodge with springs poking through the upholstery called for them. When Bell told him where he wanted to go, the man put up an argument. Then, grumbling to himself, he slid in behind the wheel. It was less than an hour's drive, perhaps forty minutes, to the railroad station. Bell and May took a train out of Mississippi, arriving in New Orleans before nightfall.

That was Lester's story. An hour and a half after he had finished talking, arrangements had already been made to release Lester from the New Orleans parish prison to the custody of United States marshals, who called ahead to Jackson to secure accommodations for him at a federal prison there. At three o'clock, a convoy set out from downtown New Orleans. Cliff Fenton and Ken Klein rode with L. J. Delsa in an ummarked New Orleans police car. They were followed by a second car containing three FBI agents, a third with two U.S. marshals, and a fourth with one marshal driving and Lester May in the back seat between two others, who sat stiffly at attention, as though the security of their prisoner depended upon the rigidity of their posture. Yet even if they had slept, Lester could have gone nowhere, for he wore both handcuffs and leg irons.

The caravan circled Lake Pontchartrain, then sped north for the Mississippi border on Interstate 55. In the first car, spirits were high, for all three men were buoyantly optimistic, none of them yet having fully comprehended the enormity of the task ahead of them. From FBI files they had learned that Herman Bell's paternal grandmother lived on a small farm in Yazoo County, Mississippi. They were confident that she was "Nana" and that when they got to her yard Lester would show them where to dig. They joked lightly among themselves, their laughter marking their restless eagerness to get to Nana Peel's farm and accomplish their mission. Two or three times Cliff asked anxiously if they were in Mississippi yet.

Finally Delsa said, "Take it easy, Cliff. You'll know soon's we get there. When you start seeing they're selling bedsheets in the gas stations, that's Mississippi."

The hundred eighty miles between New Orleans and Jackson, Mississippi, rolled by quickly, but not quickly enough to get them there with more than a small arc of daylight left in the sky. The marshals from New Orleans turned their prisoner over to their local counterparts and headed back for Louisiana. Cliff and Ken reluctantly agreed to wait until morning to start their hunt. They checked into a motel and ate dinner. Then Ken called me at the office. "The bad news is we didn't find the gun," he said. "The good news is they let us take Lester to Jackson. He's going to show us where it's buried in the morning."

The marshals arrived at the motel shortly after sunrise. May, once again in handcuffs and leg irons, sat in the back seat of their car, on his face an almost idiotic grin of self-importance, as though his role as the occasion of so much official activity more than made up for the indignities of his situation. Cliff walked to the marshals' car and asked May if he had had breakfast.

"Made it special for me," he said. "Wasn't no other folks up when they drug me outta bed."

"Well, if you want something, just holler," Cliff said amiably, ignoring the dour scowls on the faces of the two white men on either side of the prisoner.

By nine o'clock the convoy had reached Yazoo City, the county seat, forty-seven miles north of Jackson. Cliff, Ken, and Delsa went into the whitewashed cottage that served as the sheriff's office. Lester was allowed to stretch his legs on the sidewalk. A small crowd of mixed black and white faces gathered to gawk as the leg irons were unlocked and Lester, still in handcuffs, was paraded across the street to march along the perimeter of the town square, a marshal at each elbow. Heavy rains had ended just a day or two before, so that although the sky was clear and bright, the air dry, the bare spots in the grassy park oozed like a saturated sponge.

In the sheriff's office, Cliff and Ken learned that Bell's grandmother had moved since Bell and May allegedly spent an evening with her three years earlier. A deputy who claimed to know her and to know the farm offered to lead them to the farm. "She's a decent woman, never had no trouble from her," he said, shaking his head sadly. "How do you figure a thing like that?"

For the ride to the farm, Fenton and Klein convinced the marshals to let May ride with them. They had driven only a few minutes out of Yazoo City when May shook his head and muttered, "I don't know, man, something's wrong. None of this looks familiar."

"Wait till we get there," Cliff snarled, brushing aside the doubts. "It'll come back to you."

Following the deputy, they turned off the state highway onto a county road that wandered pleasantly under an arching canopy of slender trees. Soon the deputy pulled off to the shoulder. Delsa rolled up beside him while the other cars in the convoy stopped in back of them.

"What is it?" Fenton called to the deputy.

"This is it, the farm," the deputy called back, motioning to his left, where a small weather-beaten house stood in the center of three acres of fenced land.

"No, it ain't," Lester May countered.

Cliff bristled, as though Lester were under some obligation to recognize the farm. "I thought you said you only saw it at night," he snapped.

"Can't help it," May sulked defensively. "There's no pigpen, the well ain't where it's supposed to be. I'm telling you, this ain't the place."

Ken leaned across the seat to the open window and asked the deputy, "Are you sure this used to be her place?"

The deputy was.

"Well, somebody's wrong about something," Ken concluded gloomily, suddenly aware that the clues they had been given for their treasure hunt were not leading them closer to Piagentini's gun. "You said you know where the grandmother lives now?" he asked, clutching for a straw.

"Yeah."

"Well, let's get a look at her, at least make sure she's Nana. Then we can find out what happened to her farm."

The convoy turned around on the narrow road and rolled back in the direction of Yazoo City, stopping in a muddy three-street hamlet with a listed population of five hundred. Along the way, Cliff suggested a plan. He would knock on Mrs. Peel's door and, pretending to ask directions, get her to come out onto the porch so Lester could get a look at her. Unless it couldn't be helped, he didn't want any of Bell's relatives knowing about the search until it had closed in on its objective. If word got back to Bell that the New York Police were scrabbling around Mississippi looking for something, Bell could get a message to a friend who might be able to get to the gun first.

Cliff's plan accomplished its purpose only in the negative sense that an experiment can be considered a success when it proves a theory wrong. Asking for directions and pretending not to understand, Cliff induced Bell's grandmother to come outside and point out the turn he should take. Seated next to Ken in the back seat of the car, about fifty yards down the road, Lester May confirmed the young assistant D.A.'s worst fears. He had never seen that woman before in his life. She wasn't Nana.

For a moment, the thought crossed Ken's mind that there had been no truth to Lester's story, although it wasn't at all clear what May could hope to gain by making up such a tale. Maybe the pleasure he took from the attention he was getting now, out of jail for a couple of days, with agents and marshals and deputies and cops driving him around and doing his bidding, was his only motive for this whole charade.

If it was all a hoax, Ken wasn't yet ready to accept that conclusion. He still believed May, or at least wanted to. He still believed they would be able to find the woman Bell called Nana, only now they would have to do it the hard way. They would have to work backward from the train station to the woman in white to Nana's farm, where Joseph Piagentini's gun was buried. They would start by riding up and down the railroad lines until they found the station where the driver took Bell and May when they left the woman in white. Then they would draw a circle around the station with a radius of forty minutes of traveling time. Somewhere in that circle, over two thousand square miles, was the middle-aged woman who sheltered two terrorists after they buried the gun. When they found her, the farm and Piagentini's service revolver, five feet under the earth, would be only fifteen minutes away.

By this time it was well past noon and the convoy skulked back toward Yazoo City for lunch, considerably crestfallen. Even Lester, whose confidence had remained unshaken under the impact of the morning's failures, was beginning to entertain doubts. One of the federal marshals deepened the gloom by suggesting the search be called off. From the start, his attitude had been critical and negative, as though the job of guarding Lester were a personal affront to his dignity. Now he declared openly that there was no use going on, that they were all being hoaxed.

Fortunately, the rest of the marshals and all the local people called upon for help were willing to push on until all possibilities had been exhausted. Huddled with Ken and Cliff over a large-scale area map spread across the only table in the roadside fried-chicken joint he had recommended, the Yazoo County deputy carefully marked out all the railroad stations in Yazoo, Holmes, and Madison counties, then traced a route connecting them. "I reckon if we go till dark tonight and get at it again by sunup, we can cover all of them by tomorrow night," he said. "That oughta tell us if your boy knows what he's talking about."

"Fine," Cliff said, wiping his hands on a paper towel, standing, and stretching. "Lemme just go out and tell the others what we're gonna be doing."

The deputy reached out to put a hand on his sleeve. "Do yourselves a favor," he said. "Let Kenny tell them. It's pro'ly none of my business, but some of those guys out there have got enough problems with your prisoner. If they start gettin' their orders from a black man, they're gonna pack it in."

Cliff motioned with a nod of his head for Ken to go.

"No offense?" the deputy asked.

"None at all," Fenton reassured him. "You didn't invent it."

After packing up and discarding the chicken bones, the convoy retraced its path, this time driving straight to the railroad station at the east end of town. A few old men shook their heads and scratched at their whiskers as they watched about a dozen heavily armed lawmen lead a black prisoner in leg irons along the muddy sidewalk to the front of the old brick station. Then the prisoner conferred briefly with a thickset black man in a nylon windbreaker, who asked a few whispered questions and then ordered everyone, including the white lawmen, back to their cars.

"If that don't beat everything," Ken heard one of the old men mutter as he passed.

The spectacle repeated itself at Evans, Midway, Brozville, Eden, Anding, and Bentonia, as the convoy spiraled around Yazoo City in a widening arc that took it deeper and deeper into the bleak November farmland, where the wet gray soil, bare and hungry-looking, seemed to reflect the dull and listless poverty of the people, the weather-worn grimness of the bare and splintered wood houses. Everywhere they got the same answer from Lester. A few of the stations were built in heavy, rough-hewn stone, a few in plain planks. Lester was able to reject them without even leaving the car, although he left the car in any case, not so much to make sure as simply to get out and stretch for a few minutes. Once there was a delay when Lester declared he had to use the bathroom and refused to go unless the shackles and handcuffs were removed. Twice they came to stations made of old, irregular bricks, their surfaces polished smooth to the mortar. Each time, hopes soared that this would be it, but each time Lester shook his head glumly. "It was brick, like this," he said. "But this ain't the one."

Then, with the sky darkening behind them, going to crimson ahead as they pulled into Berryville from the east, Lester said, "Man, that's looking good. Let's go take a look."

Ken was sitting beside him in the back seat when he said it, a marshal on the other side. Cliff was in another car.

"C'mon, let's go. Get those things off him," Ken ordered, eager to get into the station as quickly as possible. The marshal glumly obeyed. Carrying the heavy irons in his hands, he trotted briskly beside the young Yankee lawyer and the prisoner as they virtually jogged at a quick triple time through the narrow station house and out onto the platform, where they stopped until Cliff caught up with them.

"Well?" he asked.

"I think so," May said tentatively. "Gimme a minute."

He paced off a few steps, studying the track, then turned to examine the building. The marshal made a move to follow him but Cliff stopped him with a softly growled command that promised trouble if it weren't obeyed. Lester sauntered back, the slightest trace of a swagger in his gait.

"I tol' you I'd rec'nize it, my man," he said, speaking only to Cliff. "This is where me and Herman got the train. Right here."

When Ken called me with his daily report that evening, he said, "The bad news is we didn't find the gun. The good news is we found the station."

With darkness setting in, it was too late to start prowling the countryside. Lester was turned over to the marshals, who took him back to his cell in Jackson. Ken, Cliff, and L. J. Delsa ate dinner with the Yazoo County deputy, taking a few hours over murky coffee to plan the next day's campaign. Late in the evening an FBI agent joined them with a report on the bureau's efforts to track down Bell's family. I think you're getting warm," the agent said encouragingly. "His father's people, the Peels, all live around here. We've got about a dozen names of relatives in the county and just over the county line in Madison."

"What about his mother's side?" Cliff asked.

"No," the agent answered quickly. "She lives in Jackson, and all the kinfolk we know about live right around there. Most of them are in Hinds County, just a few miles outside Jackson. Cynthia, Ridgeland, Cordelia—down in there. It's way south of here."

There was general agreement that in the morning they would concentrate on the farms and homes on the Peel side of the family. They would check out each one, and as many others in each neighborhood, on the assumption that Nana, the old farmer, and the woman in white were at least friends of the family if not actually relatives. In rural Mississippi, where the horizon marks the end of the world, especially for the older generation of poor blacks, anyone close enough to the family to have boarded Jethro Peel's boy and a stranger he brought with him probably lived within walking distance of one of Bell's numerous uncles and cousins.

The conference broke up around ten o'clock. Delsa, Fenton, and Klein climbed into Delsa's car for the ride back to their motel in Jackson. Before calling it a night, they decided to stop by the U.S. marshal's office, just to check in. The news waiting for them was devastating. "Take a look at this," the marshal on duty said dourly, handing Cliff a sheet of paper.

The paper was a teletyped communication forwarded from New Orleans to the Jackson marshal's office. It informed the marshal that Lester Bertram May, temporarily assigned to his custody from the New Orleans parish prison, had been called as a defense witness at a trial scheduled to start in Los Angeles on November 19. May would have to be returned to New Orleans for a flight to California no later than the evening of the 18th.

Cliff crumpled up the message and stormed out of the office. When you've got to dig up two whole counties in the most godforsaken part of the country, there's nothing like hearing you've only got four days to do it in.

Friday was a disaster, thirteen hours of unrelieved futility, rendered all the more poignant by a haunting awareness that the search was now a race against the clock, in which the winner might well turn out to be Herman Bell. As the miles piled up and the hours slipped away, Ken, Cliff, and all the others on the hunt grew increasingly to suspect they weren't even getting close. "None of this looks familiar," Lester kept saying. "It's not even the same kind of farms. The land looks different. It's hillier, it wasn't like this at all, and I think there was more cotton."

They drove on and on, each disappointment crushing their hopes that the next bend in the road would disclose the farmyard they were looking for, or the house of the woman in white. By the end of the day they were only dragging themselves through the motions, numbly aware that somewhere their thinking had gone astray.

Then, over their scarcely touched dinners, when Lester had already been returned to his cell, the answer came to them. Stirring absently at gummy mashed potatoes coated with a thin gravy the color of a manila envelope, Ken suddenly broke the long silence at the table by asking, "What was that thing Lester said about the driver?"

Cliff shook his head. "He said something about the driver getting pissed off at Herman."

"That's right. What were they arguing about?"

"I don't know. He didn't say, did he?"

For an answer he got a long silence, while Ken and Delsa and Cliff all tried to figure it out, as though it were a riddle. Then Ken said, "Listen to me a minute, we're doing it all backwards. We know Bell's got relatives down around Jackson and he's got relatives up here, right? So we're looking for the farm and the lady in white up here because the train station's up here. But let's just back up a little and see if that makes sense. Bell calls a friend and says he wants a ride to the station. When the guy gets there Bell tells him where he wants to go and the guy gets upset. Why?"

Cliff and Delsa both saw the point at the same time. "Because Bell says he wants to go to the station at Berryville," Delsa answered quickly.

"And the old guy says he's not going all the way up there when there's a station just a few miles away in Jackson," Cliff chimed in.

"Exactly," Ken beamed triumphantly, Sherlock Holmes explaining a mystery to Dr. Watson. "Look, Bell is hot. The FBI was just at his mother's house asking questions. He knows they're looking for him. He figures maybe they've got the train station covered in case he tries to get out of town. But they're not going to cover every little whistlestop up and down the line. So he argues with the driver, maybe he has to give him something extra, and the guy takes him to Berryville. But Berryville's got nothing to do with it and Bell's relatives near Berryville have got nothing to do with it. Tomorrow we start checking out his mother's family near Jackson."

Cliff smiled benignly. "Not bad," he said approvingly. Then he chuckled and added, "For a kid just out of law school."

Ken didn't call me until almost midnight that night. He got me at home. "The bad news is we didn't find the gun," he said. "The good news is I think we know where to look."

Nineteen

WITH THE CLOCK NOW DOWN TO THREE DAYS, Cliff and Ken decided they would have to risk an interview with Herman Bell's mother. While Delsa and the team of marshals and agents cruised with Lester through the area north of Jackson where Bell's relatives lived, the two New Yorkers drove to Mrs. Mitchell's house in the town's sprawling ghetto. It was before eight-thirty and they parked a short way down the street where they could see in through the kitchen window at the side of the house and the living-room window to the front. Bell's brothers, both youngsters in their teens, were still home. Cliff decided to wait until they left, figuring that if they were anything like Herman they might prevail upon their mother to refuse to talk to the police.

He and Ken used the empty time while they waited to devise a cover story to give her that would induce her to help. According to the FBI and local authorities, she was a hard-working and law-abiding woman who genuinely despaired over her son Herman's lawless militancy and rebellion, although she undoubtedly refused to believe how deep into criminality he had plunged. She was aware that Herman was being held on a murder charge in New York, yet she could not see her son as a killer and accepted the accusation as neither more nor less than a tragically inevitable consequence of the evil ways he had gotten into.

At five minutes to nine, the two brothers left the house by the kitchen door and hurried down the street, breaking into a run as they raced each other for the corner. One of them bore a striking resemblance to his older brother, so much so that Cliff couldn't help wondering if he was perhaps seeing a picture of what Herman Bell might once have been before something went terribly wrong for him. With an involuntary shiver, Cliff pushed that thought from his mind. "C'mon, let's go," he said, reaching for the door handle.

A pleasant, sturdy woman in a plain housedress opened the door a few seconds after Cliff knocked. Her smile changed to a look of simple curiosity when she found herself facing two strangers, one of them a white man, but there was neither hostility nor suspicion in her face. "Yes?" she asked.

"Mrs. Mitchell," Cliff said, "I'm Detective Fenton from New York, and this is Assistant District Attorney Klein. We'd like to talk to you about your son Herman, if you don't mind."

Her eyes darkened and the heavy lines of her brow seemed to grow deeper. "Yes," she said. "Please come in."

She led them into the living room, a modest and decently furnished room that offered an unfathomable contrast to the sharecropper poverty in which she had raised Herman. Apparently she had improved herself considerably since Herman's childhood.

"Mrs. Mitchell, I suppose you know that Herman is in custody in New York. He's facing a very serious charge," Ken began, following the script he and Cliff had outlined in the car. The two New Yorkers were seated side by side on the slip-covered couch, Mrs. Mitchell on an upholstered chair facing them. "Now, it's just a charge, he hasn't been found guilty. He claims he was in Mississippi in November nineteen seventy-one. We were sent down here to check out his story, to see if he's telling the truth."

Her face brightened noticeably, filling Ken with confused, ambivalent feelings. He was confident she would tell them what they needed to know, yet it was difficult not to feel shame at practicing such a deception on an honest and trusting woman tricked into believing the truth would help her son.

"Well, yes, he surely was here," she said eagerly. "Right here in this house."

"Do you know the dates?"

"The dates? You mean just exactly when he was here? No, I don't, but it was from, oh, about October to November. He was with a friend of his, a boy, I don't exactly recollect his name. Lucius, I think it was."

"Lester?"

"That's right."

"Okay, good," Ken said. "So far it all checks. What else have we got, Cliff?"

Fenton flipped open a small, spiral-bound notebook and pretended to be looking for the right page. "Yes, here it is, ma'am," he said. "He told us that when he left here he went to stay with a woman he called Nana."

"Yes, that could be, it certainly could be. That would

be Nana . . . Nana . . . Isn't that the foolest thing, I don't know her name. She's some kin to my brother's wife, but I don't know. She lives up to Cordelia, though, I know that. Oh, I feel terrible, Mr. Fenton. It's foolish not to know, but I don't. If you can wait jes' a minute, Mr. Fenton, there's some folks I can call, find out for you."

Ken and Cliff stood as Mrs. Mitchell excused herself and went into the kitchen to use the telephone. She returned in a few minutes, her face lit up with a hopeful smile. She had spoken to a cousin who suggested that the woman she was thinking of was Nanny Closter. She also mentioned a couple named Tatum who had raised Herman for a year or two when Herman was a boy.

Ken and Cliff thanked her and told her they might be back if they had more questions.

"You'll find her, I jes' know you will," Mrs. Mitchell said at the door. "I certainly do hope I been able to help."

"Yes, ma'am," Ken said. "I'm sure you've been a lot of help."

The population of Cordelia, Mississippi, is exactly thirty. At what passed for the local post office, a four-foot section of counter space in the tiny hamlet's one general store, the clerk knew of a woman named Nana. "Nana Tucker," he said. "A colored lady, but she don't live here no more." He told Cliff and Ken how to find the farm where she used to live.

Using the radio in the car, Cliff called Delsa and asked him to bring May around to Mrs. Tucker's former farm. Then he and Ken drove there themselves to wait. A storm had moved in, and rain was falling heavily by the time they got there. Ignoring it, Ken and Cliff prowled the farmyard to check it out. The details all seemed right—well, cistern, fence, pigpen out back. But without Lester's confirmation it was just an exciting possibility. God knew, there had to be hundreds of farms in the area, each with its well, each with its cistern, each with its fence and pigpen. Still, they waited for Lester with a sodden but nonetheless cheerful expectancy.

A half hour later Delsa's car slid to a stop in front of the farmyard and Lester climbed from the back seat, handcuffed but without the leg irons. He walked to where Cliff and Ken stood waiting in the rain.

"Which one?" he asked, shattering the detective's hopes with his simple question.

"You tell me," Cliff said coldly.

Lester scanned the countryside, making a full circle. There were four farmhouses along the short stretch of road where they were standing and two or three others visible off a side road a fair distance away. "You mean this one here?" Lester asked, a note of petulant disbelief in his voice. "No, man, it wasn't like that."

"What d'ya mean, it wasn't like that?" Cliff challenged. "It looks right to me. Maybe you better take another look."

Lester tossed his head scornfully. "Looks right to you," he snorted. "What's that supposed to mean? You wasn't there, my man. I mean, shit, like the well's even on the wrong side."

Cliff took a deep breath and let it out slowly. "All right," he conceded wearily. "Let's get back in the car. We've got some more looking to do."

Reluctantly, the prisoner and the lawmen piled back into their vehicles. When Cliff bent to the window to confer with Delsa on the plans for the rest of the afternoon's search, Lester stopped him before he could say anything. "Y'know something funny, though," he said laconically, as though he attached no particular significance to the observation he was about to make. "We passed a house on the way down here that looks kinda like the place that lady in white lived."

"Jesus Christ," Cliff groaned. He had just about had enough. But he yanked open the rear door and slid in next to the marshal on May's left. "Awright, we'll take a look," he sighed.

Delsa eased the car off the slippery shoulder and turned it around. They drove for about five minutes, until Lester told them to stop. Two other cars in the convoy pulled in behind.

"Well?" Cliff asked.

Lester leaned across the seat for a better look, his head almost resting on the chest of the marshal to his right, who squirmed uncomfortably. Then he straightened up and said simply, "Yup."

"You're sure?"

"Could be another house jes' like it, but that's what it looked like awright."

Motioning with his hand at the rear window, Cliff signaled for Ken to come up. "Lester says that's the house," he told Klein. "Stay here with him. I'm gonna knock on the door and find out what I can."

Cliff hurried up the muddy, unpaved walkway to the front door. He was kept waiting almost a full minute after he knocked, but then the door opened and he disappeared inside. Ten minutes later the door opened again and he stepped onto the narrow front porch that ran the length of the house. A middle-aged black woman stood next to him.

"That's her," Lester said in the car. "Jes' don' ask me are you sure, huh. I'm tellin' you, that's the lady."

Ken started to ask anyway but stopped himself, and the young lawyer and his prisoner exchanged laughing glances. Cliff, meanwhile, hurried down the walkway to the car, circling in front of it to the driver's side. Ken tried to read his face but couldn't.

Stooping at the window, Cliff said, "She says she never heard of Herman Bell or Lester May. She says she never had anyone staying with her since her husband died in nineteen sixty-eight."

Lester said, "I don't give a shit. That's her."

From beyond him, one of the marshals pointedly asked, "Well, who yuh gonna b'lieve, this guy or her?"

Cliff crouched even lower to look straight across the back seat at the marshal. "Her name is Adela Wine," he said. "She works as a maid and wears a white uniform. She's got a son in the army. I don't think Lester guessed all that. She's the lady in white all right, and she's lying about it. That's her business, I don't care. All I care about is that Bell buried that gun on a farm just fifteen minutes from here."

At that moment, finding the woman in white seemed an enormous breakthrough. But knowing that Piagentini's service revolver was only fifteen minutes away meant that Ken and Cliff could have their hands on it in fifteen minutes only if they knew where it was. The area they had to search suddenly had shrunk from a mind-numbing two thousand square miles to a more manageable three hundred square miles—which was still over ten times the size of Manhattan, about the area of all five boroughs of New York City. And the sun was already sliding low in the western sky, and it was Saturday, which meant they have only a little over two days in which to find the gun Lester swore was there.

The rest of the day was spent going nowhere. Although Mrs. Wine had denied any involvement with Bell and had been generally resistant to questioning, she did offer the name of Nanny Closter in Cordelia as possibly the woman they were looking for. This was the same name Bell's mother had given them in Jackson, and the fact that suddenly they were being pointed in the same direction by two independent sources raised their hopes to a higher pitch. But when Lester May was taken to the Closter farm, he dashed those hopes in an instant.

"No dice," he said laconically. "Not even close."

At dinner that night, after the marshals had taken Lester back to Jackson, Ken and Cliff took stock of the situation. Despite their disappointment about the Closter farm, and despite the fact that the time clock was now down to a mere two days, there were still grounds for confidence. For the first time, I thought I heard a note of guarded optimism in Ken's voice when he called me that night for his report.

"The bad news is we didn't find the gun," he said. "The good news is we found the lady in white."

On Sunday morning Ken and Cliff decided to leave Lester in the Jackson jail for the day. "All we've got left is today and tomorrow," Cliff pointed out. "What we need now is some good, old-fashioned detective work. There's nothing we can do with Lester until we got something to show him. He'll only slow us down. A few hours of looking in the right places are going to do us a lot more good than cruising around with him."

Accompanied by a team of FBI agents, Ken and Cliff returned to question Mrs. Wine, while L. J. Delsa and a few other agents, joined by local Hinds County lawmen, drove to the farm owned by Ulysses Tatum, the man Mrs. Bell had mentioned as a long-time friend of the family.

Mrs. Wine started out as recalcitrant as she had been the day before, despite ominous reminders from Cliff that the withholding of information from police officers conducting a major murder investigation was a serious act with appropriately serious consequences. After almost an hour of questioning, she finally conceded she had known Herman Bell as a boy. Bit by bit, she acknowledged knowing almost everyone on the FBI's list of Bell's relatives, and finally she confessed that she once had been married to one of Bell's uncles. Still, she denied that Bell and Lester May stayed with her for two weeks in November 1971, persisting in the denial even when Ken suggested they bring May to her house so she could tell him to his face she had never seen him before.

"You do that," she challenged.

There was no point in calling her bluff. Cliff stood up and walked to the door, Mrs. Wine and the other lawmen following. He let the others pass and then turned to look straight into the woman's eyes, his own eyes communicating his stern tenacity. "We're going now, Mrs. Wine, but we'll be in Mississippi as long as it takes us to find what we're looking for," he said firmly. "You can help us or not, it's up to you. I want you to think it over because I'm going to call you every morning and I'm going to ask you one question. I'm going to ask you, Mrs. Wine, are you ready to tell me the truth now? And when you're ready, I'll come back."

He walked to the car and joined Ken and the two FBI agents. It took about ten minutes to raise Delsa's team on the radio. When they finally got them, the excitement in Delsa's voice sliced cleanly through the heavy static. "I think we're onto something," he said. "Get over here, have a look for yourselves."

The directions he gave took them to a farm about fifteen minutes beyond the other side of Cordelia, a little over twelve miles away on the narrow, mud-caked county roads. Cliff checked the time on his watch. Lester had said the woman in white lived fifteen minutes from the farm, so the distance was just about perfect.

The farm was right, too. The cistern, the well, the pigpen and fence—all exactly where Lester had said they would be. There was a tool shed at the side of the house, and Cliff Fenton was certain that in it he would find the post-hole digger Herman Bell had used to bury the gun he ripped from Joseph Piagentini's side. He radioed back to Jackson and pleaded with someone at the marshal's office to bring Lester out, getting no more than a promise that the marshal could see what could be done. Then he and Ken went inside to talk to Ulysses Tatum, the stoop-shouldered sixty-year-old black man who had been watching the lawmen in his front yard from a cracked living-room window.

Tatum played as dumb as Mrs. Wine, although it was unlikely that they had rehearsed their stories together. Both probably knew that Herman Bell was in jail in New York, charged with killing cops, and neither wanted to get entangled in his troubles. They were simply trying to protect themselves, even though they had done nothing wrong, for they probably could not think of a single instance in which any good had come to a black man out of involvement with the police. But a white Hinds County deputy who knew the names of a lot of the local blacks was able to ask the right questions and finally got Tatum to admit that years ago he and his wife had raised Jethro Peel's child.

Still, Tatum didn't recollect a visit from Bell in November of 1971. On the other hand, he made every effort to be cooperative and offered no objection when Cliff asked permission to look around his property.

The whole of Tatum's land was no more than three or four acres, and for an hour or so Ken and Cliff paced it like bloodhounds on a cold trail. Twice Cliff radioed back to Jackson to see what progress was being made in the effort to get May out of jail, and both times he was given assurances that the marshal's office was working on the problem.

So he waited, tense and optimistic. He felt a gut-deep confidence he finally had found the farm, but he wouldn't know for sure until May arrived to confirm it. His impatience urged him to question the old man some more, but prudence warned him not to. If Ulysses Tatum learned what they were looking for, they would have to put a guard on the property all night to keep him from digging up the gun. He probably didn't know what Bell had buried, but he must have known exactly where Bell dug the hole, for simple curiosity would have led him to look for freshly turned earth the morning after Bell and May borrowed a post-hole digger and then fled in the night.

In an excruciating moment Cliff Fenton would remember years later, a sickening thought suddenly jolted him with the impact of a hard punch in the gut. What if they had come so close, only to find that the gun was no longer there? What if Lester showed them exactly where to dig and there was no gun? If the old man did indeed find the newly turned earth three years ago, mightn't he have dug down to recover the mysterious treasure his young guests had cached on his property? *Perhaps they had come this far, meticulously tracing May's path backward to the Tatum farm, only to find an empty hole.*

It was after five o'clock, well past sunset, when a team of U.S. marshals arrived at Ulysses Tatum's farm with Lester May. Lester didn't hesitate a moment. As soon as he stepped from the car he told Cliff Fenton and Ken Klein, "This is it."

They led him to the back yard.

"Shit, man, something's wrong," he muttered, surprised and disappointed. "I think something's changed. Like I don't know. It ain't just the same. See, it was dark and I didn't really get a good look at the place, but it don't look right."

"Well, it's dark now, so that oughta make it just about perfect for you," Cliff suggested with a slight edge in his voice, realizing even as he spoke that May had done nothing to deserve his sarcasm.

Lester's head bobbed up and down as he contemplated the detective's statement, not quite sure if he were supposed to take it seriously. "Nah," he drawled at last. "I'll have to see it in the daytime."

"Fine with me. We'll come back in the morning," Cliff said.

He motioned for the marshals to take May away, and, when their car had disappeared down the road, he crossed to Ulysses Tatum's front door and called for the old man to come out. "I don't know if you know what that was all about," he told Tatum. "But that kid in the handcuffs is the one who said he was with Bell. We wanted him to have a look around and he said this isn't the place. Sorry we put you to so much trouble."

He turned and walked away, leaving the speechless old farmer open-mouthed on the front porch. Ulysses Tatum *knew* this was the place, and he was trying to figure out why the boy in handcuffs would say otherwise. Could be a million reasons, he concluded indifferently, simply accepting his good fortune in being rid of them so easily. "Never you mind, officer," he called after the retreating detective. "You'se jes doin' yo' job. 'Twasn't no imposition on me."

Cliff was laughing as he slid into the front seat beside Ken. "That oughta keep him from digging around tonight," he said. "Right about now he's figuring that whatever's down there, he doesn't want any part of it."

Ken's good-news/bad-news message that night raised my hopes higher than they had been. With only one day left before Lester May had to be returned to New Orleans for shipment to California, he said, "The bad news is we didn't find the gun. The good news is we found the farm."

"Did I say that? I guess I was wrong," Cliff grinned sheepishly when old Ulysses Tatum came running up to greet the convoy, protesting that he had been told his farm was not the place.

From the trunks of their cars, deputies, agents, and U.S. marshals began unpacking shovels and hoes while Lester May followed Cliff Fenton and Ken Klein around to the side of the house. Along the way, he confirmed to them that Tatum was indeed the old man who lent Bell the post-hole digger three years earlier. It was no surprise.

What was a surprise was Lester's reaction when he got his first good look at the yard in daylight. He turned completely around twice, obviously confused and disoriented, unable to get his bearings. "I tol' you las' night, something was wrong, but I kinda figured when I saw it today it'd all come to me. It ain't right, though. It ain't the way I remember it. Look for yourself."

Ken and Cliff looked but didn't know what they were looking for.

"See," Lester explained. "When we got the digger we walked 'longside the fence to the corner. That's where we buried it, right at the corner. 'Cept there ain't no corners. See, it jes' like curves."

He was right. The fence arched around the property in a long shallow curve, with nothing anywhere that could have been described as a corner. Apparently, when he accompanied Bell from the shed in the dark he assumed he was walking in a straight line, when in actuality he was following the rounded perimeter of the property. At the fence he must have noticed that his angle in relation to the house had changed and thus assumed he had turned a corner. Either that or Ulysses Tatum had moved the fence in the last three years. Cliff didn't much care which it was, because he was prepared to dig up every inch of the Tatum property if he had to.

"Well, pick a spot that looks good to you, and we'll get to work," he said.

Lester said, "You pick. I can't tell a fuckin' thing. Jes' start in near the fence somewhere, that's all."

The digging began at once, each man playing his own hunch and choosing a spot that appealed to him. Lester sat on a tree stump to watch, quietly smoking cigarettes, so detached from the whole spectacle that none of the onlookers who had gathered beyond the fence posts could have guessed the indolent young black man lazing in the front yard while white folks worked was the cause of all this activity.

After a while Cliff recognized the futility of such a random approach and decided it was time for another crack at Ulysses Tatum. He and Ken went to question the old man again, leaving all the others grumbling over their shovels in the yard. By this time the crowd beyond the borders of the Tatum property had grown to about twenty-five or thirty people. Their curious conjectures about buried treasure were clearly audible to the sweat-soaked lawmen. Someone with an authoritative voice that suggested wide learning tried to close the discussion with an informed-sounding announcement that the men with the shovels were looking for a million dollars' worth of silver service buried by slaves as the Yankee army closed in on the plantation. Lester, he opined, was a descendant of those slaves, who had faithfully passed on the secret of the treasure from generation to generation.

"Weren't no Yankees in these parts," a skeptic countered. "Weren't no plantations neither."

Inside, Cliff and Ken pushed Tatum harder than they had before, reminding him that the withholding of information constituted a crime known as obstruction of justice. The old man was cagey enough to know he could no longer bluff it out by denying that Bell and May had been at his farm. But he wasn't ready to admit anything yet.

"Lemme talk to the judge," he said.

"You don't need a judge, we're not charging you with anything," Cliff told him. "But unless you start giving us some answers, you're gonna need a lawyer."

Ken explained carefully that there was no crime and no shame involved in having let Bell bury something on his property. "You're not going to be in any trouble if you just tell us where it is," he said. "We'll dig it up and go away, and that'll be the end of it."

"Lemme jes' talk to the judge," the old man repeated.

The questioning went on for another fifteen minutes, but all Cliff and Ken could get from him was the same statement. Finally Cliff gave up and returned to the yard. "The old man knows but he's not saying," he explained to one of the Hinds County deputies. "All he says is he wants the judge. What the hell's he talking about?"

"Walt Dennis," the deputy said, leaning on his shovel.

"Who's Walt Dennis?"

"That's our judge, justice of the peace actually. To most of the folks round-bout here, I reckon he's about all the law there is."

"Think the old man would talk to him?"

The deputy laughed. "Nobody don't answer Walt when he asks 'em something."

"Okay, where do I find him?"

"You passed him on the way up. 'Member that road gang back apiece? Convicts, y'know. The sheriff was with 'em, and so was Walt. If y'all want, I'll fetch him in a minute."

Cliff thanked him, and the deputy, only too glad to be rid of his shovel, sprinted for his car.

Fifteen minutes later he returned, followed by a county car with a sheriff's star emblazoned on the door. Sheriff Sammy McGee, a tall, broad-shouldered man in his middle fifties, climbed from the passenger side of the front seat. He wore civilian clothes, and for three days now Ken, Cliff, and L. J. Delsa had been mystified by the flawless shine of his boots, which gleamed like patent leather and bore not the slightest trace of the gooey Mississippi mud that coated every other surface less than ten feet above ground level. Ken had suggested that Sammy McGee knew where the stones were, and it was the only hypothesis they came up with that made any sense.

The sheriff pulled open the rear door of his car, and an almost aristocratic-looking man in a linen suit glided out. For a moment he surveyed the scene with the detached curiosity of a prince inspecting the provinces. Sheriff McGee motioned for Cliff to come up.

"This here's Judge Dennis," the sheriff said. "I hear ol' Ulysses is askin' after him."

"Says he wants to talk to the judge."

"Natural enough," the sheriff agreed. Turning to the man at his left, he said, "Y'Honuh, this is Detective Fennuhn from N'Yawk City. You c'n take my word for it, he's one fine lawman. These fellas is down here lookin' for a gun one of our local boys took off'n a police officer he killed in N'Yawk. Seems he buried it on Ulysses' property. So I reckon they figure ol' Ulysses knows where it's at, 'cept he ain't tellin'. That about the size of it?"

"Couldn't have said it better," Cliff agreed.

The judge nodded. "If you'll wait here, Mr. Fenton," he said, walking quickly toward the house. Cliff and the sheriff swung in after him, with Ken joining them along the way. In the yard all digging had ceased, and beyond the fence the eyes of all the onlookers followed the judge as he ascended the three steps to Ulysses Tatum's porch.

Judge Dennis paused at the top of the stairs, then stepped through the doorway into the house. Sammy McGee stepped in after him and the door swung closed behind them. In less than half a minute, perhaps no more than ten or fifteen seconds, the door opened again and the judge reappeared, stepped just clear of the doorway, and raised his right hand in a dramatic gesture, like Babe Ruth calling the shot. "If you start digging right there," he called in an unexpectedly loud voice, "right where that tree is lying on the ground, I think you'll find what you're looking for."

Everyone turned to the spot he had pointed at, as though they would see the earth part and the long-buried gun rise to the surface. Ken immediately looked to Lester, who was intently studying the location, nodding approvingly. Meanwhile, Sammy McGee hurried from the house and crossed the front yard to his car. "Jes' goin' for some he'p," he called to Cliff.

Agents and deputies had already begun clearing the area where the judge indicated they should dig. Ken and Lester May watched from a few feet away. For the first time, the usually phlegmatic prisoner showed unmistakable signs of excitement. "I guess that's how come I missed it," he said, shaking his head but smiling as he spoke. "That hickory there was standin' then, it was jes' on the other side of the fence. It looks dif'rent down."

"Don't sweat it, Lester. You did just fine," Ken told him.

"Le's see, le's see," Lester muttered softly, his eyes rivited to where the diggers were just beginning to remove the first shovelfuls of sodden dirt.

Even the marshal who has been so pessimistic ever since they got to Mississippi couldn't help getting caught up in the sudden surge of enthusiasm. "Reckon mebbe I was wrong 'bout you, boy," he conceded graciously to Lester. "You jes' don' run away, hear. I think I'm gonna do me some diggin'."

Moving from the prisoner's side for the first time in a week, he threw himself into the work. In all, four shovels bit rhythmically into the soft, crustless earth, cutting a furrow about the width and breadth of a good-sized grave that deepened slowly with the passing minutes. As the mound of glistening dirt by the graveside grew, three other men with rakes and hoes began sifting through it, smoothing it out over the mushy grass, stooping from time to time to break up large clots with their hands.

In half an hour the hole had grown until it was at least ten feet long and five or six feet wide, but still no more than a foot or foot and a half at its deepest. Farther down, the earth grew denser, heavier, more resistant, and the diggers were taking the easier course, simply enlarging the mouth of the hole. Not wanting to criticize, Ken decided that the best way to get them moving in the right direction was by example. Jumping to the center of the hole, he grabbed a shovel and started digging strongly, forcing the tip of his spade into the dense clay with the sole of his shoe, then tearing free a great chunk of mud that whooshed with a sharp sucking sound as it came free. In a minute or two he had deepened the hole another foot.

Lester, alone now in the yard while all attention was focused on the digging, sauntered off to sit on a tree stump a few feet from Ulysses Tatum's front porch. With his elbows on his knees, he rocked slowly back and forth, pleasantly contemplating the labor he had set in motion.

Ten minutes later the digging stopped suddenly as everyone turned at the sound of heavy engines. Sheriff Sammy McGee's county car eased into the front yard, followed by an old and wheezing flatbed truck with sixteen denim-clad men standing on the back. Two uniformed deputies sat on the roof of the cab facing backward, shotguns cradled across their laps. Behind the truck, a sturdy backhoe lumbered into place, waddling like a hippopotamus on the rutted drive.

"I figgered mebbe it'd go a mite faster if you guys

had a little he'p," Sammy McGee called cheerfully as he climbed from his car. "Route Twenty-two c'n wait a day, I reckon."

One of the guards swung his legs over to the side of the cab and leaped to the ground. Gesturing with his shotgun, he signaled to the convicts on the back of the truck, who filed out one by one. The last man in the truck passed tools down to the others.

On the porch, Judge Dennis surveyed the scene appreciatively. "I think they're going to have to take down a couple sections of your fence to get that backhoe in the yard, Ulysses," he said softly. "That's all right with you, isn't it?"

"Ah've had fence down befo' an' it seems to me Ah's gonna have fence down agin," the old man conceded.

While the road gang set to work ripping out fence posts to clear a lane for the wide backhoe, Ken and Cliff conferred with Sheriff McGee. It was Ken's idea not to tell the convicts what they were looking for. If they thought they were after some sort of treasure, they would work well and swiftly, digging and sifting as though their labor were some kind of holiday game. But if they knew the end of their search was a gun, most of them would guess it was going to be used as evidence against someone—and Ken didn't want any of them deciding to do some unknown fellow prisoner a favor by passing over the gun when he found it.

By two o'clock the backhoe was in place and Sammy McGee explained the job to the convicts. "You get them shovels and them big sieves," he said, "and sift through every mol-li-cle of dirt that machines pulls up. You find anything, give a holler."

"What are we lookin' for?" one of the convicts, a wiry, weathered white man in his forties, asked.

"You're lookin' for anything that ain't dirt," the sheriff answered crisply. "Now git to work."

Cliff Fenton watched in admiration as the convicts, a mixed group of a dozen black and four white prisoners, set to their task with shovels, rakes, and large basketlike sieves. With the digging now in capable hands, there was little for him to do, so he took advantage of the lull to satisfy his curiosity about something. "Maybe it's none of my business, Sammy," he said, joining the sheriff at the fence. "But you know, we weren't able to get a thing out of Tatum for two days. When you and the judge walked in, he told you right away. I was wondering what you said to him."

Sammy McGee's eyes sparkled with laughter. "Didn't say nothin' to him," he chuckled. "Didn't hafta. See, there's folks 'round here say ol' Ulysses is a moonshiner. Can't prove it by me. Over the years we raided that ol' boy plen'y, never did find no still. But it could be he don' want a whole passel of po-lice and federal agents and whatnot lookin' around his property too close. So we jes' walk in the door and Ulysses says, right quick enough, 'You tell 'em to dig around the west fence, over where that hickory's down,' Is that about what you wanted to know?"

"That's about it," Cliff said.

Meanwhile, out in the yard, the work proceeded, each mounded scoop of earth offering a glistening promise of success. Gradually, as an hour, then an hour and a half passed, the boisterous spiritedness of the first onslaught of digging gave way to a more sober expectancy. The lawmen, who at least knew what they were looking for, still felt confident it would be found but no longer seemed to believe it would turn up any minute. For the convicts, on the other hand, who didn't know the object of their search, what had begun as an adventure slowly degenerated into a grim and listless routine that transformed Ulysses Tatum's grassy yard into a sea of runny mud.

Three o'clock came and went, three-thirty, then four. In the course of the afternoon the warm and gentle November sun had inched its way across the Tatum farm and was now picking up speed as it headed for the horizon, throwing the yard into deep shadow. At four o'clock Ken and Cliff began rounding up volunteers to guard the excavation overnight when darkness closed down the digging.

"If we're gonna get May back to N'Awlins to catch that plane, we're gonna hafta be leavin' pretty soon," one of the marshals announced apologetically.

"Just give us till five o'clock," Fenton urged.

The marshal checked his watch. "You know where the gun is now," he reminded Cliff. "You can find it without him."

"I know that," Cliff said softly. "Just another hour if you can. I want him to be here when we find it."

"You got it," the marshal consented. "We're just gonna hafta go like hell, that's all."

And so the digging went on in deepening gloom. By this time all the lawmen, knowing the day's work was almost done, had gathered in a tight circle behind the backs of the squatting convicts, who poked at the mounded earth like soothsayers probing for omens among piles of shiny entrails. Their sifting movements had by now become automatic, their hands flitting crablike in the dirt like the hands of practiced women at a loom. Then, unexpectedly, the fingers of one of the prisoners stuttered and stopped, a sudden cessation of movement that caught everyone's attention. His black fingers disappeared into the dirt, looking for something, then came out with a solid chunk of soil which he turned over slowly in his hands.

"Hey, man," he said, his voice curious and amused, "looks like I got me a roscoe."

It took one or two seconds which later, replayed in memory, seemed like a long time for the meaning of his words to sink in. No one said *roscoe* any more, the word went out in the '40s with *heater* and *gat*. But that was what he said, and already, even as the import of what they had heard was becoming clear, Ken Klein and Cliff Fenton were sprinting toward the bemused prisoner, shoving people aside, deputies as well as convicts, as they pushed through what suddenly felt like a crowd.

The object the prisoner held out to them, cradling it in both hands as innocently as a small child bearing a gift, looked more like an apple turnover than a gun. It was a rounded lump of dirt a few inches thick, roughly triangular, with one end tapering to a blunt point. As Ken took it from the black man's hands, some loose mud fell from it, clarifying the shape even further. The dirt that remained was hard, as though it had been baked in a kiln, and there was no metal visible anywhere.

But there was no doubt either that inside that solid

earthen casket lay a gun. Joseph Piagentini's gun. The slender tendril of a tree root clung to the thick part of the triangle covering the stock of the revolver, weaving in under the surface of the mud, just as in Deer Park, Long Island, roots had long since clutched the coffin of the young man who once wore this weapon on his hip. If there is no resurrection of the flesh, there is at least a resurrection in steel, for Joseph Piagentini's gun had risen from its Mississippi grave. It was a lawman's gun and it would demand justice.

Twenty

THE YOWL OF POLICE SIRENS STARTLED THE cold Manhattan morning. Four patrol cars, their dome lights flashing, their sirens shrieking commuters out of the way, sped south along FDR Drive. In the middle of the keening caravan, a large Corrections van painted police-department blue bounded down the potholed highway. At the Canal Street exit the convoy pulled off the drive, turned at Lafayette, circled around Foley Square, and pulled to a halt on Centre Street in front of the massive granite Criminal Courts Building.

It was January 6, the first Monday of 1975, opening day in the second murder trial of Bell, Bottom, Washington, Torres, and Torres. Before the rear doors of the Corrections van opened, a dozen heavily armed patrolmen scrambled from the cars, exchanged greetings with another dozen already on the sidewalk, and formed a protective cordon from the back of the van to the courthouse door. At opposite ends of the block, teams of uniformed officers detained pedestrians with perfunctory apologies while patrol cars at the intersections with Leonard and Franklin streets took up broadside positions blocking access to Centre Street from either direction.

Four days a week, for four months, five months, six months, however long it would take, this same caravan would howl its way along the five-mile course from the Rikers Island prison to the courthouse in the morning, from the courthouse to the prison at night. As in the first trial, there would be no sessions on Fridays, for Bell, Bottom, and Washington claimed to be Muslims and the court was bound to respect their religious scruples. These scruples, I couldn't help reflecting, hadn't prevented them from murdering Jones and Piagentini on a Friday and hadn't prevented Bottom and Washington from attempting to murder Sergeant George Kowalski on a Friday.

At the thirteenth-floor courtroom, security precautions were as intense as outside on Centre Street. All the staircases had been sealed, and the corridors were patrolled by uniformed officers and detectives. An airline-style metal detector had been set up opposite the bank of elevators, and everyone coming onto the floor, including even veteran reporters personally known to the courthouse staff, was closely screened. Pockets were emptied, pocketbooks searched, and policewomen administered intimate body searches to the women spectators, many of whom were militants who had come to demonstrate their solidarity with the killers. Downstairs, in the cavernous lobby, militants proselytized openly among all those arriving on court business, passing out extremist literature, some of which found its way to the hands of prospective jurors.

We were going to have a new judge for the second trial. As soon as the hung jury returned in May, Justice Melia indicated his reluctance to preside over a second trial. For a while the case kicked around from judge to judge; most of them didn't want it, and the few who were willing to take it on seemed to want it for the wrong reasons. Finally, Justice Edward J. Greenfield, the chief of all criminal trial parts in New York County, settled the judicial wrangling by assigning the case to himself.

I couldn't have been happier. No magistrate in the New York criminal justice system was more highly regarded than Judge Greenfield, a tough courtroom disciplinarian whose knowledge of the law was unmatched by any attorney or judge I have ever met. A tireless worker, he did prodigious amounts of homework on every case that came before him and reserved the most cutting specimens of what was at times a cruelly sarcastic wit for lawyers who came into his courtroom less well prepared than he. More than one brash and arrogant young assistant district attorney had learned humility in his court. Yet in all my years in the district attorney's office I had never heard a single complaint about his fairness either from the lawyers on our staff or from the defense attorneys who opposed them.

Indeed, when it was announced that he would be presiding over the second Piagentini-Jones murder trial, the defense attorneys were as delighted with the news as I was. A liberally tolerant man, he would grant them a wide latitude to explore the peripheries of the case, where the defense's only hope lay. That was all right with me, because this time I was sure I knew what was coming and was willing to let them lay down their smokescreens, confident I could blow them away easily. What gratified me about trying the case before

Judge Greenfield was my awareness that his comprehensive grasp of the law rarely opened him to reversible error. If I won in his court, I knew I wouldn't lose on appeal.

After disposing of a few preliminary matters, we set to work selecting a jury. At the first trial, no less than a month had been consumed as we questioned over six hundred prospective jurors. Yet in looking back at that trial, I now felt I had let myself be rushed and hadn't been careful enough. I had been afraid of boring and antagonizing the jurors by haranguing them as intensely as the defense did. This time around I was determined not to make the same mistake. No matter how long it took, I was going to make sure that every man and woman in the jury was as thoroughly indoctrinated by the prosecution as the defense. As a result, jury selection took almost twice as long as the second trial. For seven grueling weeks, through January and well into February, we went over and over the same questions with candidate after candidate. In all, more than eight hundred men and women were examined by Judge Greenfield, myself, and the team of defense lawyers before we finally settled on twelve.

In choosing a jury, a prosecutor cannot afford to think only in terms of each individual juror's qualifications. He also must consider the composition of the panel as a whole. Twelve intelligent and unbiased men and women, each capable of weighing the evidence and returning with an appropriate verdict, may end up as a hung jury if they cannot get along together. This was one area in which I had made a bad tactical error at the first trial, where the jury consisted of eleven men and one woman. In my experience, I haven't found men preferable to women or women preferable to men as jurors in murder cases; neither sex seems more likely than the other to be a "prosecution juror." Nor have I found whites preferable to blacks, working-class people preferable to professionals, or vice versa. But the point is that one never does get a homogeneous jury; there is always a mix. And when there is a mixture, one of anything means trouble for the prosecutor. A solitary woman among eleven men, a single black impaneled with eleven whites, tends to feel isolated, and the last thing a district attorney wants is an artificial line of cleavage splitting a social unit from which he must demand absolute unanimity.

Getting the right balance and the right jurors sometimes requires the patience of a chess master and the nerves of a high-rolling craps shooter. The stakes are justice itself. At the first trial I had let myself get boxed in by not balancing the jury as I went along. Not willing to make that mistake again, I made up my mind to gamble some of my precious challenges early in the game to make sure I didn't get myself in a situation where I would have to make all of my last selections men or women, blacks or whites, in order to achieve a decent integration. To do it right, of course, I had to cut it very close, so close in fact that when the seven weeks were over and the last juror sworn, I had only one unused challenge left. But I also had a nicely mixed panel consisting of seven men and five women, eight whites and four blacks, ranging in age from their twenties to their sixties.

A few of the selections throw some light on the type

of thinking that goes into choosing a jury. For example, from the way the questioning had gone I knew the defense liked an attractive young blonde who had been antiwar and then an anti-Nixon activist, who was a member of the New York Civil Liberties Union, and who had been a psychology major in college. On each count, she seemed to be a solid defendants' juror—an active liberal who undoubtedly disliked the penal system and might be reluctant to send anyone to jail, who apparently sympathized with the plight of blacks and might be taken in by the radical rhetoric of the defendants, who might try to excuse the actions of the defendants in terms of all sorts of "psychological" variables.

On the other hand, when I asked her if she ever had been the victim of a crime, she said she had been raped a number of years ago. She had gone to line-ups, she had picked out her assailants, she went over her testimony with an assistant D.A. before going into court, where she was cross-examined by a defense lawyer who tried to impugn her sexual ethics. Because she had attended a line-up, it seemed to me she would be able to put herself in the place of Ruth Jennings and Gloria Lapp. She had spent hours in the district attorney's office and knew we didn't pressure witnesses to alter their testimony in order to strengthen a case. She also knew what it felt like to be badgered by a defense lawyer who must discredit a witness in order to make the truth seem like it is not the truth. I was confident she would be able to identify with the five women who were my key witnesses.

Weighing one side against the other, I decided to take a chance on her. When the challenge board was passed to me, I left her card in place, hoping it would still be there after the board was handed around the defense table. It was. I still remember the reaction in the courtroom when the clerk read the names of the challenged jurors and hers wasn't included. A newspaper reporter with fifteen years' experience on the courthouse beat threw down his pencil in disgust and there was a clearly audible murmur of disapproval from the knot of courtroom buffs who always fill the first few rows of seats. Perhaps I imagined it, but it seemed to me that even Judge Greenfield was looking at me with a stern scowl of puzzlement if not dismay. I wasn't surprised by the reaction, which simply meant that the others in the courtroom didn't have the same hunch about her I did.

To some extent the job of selecting a jury was made easier for me by the remarkable tactics of the defense team. Because the defendants were black and because they fancied themselves as revolutionaries in the forefront of the black movement, they must have imagined that any blacks exposed to their rhetoric for a few weeks would automatically rally behind them. This was exactly the same brazen miscalculation the defendants had made when they assumed that by shooting two uniformed men in the back they would ignite the revolutionary passions of the black community. In 1971, if any white man had dared to suggest that the black population of America would rejoice at the ambush murder of two young men, he would have been quite rightly denounced as a depraved racist. In 1975, the inherent racism behind the assumption that a black juror would vote guilt or innocence in terms of skin color was no less appalling.

Yet that is precisely what the defense must have

assumed, for nothing else could account for the fact that the first juror they approved, and therefore the foreman of the jury, was a career soldier who had retired from the army after twenty years with the rank of sergeant. He now worked as the chief of security at a local college. Such a man would know about youthful revolutionaries and undoubtedly disliked them. He would also know the difference between radicalism and murder. He had been a soldier in the past and was practically a cop now. He would know what an army was and what one wasn't, and would have nothing but contempt for the sorry collection of skulking assassins who billed themselves as the Black Liberation Army. And above all, he knew firearms and could form a sickeningly clear picture in his mind of what a .45 fired from half a foot away could do to the back of a man's head. Yet he was a black man, and so he became our foreman. From the moment he was sworn in, I was certain we would get justice this time, for it seemed to me that the arrogance of the defendants was already starting to undo them.

By Thursday, February 13, our full complement of twelve jurors had been sworn, and we immediately began selecting the four alternates who would listen to the entire trial from the jury box and who could be brought into service at any time before the commencement of deliberation in case one of the regular jurors had to be excused. We picked two alternates that day before suspending for the long four-day weekend—Friday being our usual day off because of the defendant's religion and Monday being a legal holiday.

At about 9 P.M., Sunday, February 16, Herman Bell,

armed with a wooden stick crudely carved into the shape of a knife, overpowered a guard in the maximum security cellblock on Rikers Island. Bell managed to get the cellblock keys from the guard and apparently was attempting to free his codefendants when he was subdued by other guards. A Corrections Department spokesman credited the "double surveillance" feature of the prison's maximum-security procedures with thwarting the escape attempt.

At the very moment Corrections officers inside the Rikers Island prison were recapturing Bell, police in the Bronx received a telephone call from a man who claimed to have spotted five men armed with shotguns setting off in three rubber rafts from the pier at the foot of Tiffany Street in the Bronx. According to the caller, the rafts were being rowed in the direction of Rikers Island, a little over half a mile away in the middle of the East River.

A Harbor Patrol launch was immediately sent to investigate, followed a few minutes later by a second boat and a police department helicopter. For almost three hours the East River waters surrounding Rikers Island were searched, but no trace of the rafts or of the five armed men was found. Then, around midnight, the Harbor Patrol located a single yellow six-foot raft bobbing in the narrow channel between Rikers Island and La Guardia Airport's runway 22, which sits on a landfill causeway extending far into the river from the Queens side. On the raft, which apparently had been abandoned, were oars, a pair of diver's swimming fins, and small quantities of .38-caliber and 9-millimeter ammunition. There was also a map of the area with a pencil line tracing a route from Hunts Point Park in the Bronx to Rikers Island, then back to the Tiffany Street pier and overland up Tiffany Street to Bruckner Boulevard. Although a police department spokesman refused to speculate on any connection between the aborted waterborne commando operation and Herman Bell's escape attempt, he did tell reporters, "You can put two and two together."

I first learned about the attempted escape early Monday morning when Cliff Fenton called me at home with the news. At the time, information was still sketchy but he assured me none of the defendants had escaped or been injured in any way that would delay the trial. Nevertheless, I was worried. The story broke too late to make the morning papers, but it would get heavy play in Monday afternoon's *Post* and in the *News* and *Times* Tuesday morning, when our jurors could read it on their way to court.

As I expected, on Tuesday morning the defense lawyers immediately brought the newspaper accounts of Sunday's events to the judge's attention. Although the defense made no application for a reexamination of the jurors, Judge Greenfield, on his own motion, elected to question the sworn jurors one at a time "to see whether this has affected their ability to render a fair and impartial verdict."

The court officer brought in the first juror, who readily admitted having read an account of the attempted jailbreak in the *Daily News* and having heard about it on the radio. Judge Greenfield asked him whether his view as to the guilt or innocence of the defendants had been colored by what he heard and read.

The juror, the black former sergeant shifted uncomfortably in his seat before answering. When he spoke, it was obvious that he had known the question would be coming and had given his answer some thought. "At first, I had a complete open mind, both ways," he began. "Frankly, I don't think that anyone could have sat here with . . . with more fair and open-minded judgment than I intended to serve. But right now, I would like to decline."

"You would what?" Judge Greenfield demanded.

"I would like to decline from it."

"That's not my question, whether you would like to decline. The question is, could you no longer be fair and impartial?"

"I wouldn't say completely, it affected me that much. But if I said it did not affect me at all I would be making an incorrect statement. I would try my best, but it did have some effect, yes."

The judge then asked the defense lawyers if they wanted to question the juror. they conferred briefly among themselves, their heads nodding in agreement, before announcing, "We have no questions, Your Honor."

The second juror was summoned. A woman in her late sixties, she was asked by the judge if she could still be a "fair and impartial juror and evaluate only the evidence you hear in this courtroom with respect to the events of May 21, 1971."

"It would be very hard, I think," she answered frankly. Again, the defense was silent.

And so it went. Each juror acknowledged having heard of the incident, either in the newspapers or on the radio. To varying degrees, they confessed it made them uncomfortable, although most of them promised to try to disregard it when it came time to decide on a verdict. At the conclusion of the voir dire, the defense moved for a mistrial on the grounds that the jury had been exposed to prejudicial publicity. I waited tensely for the response from the bench, glumly wondering which of the two possible outcomes was worse. The prospect of having to go through the ordeal of jury selection for yet a third time left me numb. On the other hand, I couldn't fail to recognize that the aborted jailbreak attempt added a dimension to the trial that had always been there implicitly but was now dramatically explicit. That dimension was fear. For the ill-fated commando raid on Rikers Island reminded the jurors that the defendants had desperate, dangerous, and heavily armed supporters on the outside. Although a few courthouse wags had begun referring to the anonymous men in the rubber rafts as the "Black Liberation Navy," the jurors were too closely tied to the case to dismiss them so lightly. Indeed, a number of easily recognizable militant types, admitted to the courtroom on press credentials of one sort or another, now sat among the legitimate newspaper reporters ostentatiously sketching the lawyers, the defendants, the judge, but most especially the jury. No matter how staunchly one wanted to do his or her duty as a citizen, how could a juror in such a setting fail to consider the possibility that those sketches would end up in the hands of a team of BLA hit men?

If only one juror were so frightened by the existence of the BLA commandos that he or she refused to bring in a verdict of guilt, we would end up with another hung jury.

I have no doubt at all that Judge Greenfield fully understood this danger. He could have foreclosed the possibility of a verdict based on fear by dismissing the jury and attempting to impanel a new one. But apparently he felt that to do so would have been to endorse a cynical assessment of the jury system. Instead, he decided to keep the present panel and go ahead with the search for the final two alternates. A tough and courageous call, his ruling reaffirmed his belief in the integrity and courage of the fourteen men and women who had already taken their oaths to serve impartially and to vote the truth as they saw it. I felt better knowing he trusted them, and I'm sure the jurors themselves, however mixed their feelings at the time, could not have been unmoved by his clear declaration of confidence that they would do their duty.

Both sides delivered their opening statements after the noon recess on Wednesday, February 19. As at the first trial, our first three witnesses were Jack Farrell, who prepared the diagram of the crime scene we would be using; Heinz Graumann, the aerial photographer who took pictures of the Colonial Park area for us; and Detective Phillip Ventura, who took photos of the crime scene on the night of the killings. Their testimony being merely a legally required formality that enabled me to introduce various exhibits, they were hardly cross-examined at all. In just a little over an hour all three of them had finished testifying and the decks were cleared for me to begin proving the People's case against the defendants.

I led off Thursday morning with Richard Hill, who

once again did a superb job of evoking in the minds of the jurors a vivid picture of the scene at Colonial Park during those harrowing and confused moments while Waverly Jones lay dead on the sidewalk and Joseph Piagentini suffered his final agony. In addition to setting the stage for the witnesses to follow, Hill established two important points for me. The fact that he had entered the project from the east and had seen no one fleeing from the scene indirectly corroborated the testimony of the other witnesses, who would report that the defendants ran in a westerly direction. And the fact that he noted the absence of the fallen officer's weapons before the police responded to the scene established that the guns were taken in the few seconds between the time the shooting stopped and the time Hill first saw the bodies. His testimony thus foreclosed the possibility that anyone other than the killers stole the two missing service revolvers.

Hill was followed to the stand by Mike Warnecke, who told the jury that Colonial Park was in the sector normally patrolled by himself and his partner. He told of being flagged down by a cab driver, of racing to the scene, of carrying Piagentini to a patrol car and driving with him to Harlem Hospital, where he was pronounced dead on arrival. When Warnecke concluded his testimony we recessed for lunch, after which I put Gloria Lapp on the stand.

During the seven weeks of jury selection, most of my evenings after court adjourned were spent preparing witnesses. Gloria Lapp had come to my office on several occasions during this period, and I did everything humanly possible both to bolster her confidence and to keep her recollection of the events fresh and clear. The sessions were brief, rarely as long as half an hour. Sometimes I would question her about the events of May 21, 1971; at other times I would ask her to go over the various line-ups she had attended. Once in a while I wouldn't question her at all, but would talk in a general way about the problems witnesses face on the stand. On still other occasions, Ken Klein cross-examined her, playing the role of defense attorney to the hilt.

"Don't get upset if you don't remember something," I told her again and again. "The last time, they asked you how many cars were in the parking lot. And you let yourself get flustered because you didn't remember. You can't let that happen again. If you don't remember, just say so. For God's sake don't make up an answer, that's the surest way there is to make a problem for yourself. Just say, 'I don't know,' if you don't know. They'll try to make a big thing of it, but believe me the jury doesn't care about things like that. And the other lawyers know it, too. The only reason they ask those kinds of questions is to unnerve you, to try to make you lose your confidence. I've seen it happen a thousand times. If you testify about what kind of hat the defendant was wearing, they'll ask you about his shoes. And if you answer that one, they'll ask you about his socks. Sooner or later they'll get you to say you don't know. But so what? You saw what you saw, and that's what the jury cares about."

Unfortunately, my office wasn't a courtroom and Ken wasn't a hostile defense lawyer. Going over testimony in the district attorney's office is no more like taking the stand than rehearsing a speech in front of the bathroom mirror is like delivering it in a crowded auditorium. Besides, there was more than stage fright at work here to unnerve young Gloria Lapp. She was not merely going to be asked questions about things she had observed. She was going to be asked to look directly into the face of a man she had watched kill another man, to point to him, and to declare he was the killer. No one who has not undergone such an ordeal can imagine the courage it takes. As she looked at Tony Bottom, seated barely twenty feet from her, her mind would be filled with pictures of him stalking Waverly Jones, raising his gun to the back of the handsome young officer's head, and firing shot after shot into him as he fell. And even as she fixed those images in her mind, she would be aware that friends of this killer were at that very moment sketching her likeness in the courtroom.

I led her through her testimony that afternoon filled with the profoundest admiration for her courage. As at the first trial, she came through the direct examination superbly. I kept her on the stand less than two hours, hoping that if she could maintain her poise under cross-examination for another hour or so until we adjourned, she could take home a positive image of herself to bolster her confidence over the three-day weekend.

Then, within minutes of turning her over to the defense, I realized my calculations couldn't have been more wrong. Like the victim of a bad crash who again and again in his dreams watches his car skidding crazily toward the collision, for almost an hour and a half I had to sit and listen to an excruciatingly exact replay of the first trial. After no more than fifteen or twenty minutes her voice had become inaudible and she had to be asked to repeat her answers, sometimes more than once. Many of the questions she did not answer at all until they were repeated to her, and from where I sat she seemed to be staring somewhere over the shoulder of the attorney questioning her, her mind utterly distracted. At one point, when the judge repeated a question she hadn't answered, she leaned over from the witness chair and whispered something to him. He immediately summoned a court officer. I rushed to the bench to find out what was going on.

"It's quite all right, Mr. Tanenbaum, the situation has been taken care of," Judge Greenfield said, adopting a reassuring tone that was intended mostly for Gloria's benefit. "The witness informs me that there is an individual in the audience who is drawing her likeness, and it upsets her extremely. I sent word to that individual that he is not to proceed, so there should be no more problem."

Turning to Gloria, he said, "Would you like a few minutes to settle yourself, Miss Lapp, or are you ready to go on?"

Gloria took a deep breath, thanked the judge, and said she was ready to proceed. But it was too late for her to regain her composure. Only when we adjourned for the day did I learn that less than ten minutes after the judge ordered the artist to stop sketching the witness, a second man, seated only two seats from the first, opened a sketch pad and began to draw. Too numbed by hopelessness and despair, Gloria offered no protest but went bravely on with the cross-examination. Her hands were trembling uncontrollably when she told me about it.

Once a prosecution witness begins her cross-examination, she belongs to the defense. Legal ethics thus prevented me from meeting Gloria on Friday or over the weekend to go over her testimony again. I thought about her all weekend, frightened and lonely and far from home. Between the end of the first trial and the start of the second, her family had moved from New York—I think in part because Gloria could no longer stand living so near the scene of the murders. So she was alone in the city now and there was nothing I could do to comfort her. I just saw her briefly before she took the stand Monday morning, just long enough to tell her, "Don't worry. Try to keep calm and answer their questions, and it will all be over in a little while."

In court a few minutes later, the defense lawyer who had been examining her on Thursday picked up exactly where he had left off. Playing on her fears as expertly as he had played on her lack of self-confidence at the first trial, he began by asking, "Miss Lapp, you used to live at the Polo Grounds project adjacent to Colonial Park, is that right?"

"Yes."

"But now you no longer live in New York City, is that right?"

"Yes."

"You now live down south, is that right?"

I leaped up to object and the objection was sustained.

"What was the last school you attended?" the lawyer asked, probing for the same information in another way.

Again I objected and again the objection was sustained. The defense lawyer asked for a conference at the bench.

Gloria watched us tensely from the witness stand, unable to hear the arguments. By this time she was obviously so overwrought that I doubt she would have been able to answer if the judge ordered her to divulge her address. The defense lawyer made his points tellingly, citing a Supreme Court decision which held that the defense is entitled to the address of a witness so that it can investigate "her reputation in her present community for truth and veracity." I countered by arguing that the Supreme Court case lacked the overwhelming elements of fear and jeopardy we had here.

"We are dealing here with a situation that occurred four years ago in a different community," Judge Greenfield reminded the defense attorney.

"That's absolutely right, Your Honor," the lawyer shot back. "But she is testifying today. Her credibility is in issue today, as to whether she is telling the truth today."

Justice Greenfield couldn't help seeing the point, but he was unmoved by it. "I will permit no such questions of this witness, absolutely not," he declared. "The ruling stands."

I went back to the prosecution table greatly relieved. Gloria, though, seemed beyond help. For another hour she went numbly through the motions, mumbling her answers, becoming vaguer and less responsive by the minute. To my right I could see several jurors shaking their heads disapprovingly as they asked themselves whether this girl really was capable of the certainty they so rightly demanded in a matter of such great import.

If the defense had had enough sense to stop right there, the momentum they built up in discrediting Gloria might have carried them through the next witnesses, as it did at the first trial. They had totally destroyed one of my key witnesses, the only person at the scene of the crime to have picked Tony Bottom out of a line-up as the man who killed Waverly Jones. They had reduced her to the point of whimpering uncertainty and they had nothing to gain by attacking her further. Yet they went on and on, needlessly, cruelly. And as the questioning continued her fear and confusion gradually gave way to anger. Slowly, ever so slowly, Gloria Lapp was being resurrected as a witness.

Q: Miss Lapp, between the last trial and the present trial, this trial, how many times have you been to the district attorney's office?

A: You asked me that Thursday. How many times are you going to say that?

> THE COURT: Please answer the question, Miss Lapp.
> THE WITNESS: I don't know.
> DEFENSE COUNSEL: I didn't hear the answer.
> THE COURT: There was no answer.
> DEFENSE COUNSEL: She said something.
> THE COURT: Did she? I didn't hear.
> THE WITNESS: I said I didn't know.

Q: Was it fifty times?

A: I said I don't know. If I don't know, I don't know. You calling out numbers ain't gonna make me remember any better.

Q: All right, Miss Lapp, let me ask you this. When you were in the district attorney's office, did Mr. Tanenbaum, Mr. Klein, or any of the police officers, did they remind you of things, is that right?

A: What kind of things?

Q: Things that had to do with your testimony.

A: Certain parts.

Q: Do you remember what parts they reminded you of?

A: Not the part you're thinking.

Q: About the part where you saw the shooting?

A: I said not that part.

Q: Not that part. What part did they remind you of?

A: Little details. Like the stuff you keep asking me about.

Q: I see. Did they tell you they weren't happy with your testimony at the first trial?

A: No.

Q: Did they tell you they weren't happy with the fact there was no conviction at the first trial?

I rose to shout an objection, but before I could get the words out Judge Greenfield, as angry as I have ever seen him, roared at the defense attorney, "That is improper, sir! That is entirely improper, and I will see you in my chambers after court."

He then interrupted the proceedings to admonish the jury that they were absolutely not to concern themselves with the outcome of the first trial. "This is a separate, independent, distinct proceeding, and we are not concerned with what happened and did not happen in that case. You are not to allow yourselves to be governed in any way by anything that you may hear or suspect happened or did not happen. The only thing we are taking into account is that certain witnesses have previously testified, and therefore counsel may refer to that previous testimony to compare it to testimony on this occasion. But that is the only basis upon which we will have reference to that previous trial, and for all other purposes you will disregard it entirely." He then instructed the defense attorney to proceed with the cross-examination.

Perhaps Gloria saw in Judge Greenfield's anger a reflection of her own, and perhaps it steeled her. Or it may be that she simply had been pushed around too much. Whatever the cause, there was a strength in her voice now that I hadn't heard there before. Deaf to it, the defense attorney pushed on, recklessly badgering her, building toward an explosion. "Miss Lapp," he asked, "when did you first become aware that you were going to San Francisco to see a line-up?"

A: A day or two before we left.

Q: Were you aware at the time that two people had been arrested in San Francisco in connection with these murders that you witnessed?

A: No.

Q: Who did you go out on the airplane with? Was one of them Mr. Lankler, the assistant D.A., is that correct?

A: Yes.

Q: And you were also aware that three other people

were going, in addition to you, as prospective witnesses, to view this line-up?

A: I knew that I was going and Ruth Jennings was going. But I didn't know about the other people until I got there.

Q: Until you got where? To San Francisco?

A: To the airport. On the plane.

Q: I see. Then wasn't it in your mind, Miss Lapp, that this is it, this is the time I have to make an identification because they are going to a lot of trouble, a lot of expense, flying four people out there? And in fact didn't you also know that there were two suspects from reading about it in the *Daily News*? Isn't that all true, Miss Lapp?

A: No.

Q: All right. Now, in San Francisco, Miss Lapp, were you told there was an attorney present for one or more people in that line-up?

A: Yes.

Q: In fact, didn't Mr. Lankler tell you that you could or could not, it's up to you, whether you wanted to speak to that attorney?

A: Yes.

Q: And you chose not to speak to the attorney, right?

A: Yes.

Q: Why?

A: Because it was none of his business.

She spat the last answer at the lawyer, who only now realized he had no choice but to back off. Reluctant to dismiss the witness at a moment when she seemed to be in command, he leafed hurriedly through his notes, looking for a few closing questions. Then he said, "Miss Lapp, we'll be just another minute or two. When was the last time you saw Detective Butler?"

A: I saw him in the courthouse this morning.

Q: About how many times have you seen him since May 21, 1971.

A: I don't know.

Q: Hundreds?

A: I don't know.

Q: Well, could you estimate, is it more like ten or more like a hundred?

A: I said I don't know. You can call out all the numbers as much as you want, I still say I don't know.

> DEFENSE COUNSEL: Your Honor, I would ask that you direct the witness to make some effort to answer the question.
>
> THE COURT: She said—

He was interrupted by Gloria Lapp. "I am not answering no more things," she cried. "Stupid lawyer, I am not answering nothing else he has to say."

"Miss Lapp, you will answer the questions whether you think he is a stupid lawyer or not," Judge Greenfield admonished her.

But Gloria wasn't taking orders from anyone at this point. She was sitting straight in the witness chair and her voice rang through the courtroom, filling it with her rage. Raising her right arm defiantly, she pointed straight at Tony Bottom and shouted, "They're only doing it to get on my nerves. The only thing I remember is that that dude over there was out there and he shot the cop and that's all that matters. Don't ask me nothing!"

She lowered her arm, and for fully half a minute there was absolute silence in the courtroom. Her statement had been totally out of order, yet the defense was so shocked that it raised no objection, for what would have been the point? No one in that court would ever forget her words or could fail to understand them. So clearly that there could no longer be any question about it, her cry exposed the solid bedrock of certainty that until that moment had lain buried under layer upon layer of frustration. In a single moment she put all of her testimony and indeed the whole trial in perspective, and suddenly there was nothing more to say. "He shot the cop and that's all that matters."

Twenty-One

AT THE FIRST TRIAL, NEAR THE BEGIN-
ning of her testimony, I had asked Christine Rowe to
identify all five of the defendants, as I was required by
law to do. She had risen from her seat to get a better
view of the defense table and, indicating each defendant in turn, had given his name and the name she had
known him under as well as a phrase or two about what
he was wearing at the time in order to make her identifications clear to the jury. When she had gotten to the
last man in the line, Tony Bottom, she hesitated a
moment, put her left hand on her hip, wiggled her hips
around, and pointed melodramatically in his direction.
"And *that*," she had announced with special emphasis,
"is T.B., To-nee Bot-tom."

Small things like that drive prosecutors up the wall.
I didn't know what particular feelings lurked behind
that demonstration, nor do I know to this day, but I
saw at once that with a single gratuitous gesture she
had handed the defense a tool it could use to dis-
mantle her testimony. On cross-examination she had
been questioned closely about her feelings for the
defendants, especially Bottom, and I doubt the jury

believed her when she swore she harbored no animosity toward them. She had made it possible for defense counsel to argue in his summation that some real or fanciful grudge Christine harbored against Tony Bottom had prompted her to testify so that he would have to take the rap for these killings. He argued that in her, the police had found the perfect accomplice to aid them in their conspiracy to frame five innocent men.

After the first trial, I had called her into my office to lecture her on the danger of such careless gestures. At first, she didn't seem to know what I was talking about. When I came around from behind my desk and did a not-bad impersonation of her bump-and-grind routine, she broke up with laughter.

"Tanny," she said, "you sure got soul." She promised there would be no surprises like that the next time.

In almost every regard, Christine was an ideal prosecution witness. She was an attractive and extremely intelligent young woman who combined an intimate knowledge of the character and actions of the defendants with a deep sense of moral guilt for her own involvement in the events she would be testifying about. What is more, she was articulate enough to communicate her feelings to the jury. She knew the defense would use the ten months between the first and the second trial to sharpen their attack, and she gave a great deal of thought to the questions they would ask. She vowed that when they came at her she would be ready.

There were no preliminaries. They went after her from the opening bell.

Q: Do you enjoy this, Miss Rowe?

A: What?

Q: Trying to get one of these defendants.

A: Pardon?

Q: Trying to hurt one of these defendants, do you enjoy that?

A: No.

Q: You testified that you lived in the Torres apartment on Anderson Avenue for about a month and a half, isn't that right, Miss Rowe?

A: From the end of April till the beginning of June, right. About a month and a half.

Q: I noticed earlier, when you described the apartment, you weren't quite sure about the bedroom. Is that because you never slept in the bedroom?

A: That's true.

Q: You slept in the living room?

A: Yes.

Q: On a bed or on a couch?

A: The couch. It was a couch that opened up, a bed.

Q: Did you sleep alone?

A: Sometimes.

Q: But sometimes you didn't sleep alone?

A: That's true.

Q: Miss Rowe, did you ever have sexual relations with anyone in that apartment?

A: No.

Q: But occasionally you shared your bed, is that right?

A: Yes.

Q: With whom did you share the bed?

A: I shared the bed with everyone.

Q: Did you ever share the bed with Anthony Bottom?

A: I shared the bed with everyone.

Q: Did you ever have sexual relations with Anthony Bottom?

A: No.

Q: When Anthony Bottom left for California in June, did he leave because he was afraid he had been seen, or was it because he wanted to go back to his girlfriend?

A: I heard he left because he wanted to see his girlfriend.

Q: I see. But you're not trying to hurt one of these defendants, Miss Rowe? You don't have any animosity against any of these defendants, do you?

A: No, not really. I used to. But that's all over now. I mean, what can you do? As far as I'm concerned, they're sick, they need help.

Q: Is Mr. Bottom sick because he left you for his old girlfriend?

A: He never left me for his old girlfriend. He had his girlfriend before I got there and he had her when he left.

Q: And he had you?

A: No.

Q: On the couch, the couch that opened up into a bed?

A: Were you there, mister? Now how do you know!

The defense lawyer pulled back to regroup, then charged again.

Q: Then you have no animosity toward any of the defendants, no resentment?

A: No, not for that, no.

Q: But you do have some resentment?

A: I mean, like, they got us involved in all this, see. When they did it, if they just came back and kept it to themselves, if they just kept their mouths shut, that would have been the end of it right there. But they got us involved. My sister was in jail and Celia was in jail and I had cops living with me twenty-four hours a day for sixteen months, messed up my life completely. Like we wouldn't be here now if they were men and stood up and done what should have been done, which was to plead guilty.

Q: Are you angry with them for not pleading guilty?

A: No, I'm not angry. I have a very low regard for them, that's all. Don't respect them whatsoever.

Having gotten nowhere in their efforts to discount Christine's testimony as the product of sexual jealousy or resentment, the defense tried to suggest that she was motivated by a fear of the police. They brought her back to the Denver police station, where New York detectives had questioned her for the first time. Was she aware that her sister was in jail at that time? Did the police tell her she could be jailed if she didn't cooperate? For how many hours did they interrogate her? Was she frightened? Didn't she initially tell the police she knew nothing at all of the events of May 21, and didn't the police tell her they wouldn't accept that answer?

But Christine never let herself be intimidated, never went for the bait:

Q: From the questions the police asked you then, Miss Rowe, did you have in your mind what they wanted, what answers they wanted you to give them?

A: What they wanted? No. I only told them what I knew. It didn't matter what they might have wanted to know.

Q: But you knew at the time that Anthony Bottom and Albert Washington had been arrested, right?

A: Yes.

Q: That Gabriel Torres and Francisco Torres had been arrested?

A: Yes.

Q: Was it in your mind that the government was interested in getting evidence against those men?

A: What they were interested in? I don't know what they were interested in. I was only interested in telling them the truth about what they asked me, and that's what I did.

Q: But you were frightened?

A: Yes.

Q: You felt you were under pressure?

A: The pressure I was under was from the fact that I was going to have to deal on an open level with what had went down on May 21st. That was the pressure.

For three solid days Christine Rowe gave as good as she got. She was on the stand almost eighteen hours, and her testimony covers over five hundred pages in the trial transcript. Perhaps the most memorable part of it, providing a moment of comic relief we all needed at that point, came at the very end when Albert Washington rose from the defense table to cross-examine her himself. Loping across the well of the court, his hands clasped behind his back in a passable imitation of a lawyer, he started firing questions when he was still twenty feet from the witness.

> Q: Now, Rowe, isn't it true that you were purged from the Black Panther Party?
>
> A: No, that's not true. I left the Black Panther Party. Nobody ever told me you could be purged from it.
>
> Q: Then how come you say you was never a member of the Black Panther Party?
>
> A: I said I don't know whether I was a member or not, I never got a membership card.
>
> Q: Wasn't you ordered out of the house on Stebbins Avenue?
>
> A: No, I was not.
>
> Q: Isn't it true that you had an argument, a very bitter argument, with Tony Bottom over politics?
>
> A: Yes, I did.
>
> Q: Isn't it true that you damned near had arguments with all of us over politics?
>
> A: That's correct, because I did not agree with your politics whatsoever.
>
> Q: We are not discussing whether you agree or disagree. The point is that behind the disagreement, instead of engaging in constructive kinds of struggle, you have taken it to the level of try-

ing to give it back to us through lies in this courtroom.

A: Oh, now, you know better. No, that's not true.

Q: Isn't it true that this is another reason that you
was kicked out of the Black Panther Party,
because you had bad politics?

A: Well, you can call it bad politics if you want, but
when anyone goes around shooting other folk I
don't consider it necessarily politics.

Someone at the defense table tried to signal Washington to sit down, but either he didn't see it or he
hadn't had enough yet. "Isn't it true that we supported
you, we took you in when everybody else had kicked
you out?" he asked.

"Hell, no," Christine shot back. "It's not the truth
and you know it. I was on welfare."

"You are full of shit!" Washington roared.

Christine glanced across to the prosecution table to
see if I would object, but I was enjoying the show too
much to interrupt. "Look," she said with cool mockery,
"I got a welfare check twice a month. Why don't you
use your resources and check it out, honey?"

Washington stepped back and paced in front of
the witness for fully half a minute. Then he walked
back to the defense table, leaned against it, and
demanded, "Now, Rowe, isn't it true that you weaved
this whole case together, you weaved this whole thing
together out of your bitter vindictiveness? And now
you've come into this courtroom twice and told lies
about us?"

"I weaved this together?" Christine challenged

incredulously. "I suppose you didn't know any of these people before this time?"

Washington went on as if he hadn't heard a word she had said. "Isn't it true, Rowe, that the only reason you brought us into this, with all this shit about them guns and turning on the TV and acting it all out, is to tie us into these murders with your lies?"

On the witness stand Christine heaved a long, sorrowful sigh. "Oh, Noah, why don't you sit down and quit disgracing yourself," she pleaded. "You know better, you know better."

On the last court day in February, Detective Bill Butler took the stand. After he had identified himself and informed the jury that he was on duty in the Thirty-second Precinct on the night of May 21, 1971, I asked him if he had responded to the scene of the crime. He said he had.

"Did you find any ballistics evidence at the scene?" I asked.

"Yes, sir. I found six forty-five-caliber shells."

"Where did you find them?"

He stepped down from the stand, walked to the diagram of the Colonial Park grounds, and drew a small circle next to the green-shaded area representing shrubbery. "Right here, near the bush area, approximately four or five feet from the blood spot on the ground where the police officer had been lying."

I asked him to write the number 45 in the circle to remind the jury what it stood for. When he returned to the stand I showed him six spent shells, which he identified. They were received in evidence.

"I have no further questions of this witness," I said.

At the defense table, jaws dropped audibly. At the first trial they had singled Butler out as the evil genius behind their alleged frame-up, and I had no reason to suppose they wouldn't try to do so again. Only this time I wasn't giving them a target to shoot at.

Between trials, I had carefully reexamined every aspect of Bill's involvement in the investigation, from the moment he responded to Colonial Park in May 1971 until the arrest of Herman Bell in September 1973. Whenever other witnesses were available to detail the events to the jury, I could dispense with his testimony. Proceeding in this way, I crossed off topic after topic, until in the end I fell only slightly short of my goal, which was to make Bill Butler absolutely invisible. Except to introduce one totally uncontroverted exhibit—the six spent shells he found and marked at the scene—there was nothing for him to testify about. Indeed, if there had been any other legally valid way to introduce the bullets into evidence, I wouldn't have put Butler on the stand at all.

According to the rules of evidence, a witness may be cross-examined only with regard to matters he has testified about on direct examination. By limiting Butler's direct testimony, I thus made it impossible for the defense to cross-examine him about his activities in San Francisco and New Orleans, his relationship with Ruth Jennings and Gloria Lapp, his role in the arrests of Alie Horn and the Torres brothers. To be sure, after the People presented its case, he could be called as a defense witness and all these areas could be explored. But by then it would be too late, for the jury would have a clear picture of the entire case in its mind, a picture in which Bill Butler figured as no more than one of the countless obscure detectives who played marginal roles around the peripheries of the investigation.

I further reinforced this strategy by asking Bill to have absolutely no contact with the witnesses, even to the extent of having him leave my office whenever one of the witnesses arrived for a meeting. The defense was going to have a hard time convincing the jury that Gloria or anyone else was a pawn in Butler's hands when none of them had even seen him in a year.

It worked to perfection. The defense never got to first base with its insinuations that an insignificant cop who hardly figured in the case at all somehow managed to switch the fingerprints in order to implicate Herman Bell. Nor could the jury give credence to the defense theory that the witnesses were somehow under the malign influence of a man with whom they were no longer even in contact.

Butler was followed to the stand by Alie Horn and Celia Torres, who completed the work Christine Rowe had begun. The defense tried to smear Celia by suggesting that only an unprincipled woman would come forward to testify against her own husband and the father of her children.

Q: Mrs. Torres, you were held in civil jail for thirteen months as a material witness, isn't that true?

A: Yes.

Q: And during those thirteen months, you weren't cooperating with the police, with the district

attorney's office, right? You weren't even talking
to them?

A: Yes.

Q: And then you decided to talk to them because
you realized that as soon as you started to talk to
them again, that would be the key to your freedom, the jail doors would swing open wide, isn't
that right?

A: Yes.

Q: So that is the reason you started to talk to them
again, just to get out of jail?

A: No. That's one of the reasons.

Q: The other reason was to try and convict your
husband, Gabriel Torres, of murder, was that
one of the other reasons?

Celia didn't flinch. "I am not convicting him," she
declared firmly.

There was the slightest pause, and then the next
question hit with the impact of a punch.

"Mrs. Torres, what do you tell your children when
they ask you, 'Where is our father?'"

"They know," Celia stammered, her voice choked
with suppressed emotion. "They know where their
father is. When their father was arrested, I told them
their father was in jail. And if they ever ask me, I will
tell them what happened."

"You will tell them that you came into court because
you wanted to get out of jail and you testified against
their father, is that right?"

She shook her head slowly, as though there
were nothing in his sneering accusation she hadn't

told herself a thousand times. "I am going to tell them what happened," she repeated, her voice under control now. "What happened with their father and what happened with me. And they'll have to take it from there, think what they want. I will tell them the truth."

As they had done with Gloria Lapp, the defense again had asked one question too many. The heartfelt answer of this obviously anguished young mother rang with such conviction that it validated her entire testimony. At that point there was nothing left for the defense to ask her, so they let her go.

I called Alie Horn, who put the finishing touches on the Anderson Avenue portion of my case. A large and imposing woman with a forceful personality and absolute self-command, she dominated the courtroom with her presence the way a great actress can dominate a stage. Once and for all, she laid to rest the defense notion that the women I had put on the stand had been coerced and intimidated by the police, for the jury simply found it inconceivable that anyone could tell Alie Horn what to say.

By the end of her testimony, the defense had become so ragged that it began conceding crucial points. On direct examination she had testified that when Tony Bottom returned to the apartment shortly after the killings, he had said, "We offed some pigs." In their cross-examination the defense made no effort to suggest that Alie was putting words into Bottom's mouth. Instead, they questioned her about what the words meant, thus tacitly admitting Bottom had said them.

Q: Miss Horn, let me talk to you about something. Gabriel Torres, he was a heavy baseball fan, New York Mets fan, right?

A: Yes.

Q: And the other men, the other defendants, they were baseball fans too?

A: Yes.

Q: And they would watch baseball and talk about those games, right?

A: Yes.

Q: And if the Mets won, they would sometimes say, "We won," right?

A: Not that I recall.

Q: Not that you recall. Well, let me take another example. If one of them read something, about black people or Puerto Rican people, and it was good, would he sometimes say, We got something, something like that, using the word "we" in a collective sense?

A: Not that I recall.

Since Alie wasn't willing to oblige defense counsel with the right answer, I decided to help them out. I wanted to make sure the jury didn't miss the point. "Your Honor," I called out, rising from the prosecution table, "if defense counsel is willing to stipulate that the defendant Bottom said, 'We offed some pigs,' I will be glad to leave it up to the jury to determine what the interpretation is."

That was the last we heard in the trial about the collective use of the word *we*.

When Alie completed her testimony after three full

days on the stand, I heaved a long sigh of relief. Four key witnesses, each of whom had been badly damaged at the first trial, this time made it safely through the rapids. Gloria Lapp, Christine Rowe, Celia Torres, and Alie Horn had come through without sustaining more than a few scratches in their credibility. As I watched Alie step down from the stand, I felt comfortable for the first time in the trial.

The feeling was destined to last only a few seconds. After crossing the well of the court, Alie stopped at the defense table and said something to the defendants. It happened so fast there was no way I could stop her. Bell snorted derisively in response and Bottom shot back a sarcasm, but their lawyers leaped to their feet demanding that the witness be recalled to the stand. All the lawyers, including Albert Washington, then rushed to the bench and I hurried to join them.

Apparently there was no clear consensus about what she had said, for I could hear the defense team debating the incident among themselves. One of the lawyers thought she said, "I just buried you." Another thought it was, "Herman and T.B., you are dead."

Suddenly I felt angry and sick, for I knew that nothing can sour a jury so quickly as hearing that a witness wants to put a defendant in jail. Just when everything in the trial had been going my way, a witness was revealing an animosity against the defendants she had successfully concealed while on the stand. If only one juror said to himself, "That Horn woman sure had it in for them, I wouldn't put it past her to lie," I could find myself with another hung jury. In every case he tries, a prosecutor is playing a game of Russian roulette in which there are twelve chambers in the revolver. He loses if only one of them is loaded.

I argued that there was no reason to call the witness back to the stand, but Judge Greenfield ruled against me, as I knew he would. The court officer then led Alie back to the witness stand, and the clerk reminded her she was still under oath. I held my breath as one of the defense lawyers asked, "Miss Horn, what did you say just now to Anthony Bottom and Herman Bell?"

Alie laughed and shook her head. "I said they were both *pindahos*," she answered. "And I meant it."

There were chuckles from scattered points in the courtroom. Herman Bell and the other defendants, except for Washington, were giggling and laughing, but neither the judge nor the defense lawyers nor Ken nor I knew what the word meant.

"They were both what?" Justice Greenfield asked.

"*Pindahos*," Alie repeated. "Ask them what it means. They know."

At the defense table, Bell and the others were still laughing. Bell's hand covered his mouth and he was shaking his head at Alie, who, after all, once had been one of them. If he had spoken to her then, he probably would have said, "Horn, you are too much!"

"No, I am asking you, Miss Horn. What does it mean?" the judge demanded sternly.

Alie looked to me for help but there was none I could give her. She turned away to face the defendants and leaned far forward toward them, her elbow on her knee. "It means," she said, drawing out the syllables into a hissing sneer, "that they are a bunch of pus-sies."

The courtroom erupted with laughter that somehow

discredited the defendants, made them smaller in everyone's eyes. Only the red-faced defense attorney confronting Alie didn't seem to be in on the joke. "Miss Horn," he declared with great pomposity, raising his voice over the noise in the courtroom, "this is a murder trial. You may think it is funny, but I assure you it is not!"

"Oh?" Alie purred archly. "Then why are your clients laughing?"

In April of 1974, a few weeks before Judge Melia had dismissed the jury in the first trial, Ruth Jennings had given birth to a healthy baby boy. Two weeks later, while the accused killers of Waverly Jones and Joseph Piagentini were still celebrating their courtroom victory, the girl who had watched the murders was discharged from Harlem Hospital, the very hospital to which the bodies of the victims had been taken three years earlier. By June she had fully recovered from her difficult pregnancy.

Leaving her baby with her mother, she had come to see me during the last week in June. I was delighted with how well she looked. Her round face had filled out again and her eyes sparkled with the happiness of a new mother. I questioned her briefly about what she had seen on the night of May 21, and her account of the events squared exactly with Gloria Lapp's testimony. Then I pulled open my desk drawer and removed two photographs. The first was a San Francisco Police Department photo of the line-up she had attended in September 1971. I slid it toward her and asked her if she recognized it. She did. We talked about it, and she repeated what she had told Lankler and Butler at the time. The second man looked like the taller killer, except that his face was puffy. It lacked the "slim hardness" she remembered on the face of the man she watched kill Waverly Jones.

I took back the line-up photo and handed her the snapshot of Tony Bottom, Francisco Torres, and Lester May taken from Herman Bell's overnight case in New Orleans.

"Do you recognize any of these men?" I asked.

"That's him," she said. "The one in the middle. It's exactly the way he looked that night."

"Are you absolutely sure?"

She didn't hesitate a moment. "Absolutely," she said. "In San Francisco it looked like him but I didn't want to say for sure. But this is the same man. That's just the way he looked, the jawline, the eyes. It's the same man."

I had known then that I had a witness who would corroborate Gloria Lapp. Briefly, I had toyed with the idea of putting her on before Gloria, because I knew she would stand up better under cross-examination. But it was impossible to predict how much mileage the defense would be able to get out of her failure to identify Bottom at the line-up. To be on the safe side I had decided to hold her back, putting her on after the women from Anderson Avenue in order to give dramatic symmetry to the case, which would thus move from the blood-letting to the killers' celebration and back to the scene of the crime.

A bright and personable girl, pretty and confident, with large, serious eyes, Ruth Jennings turned out to be the kind of witness lawyers dream about. Exactly as I hoped she would do, she made an asset out of the most damaging weakness in her testimony. The defense only embarrassed itself by attempting to suggest she was pressured into identifying Bottom. In the eyes of the jury, her refusal to pick him out in San Francisco established beyond any doubt that Ruth Jennings was not the sort of girl who would make so important a decision as an identification in a murder trial simply because someone wanted her to do it.

Ruth's testimony concluded the People's case against Tony Bottom. I then turned my attention to Herman Bell. At the first trial, I realized now, I hadn't done enough to counter the defense's suggestion that Bill Butler switched the fingerprints in the case, surreptitiously inserting a set of Bell's prints into the case file in place of the latents actually lifted from the Colonial Park Mustang. I had mistakenly assumed that the utter absurdity of the argument and the fact that the defense had absolutely no evidence to substantiate it would have forced the jury to reject it.

This time I wasn't going to make the same mistake. I led off with the same fingerprint witnesses I had used at the first trial and ran them through the same questions, carefully baiting my trap. The defense walked right into it, insinuating on cross-examination that Detective Lacho, who made the lifts in May, could not prove they were the same prints Detective Bannon identified in November, and conversely that Bannon could not prove the prints he identified were precisely the ones Lacho found. The defense may have raised some doubts in the minds of the jury, but at the same time they had clearly committed themselves to the theory of a switch made sometime between September, when Butler went to San Francisco, and November, when the match was made.

At that point I called to the stand the director of the Federal Bureau of Investigation's fingerprint section. He traced in detail the FBI's handling of the fingerprints in the case. On May 28, 1971, exactly one week after the murders, detectives attached to the New York City Police Department's Bureau of Criminal Identification had hand-delivered copies of the prints found at Colonial Park to two FBI agents in New York. The agents initialed and dated these copies and drove them to La Guardia Airport where they handed them over to an Eastern Airlines pilot flying the New York-to-Washington shuttle. The pilot in turn was met in Washington by another FBI agent who took the prints from him and delivered them the next day to FBI headquarters, where the director of the fingerprint section himself personally initialed and dated them, Saturday, May 29, 1971.

The FBI copy of the prints, with the director's initials on it, was then introduced into evidence and shown to the jury, who could see for themselves that these were clearly identical to the prints Bannon already had sworn were Bell's. If there were a switch, therefore, the director of the FBI fingerprint section was in on it. To accept the defense theory, the jury would have to believe that a top FBI agent knowingly accepted a false set of prints, fraudulently backdated it, recalled all the copies of the genuine prints disseminated among FBI fingerprint analysts, and then perjured himself on the witness stand—all so that he could help a detective he had never even met frame an innocent man.

Twenty-two

THE STORY OF JOSEPH PIAGENTINI'S GUN didn't end when a black convict in Cordelia, Mississippi, handed the mud-encased revolver to Ken Klein. Despite their eagerness to confirm that it was indeed Piagentini's gun and not some other weapon Herman Bell had to get rid of, Ken and Cliff elected not to risk cleaning off the mud themselves. They would take it as they found it back to New York, where it could be photographed and cleaned by experts in the police lab.

Getting back to New York with the gun presented them with a bit of a problem, which Cliff solved with typical ingenuity. Airline regulations do not permit even police officers to carry firearms onto an aircraft and, mud or no mud, the long-buried gun was still a firearm. If the airline wanted to get stubborn about it, Cliff knew he would end up having to take a train back to New York, since there was no way he was going to let the gun out of his sight for even a single minute.

"Let me talk to them about it," Ken urged.

"Oh sure, you lawyers are good for some things, like murder trials," Cliff chuckled. "But when it comes to getting my ass stuck on the Chattanooga choo-choo for twenty-four hours, I don't take chances. I'll handle it myself."

Cliff's way out of the dilemma was pure Fenton, as characteristic as slashing Linda Gill's tires to get Herman Bell out of his house. He simply walked through the airline checkpoint flashing his badge and wearing his own gun in his waist clip. He carried Piagentini's gun in a shopping bag. Naturally, the metal detector went off and the airline clerk stopped him.

"Excuse me, officer, do you have a weapon on you?"

Cliff admitted he did. The clerk asked for it. Cliff said he would keep it. The clerk told him it would be returned to him when he disembarked, but Cliff refused. The argument started to heat up. Finally Ken, catching the drift of the game, stepped in. "C'mon, Cliff," he pleaded. "Give him the gun. What difference does it make?"

Cliff shrugged with mock disgust, unbuttoned his jacket, and removed his revolver. The clerk took it, gave him a receipt, and sent him aboard, so pleased to be rid of him that he never thought to make him walk through the metal detector a second time.

With this little subterfuge, Cliff and Ken solved the last of their problems with Piagentini's gun. Mine, though, were only beginning. In January while we were still selecting the jury, I had Lester May flown to New York so I could interview him before putting him on the stand. Without May's testimony, I would not be allowed to introduce the gun into evidence, for he had been the only one with Bell when Bell buried it.

On the first Friday after May's arrival from New Orleans, federal marshals brought him to my office. We talked for about forty-five minutes but didn't get into the specifics of the case. I wanted to use the first meeting to get acquainted with May and to let him get to know me. He was being held at the time in a federal penitentiary outside New York City, and he indicated to me that he was afraid he would be killed if black radicals in the prison learned he was there to testify against Herman Bell. I asked him if he would feel more comfortable if we moved him from prison to prison every few days.

"Yeah, that'd help," he said. "Thanks."

Then he went over the terms he was asking as the price for his cooperation. I reminded him that he was facing no charges in New York and that I had no authority to make any deals in any jurisdiction outside New York. All I could give him was my word that I would appear before any judge when he came up for sentencing and inform him that May had been cooperating with New York authorities in their investigation of two police murders and had testified truthfully. He was satisfied with that answer.

"Okay," I said. "Do you have any other questions, anything else that's bothering you?"

"No, man, not at all," May said. "You folks is the only ones ever treated me like a human being."

I promised I would arrange with the marshals to have him moved and reminded him I would be seeing him again in a week. "Meanwhile, if you think of anything that's troubling you, save it and we'll talk about it next Friday. If it's anything urgent, ask to see the warden and ask him to put you through to me."

May thanked me, and I rang for the marshals.

Before they arrived, he said, "Yeah, there is something I been thinking about. Like I don't wanna get hit with charges out of anything I tell you, see."

I assured him that wasn't a problem. "Look, Lester," I told him, "all we're interested in is this case—I'm sure you realize that. From everything we know, you're not involved in it, so you've got nothing to worry about. But if it makes you feel uneasy, we can get you a lawyer and he'll advise you. Or I can even get you to see the judge if you want his assurances."

"Lemme think it over," Lester said. "I'll let you know."

When May was brought back to my office the next Friday he had already been moved twice and was satisfied with the precautions being taken for his safety. I asked him if he had made a decision about a lawyer.

"Yeah. Y'know what I'd like to do, man, is talk to the judge, get myself straightened away," he said.

"No problem," I told him, reaching for the phone and calling Judge Greenfield. The judge said he would see Lester immediately. The marshals then escorted him from my office to the judge's chambers.

An hour and a half later my phone rang. It was Judge Greenfield. "Bob, I have just finished talking to Mr. May. I think it advisable for you to speak with him."

Judges usually don't call lawyers with messages like that, and I knew something was wrong. I slammed down the phone and raced from the office, hit the fire stairs at full speed, and got to the thirteenth floor just as the elevator doors halfway down the corridor were starting to close. I called out. Even at that distance I could hear Lester say, "C'mon, let's go," but one of the marshals put out his arm to stop the doors. I got in the elevator with them.

"What the hell happened in there?" I demanded angrily.

May looked away from me. "I told him I buried it," he muttered.

"What?" I shouted. "How could you do a thing like that?"

"I don't wanna talk about it," Lester mumbled, looking at the floor.

I couldn't take an answer like that from him. "Why did you do it?" I demanded.

Lester looked up at me with sorrowful eyes. He had meant what he said when he told me a week earlier that Cliff and Ken and I, the three New Yorkers who had worked with him on this case, treated him well. His eyes told me it cost him something to turn on us, but he was a confused and frightened young man, and he was in deep trouble.

"Look, man," he said at last, almost pleading, "I'm facing a murder rap in Frisco with two of these cats. How the hell can I be a defendant with them out there if I testify against them here?"

I took a deep breath to get my anger under control. "All right, look, the judge must have assigned you a lawyer, right?"

"Right."

"Okay. You talk to your lawyer. Lay the whole thing out for him. Then come see me next week and have the lawyer come too. In the meantime, you listen to what he has to say and you think it over. Think about who's been good to you. We'll be straight with you all the way, Lester, you know that, right?"

He smiled a thin, apologetic smile. "Yeah, man, I know that," he said.

I stepped off the elevator and the marshal released the door. As it closed, I said, "Just one thing, Lester. Who buried the gun, you or Herman?"

"It was Herman, man. I told the judge it was me, but it was Herman."

In the presence of his lawyer a week later, Lester May rescinded his recantation. He also told me a great many other things about the case that greatly complicated the decision I would have to make about whether to put him on the stand. He began by taking me back to the early spring of 1971, when Joseph Piagentini and Waverly Jones were two obscure young patrolmen in Harlem and their future killers were three thousand miles away in San Francisco, as remote from their lives as any strangers could be. May was then part of a cell that met regularly in Tony Bottom's Divisadero Street apartment for what May called "political education" classes. Herman Bell and Francisco Torres were there, and the discussions were led by Albert Washington.

"What about Gabriel Torres?" I asked. "Was he there, too?"

May drew on his cigarette and squinted through the smoke. "Gilbert?" he asked. "Nah, he wasn't there, wasn't around at all. Like I didn't meet Gilbert till the summer, y'know, when they all come back."

I asked him to go on.

"So we talked about gettin' down, an' what we had to do. We talked about scoping pigs, which means like surveillance, following the pigs, scoping the pigs to kill them. And then they all split, an' after a while I got a message, T.B. wants his piece. See, he had this piece he loved, this beautiful motherfuckin' forty-five with a pearl handle, hell of a piece. But he took a plane when he split so he couldn't take it, see."

He turned to his lawyer, an exceptionally able defense attorney named Herbert Adlerberg. "Can I tell him that?" he asked.

"Tell him what? About Bottom's gun? I don't see why not," Adlerberg said.

"No, I mean—" May motioned for Adlerberg to come closer and then whispered in his ear.

"Don't go into specifics other than what pertains to this case," Adlerberg advised him. "Tell him anything you can about the guns in this case, that'll be okay."

Lester nodded. "So I get this message, T.B. wants his piece. So I stop by his pad an' I get it an' I ship it to New York."

"Who did you send it to?" I asked.

"Shit, man, I don't remember that. I sent it, right, like they give me an address. Wasn't T.B., I know that. Some other name."

"Okay, fine. Then what happened?"

"Then nothin' happened, man. Like in the summer they come back. T.B. and Cisco and Herman and a couple of foxes. There's Christine. You know Christine, man?"

"Yeah, I know Christine."

"Okay, so there's Christine and there's Horn. So they're all back, see. 'Cept Noah, he doesn't come back, right. But Herman and T.B. and Cisco, they all come back."

"When was this?"

"Like summer, early summer. June."

"Did they say anything to you about where they had been?"

"Yeah, man, sure, they tol' me."

"What did they say? Try to remember very precisely. It's important, Lester."

"Well, see, I knowed where they been. Like I met them at the airport, dig, so I know I'm meetin' a plane from New York. An' I say, 'Where you cats been?' An' they say—"

"Who said?"

"Herman, it was Herman. He says, 'New York,' An' I say, 'What you doin' in New York?' An' Herman says, 'Taking care of business.' "

"Was that all that was said?"

"Yeah, man, I don't ask no questions. It ain't that kinda thing."

Lester then went on to repeat to me what he had told Cliff and Ken in New Orleans about meeting Bell in Jackson, about FBI agents calling on Bell's mother, about burying a gun on Ulysses Tatum's farm. I cut him off when he started to tell about his activities in the New Orleans area prior to his arrest. "Herb, he's already been convicted and sentenced for bank robbery in New Orleans," I pointed out to the lawyer.

"One count?" Adlerberg asked.

"Yeah," Lester said.

"All right, let's skip ahead," Adlerberg advised. "Then you were arrested, right? Pick it up there."

"Well, they come down pretty hard," Lester said. "You sure you wanna hear about it?"

"I think I'd better hear about it," I said. If he was going to take the stand for me, I didn't want any surprises. I had to know everything.

"Well, see, I was in my car when they busted me. An' these fuckin' pigs stop the car and they drug me out. I had my kid with me and the old lady."

"You're married?" I asked.

He shrugged. "Yeah, I guess. So my old lady's there and the kid. And the pigs is all got shotguns, see. They put a shotgun upside my head, they even put a shotgun upside my little boy's head. Like he's three years old, dig. So I know it's gonna be heavy."

He then went on to recount, in excruciating detail, how the New Orleans police systematically tortured him in an attempt to learn the whereabouts of Herman Bell and other members of the BLA bank-robbery gang. He told a harrowing story of cattle prods applied to his skin, of needles stuck into his penis, of having something rammed down his throat until he choked and then passed out. He claimed he was beaten on the very day Detective Lyons first came down from New York to question him. "It was the day that white cop from New York shows up," he said. "They work me over real good, I mean they really stomp me, y'know. An' then they kinda straighten me up an' they send me in to see him. They say, like, 'You better act right, boy.' "

May also claimed he was locked in a cell with a psychopath. "This was an unbelievable bad nigger," he said. "Not mean, just crazy, dig. Psycho-crazy. An', see, I know they done that on purpose, 'cause when I tol' them I gotta get outta there 'fore he chops me apart, they say, 'Look, boy, if we put him in another cell he's only gonna chop somebody else apart. Now maybe if you could give us a reason to care, we could fix that up."

I had no idea whether May was telling the truth

about any of this. If he wasn't, then he was a convincing liar. From my point of view it was immaterial, because in either case the defense would be able to capitalize on May's allegations when they cross-examined him. Considering they had won a hung jury at the first trial with their vague suggestions about more or less subtle forms of psychological pressure applied to the witnesses, there was no telling what they could do if we let them bring cattle prods, chokings, and psychopathic cellmates into the case. If I put May on the stand, I would be handing all this ammunition to the defense.

On the other hand, there was no getting away from the fact that Lester was an invaluable witness. He could set the context of the case as no other witness could, for he would testify that he was present when Albert Washington, Herman Bell, Tony Bottom, and Francisco Torres discussed "scoping pigs, scoping them to kill them," a month before the murders. Lester and Lester alone could testify he had seen the pearl-handled .45 in Tony Bottom's possession in California before the killers came east. Lester could corroborate Christine Rowe's account of picking up the gun at the Greyhound station because it was he who had sent it. But most of all, without Lester's testimony, it wouldn't be possible for me to introduce Joseph Piagentini's gun into evidence. In my mind Piagentini's service revolver was a crucial piece of evidence that had to go before the jury.

Still, the risks were so great that I did something I usually don't do. I purposely put off making the decision until the last possible moment. When the FBI fingerprint expert left the stand, Judge Greenfield asked if I had any more witnesses. I requested a recess until the next morning, when I would either present my last witness or rest my case. The judge agreed to the recess and I asked Cliff Fenton, Ken Klein, and Bill Butler to meet me in my office.

"Tomorrow I intend to put Lester on the stand," I told them. "But first I want your thoughts on it."

We argued the pros and cons well into the night. On one side was the fear that Lester's account of torture and brutality could taint our entire case. "You're winning," Ken said. "You've got them on the ropes. They've had two months to convince the jury the girls were pressured, and so far they haven't laid a glove on us. Once Lester starts talking about being tortured, there's no telling where it's going to lead."

I played devil's advocate. "You're right, I've got them on the ropes," I said. "Doesn't that mean I've got to go for the knockout?"

Bill said, "No, they'll take him apart. If you let the defense get that cattle prod into the case, they're gonna stick it up your ass and you know it."

I countered with all the arguments I could think of. I would steal the defense's thunder by letting Lester testify about the torture on direct. I would make it clear that he hadn't cracked under the torture, that he said nothing about the gun until fifteen months after the torture stopped. "Look," I said, "I can't apologize for every police department in the country. Does it make sense to hide Piagentini's gun from the jury because some cops we had no control over did a number on Lester? The fact is we didn't torture him and we're the ones he told about the gun. We've treated him right and he'll say so on the stand."

"How the hell do you know what he's going to say on

the stand?" Cliff snapped. "He flipped once already and then he flipped back. What if he flips again?"

"He won't."

"He won't, huh?" Cliff challenged. "And so what if he doesn't? Are you going to be able to let him tell why he flipped?"

"No," I had to admit. Lester had recanted because he didn't want to be a codefendant in California with men against whom he had testified in New York. But he wouldn't be allowed to say that on the witness stand because information about other charges against the defendants was considered prejudicial. Lester, though, would have to admit he was facing a murder charge in California. "All he can say," I explained, "is that he recanted because he thought it inadvisable to testify against the defendants."

"Well then, Jesus Christ, what are we talking about?" Ken moaned.

"We're talking about Joseph Piagentini's gun," I said. "We're talking about the gun Herman Bell emptied into Piagentini. That's the bottom line. Does the jury get to see that gun or don't they? What do you think, Bill? You said from the start the guns were the case. Find the guns and you find the killers, right? Do I put it on?"

Butler shook his head. "It's too big a gamble," he said.

"Cliff? You were in Mississippi, you've got a stake in this. Does the gun go in?"

"No," Fenton said. "Not if Lester has to take the stand."

"Ken? You're the one who found it. What do you say?"

I knew how much finding the gun meant to him. He swallowed hard. "You're winning," he said. "Don't blow it."

"All right," I said. "Thanks. Now let's try to get some sleep."

The clerk's voice rang like a judgment through the courtroom.

"The People call Lester Bertram May."

Lester entered the courtroom from a rear door that led to the holding pens. He moved slowly, as he always did, an ambling, shuffling gait that communicated a strange indolence in one so young. Before stepping up to the witness chair, he paused to survey the courtroom, offering a perfunctory nod in my direction. Then he looked at the defendants hard, for a long time, and I hoped the jury was watching his eyes, which fixed in turn on each of the five prisoners at the defense table. Three of the defendants—Gabriel Torres, Albert Washington, and Tony Bottom—looked away, while Herman Bell scowled at him darkly from under heavy, threatening brows. Francisco Torres muttered to himself but kept his eyes on Lester the way one watches a snarling dog. After the clerk administered the oath, I rose and approached to begin the examination.

Speaking softly but audibly, his diction polite and almost deferential, Lester spelled out to the jury all the things he had told me in my office. He came across as slow-witted although not necessarily stupid, a man whose natural indolence was offset by a sort of listless cunning. As lethargic as a turtle, as cautious and as self-contained, he gave the impression of knowing more than he told and of measuring his words carefully. Often, at key points in the testimony, he would respond to my questions by repeating them, so that the record reads from time to time like the script of some ancient vaudeville turn, with me as the straight man.

Q: Directing your attention to the spring of 1971, Mr. May, would you tell the jury what was discussed in your presence by the four defendants—that is, all the defendants excluding Gabriel Torres—what was discussed concerning police officers.

A: Scoping pigs and bombings.

Q: Scoping pigs?

A: Yeah. And bombings.

Q: What does the term "scoping pigs" mean?

A: It is like surveillance, see. Like which streets they go down, how many of them, if there is a backup unit, where do they stop, what time do they stop.

Q: Did any of the defendants say anything about scoping pigs, their purpose, what they would be doing when they were scoping pigs?

A: Yeah.

Q: What was said?

A: What was said?

Q: Yes, about scoping pigs.

A: About scoping pigs?

Q: Yeah, right.

A: Scoping them to shoot them.

May then told about shipping Bottom's gun to New York, about the return to California of three of the defendants—Bell, Bottom, and Francisco Torres—early in June. Gabriel Torres and Albert Washington arrived later in the summer. When I asked May if there were further discussions about scoping pigs with all five defendants present, his lawyer advised him to invoke the Fifth Amendment.

"This witness is currently under indictment for the crime of murder in the first degree involving the shooting of a police officer in the Ingleside police station in the late summer of 1971," Adlerberg explained at the bench. "The question Mr. Tanenbaum asked is very broad, and the answer could as well be deemed relevant to the August shooting in San Francisco as to the May shootings in New York. That is why I advised my client not to answer the question."

The defense then approached the bench and moved for a mistrial, arguing that the question and May's failure to answer it were prejudicial. By taking the Fifth, they contended, Lester implied that his conversations with the defendants might implicate him in the Ingleside attack, in which case it seemed reasonable to infer that they also implicated the defendants. "Mr. Tanenbaum asked the question knowing it wouldn't be answered because he's trying to get in by the back door something he perfectly well knows he can't get in by the front," one of the defense lawyers charged.

"This whole argument is absurd," I shot back. "If Mr. May's refusal to answer this question gives rise to an implication in the minds of the jury, that can't be helped. The implication arises because of the nature and acts of these defendants. The nature and acts of these defendants obviously are not going to inure to their benefit because they were going around the country murdering police officers, and that is what gives rise to the implication."

Judge Greenfield nodded appreciatively and denied the motion for a mistrial as well as a subsequent motion that all of May's testimony be stricken from the record. The defense, though, had a found a new toy to play with. After I concluded Lester's direct examination by leading him through an account of the sequence of events that culminated when Herman Bell buried Piagentini's service revolver in Mississippi, I turned him over to the defense. They cross-examined him for two full days, studding their interrogation with questions they knew he would refuse to answer and then protesting that his testimony should be stricken from the record because they were precluded from a proper cross-examination. Almost half of the fourteen hours Lester was on the stand were consumed with legal arguments at the bench.

Most of these shenanigans concerned May's possession of guns in the summer of 1971. The defense wanted to make out that May was the BLA's "armorer," that he regularly procured guns for Bell, Bottom, Washington, and "anybody else in California that needed a gun." Whenever May took the Fifth, the defense renewed its claim that they were being prevented from establishing the plausibility of their contention that it was May who gave Albert Washington and Tony Bottom the two weapons they had on them when they were arrested, that it was May who buried a hot gun on Ulysses Tatum's farm.

Finally, Judge Greenfield ran out of patience and ordered the defense either to ask May directly whether he had possessed any of the guns in evidence in this case or to find a new line of questioning. "I have made enough rulings about his possession of guns in general," the judge growled. "Obviously, he is not going to answer such questions. Either you ask him about these particular guns or you get off the subject of guns entirely, is that clear?"

"He won't answer that either," defense counsel complained.

"Oh yes he will," Judge Greenfield responded. "If you ask it, I assure you he will answer it."

This being the case, the defense prudently elected not to ask it.

Instead, Albert Washington rose from the defense table to cross-examine the witness. Lester's eyes followed him as he approached the witness stand, and a small, half-apologetic smile played at the corners of his mouth.

"It's been quite a while since we rapped, right?" Washington began.

Lester's smile broadened as he remembered. "Right," he answered quickly. In California he had been eighteen years old and he had admired Albert Washington, whom he regarded as a leader. In those days they were making a revolution.

"Since we first met, like back in the winter of nineteen seventy, we have had many discussions, right?"

Lester nodded. "Right."

"Francisco, Herman, and T.B.?"

"Yes."

"And some of these discussions, right, were about how the police was treating people in our community, right?"

"Yes."

Washington pursed his lips and nodded sagaciously, pacing in front of the witness. "So our discussions about the police," he went on, "basically we talked about like how the police was brutalizing black people, right?"

"Yes."

"And our sole purpose for being together, right, was to try and stop that?"

"Yes."

"Now you knew, right, the kind of things that they'd do to people, brutalize and torture them, right?"

"Yes."

"And now you've experienced it yourself, right?"

"Yes."

"And you know that others will experience it after you, too, right?"

"Yes."

Lester's head bobbed with each answer, as though he were once again in Tony Bottom's kitchen listening to the Old Man unfold his dreary liturgy of police oppression and revolutionary counter-violence. What accounted, I wondered, for the strange hold this shallow and undramatic ideologue seemed to have on young men like May and Bottom? Was there some magic in his words my ears couldn't hear? For Lester seemed to be once again under his spell. I didn't know where it would lead, but what I feared most was another recantation.

"So, in essence," Washington went on, "like the talks that we had was to watch the cops, watch their behavior, keep check on them, to try and stop them from that. Like we had legal aid classes, too, right?"

Lester smiled and nodded. "Right," he said.

Suddenly I understood what Washington was driving at.

"Okay," he said, moving in close to the witness. "So I mean, like, when we say scoping pigs, right, it's no more than we know they're dangerous, they have to be watched, right?"

Something in May snapped and he sat up rigid, his head cocked, a look of quizzical disbelief in his eyes. He shook his head slowly from side to side, like a child who has just caught his father in a lie. After all Lester had been through in the cause of Noah's revolution, after the shootings and the beatings and the prospect of the rest of his life in jail, Noah was standing in front of him and saying there was no revolution, asking him to say it too.

"No, man," Lester protested. "It meant that and it meant the other thing, what I stated."

Albert Washington said nothing. Judge Greenfield asked, "What was that?"

May turned to the judge. "Scoping pigs is surveillancing. It's watching the cops."

"For what purpose?"

"To shoot them."

As the last defense lawyer rose to examine the witness, I knew the crucial test was still to come. They had saved their best shot at him for the end, for they were hoping to discredit not only Lester May but the entire prosecution case by exposing the brutal methods used in New Orleans to coerce this witness into talking. Just the night before, I had told Bill, Ken, and Cliff that I would try to steal the defense's thunder by questioning him about the torture myself, for there is a courtroom axiom that says it is better to introduce damaging material oneself than to let the defense spring it on the jury during cross.

But a trial lawyer is by nature a gambler, and since I knew I was playing a high-risk game merely by putting Lester on the stand, I decided to go all the way. I left out all references to torture in my examination of the witness, staking everything on a ruling from the court that would severely restrict the defense's latitude for cross-examination in this area. I knew they would approach the subject obliquely, hoping to build slowly toward a crescendo, so I figured I could afford to let them play a few low cards before I trumped them.

Q: After your arrest, Mr. May, were you threatened in any way?

A: Yes.

Q: What kind of threats?

A: That I was going to spend the rest of my life in jail.

Q: Did they also tell you there may come a time when we will take you out of your cell and kill you?

A: Yes.

Q: And you believed it, didn't you?

A: I believed it.

Q: Now let's go back to the time of your arrest for a moment. You were with your child at the time, is that correct?

A: Yes.

Q: And when the police stopped your car and arrested you, what did they do to your child?

A: Stuck a shotgun to his head.

Q: How old was your child at the time?

A: Three.

Q: Three years old. Was your child armed?

A: No.

Q: And did this child, this three-year-old child, did he threaten the police in any way?

A: No.

The defense lawyer paused for effect, and I decided it was time to make my move. I waited for his next series of questions—"Were you then taken to a police station? Did they question you? Did they beat you?"—to interrupt with an objection.

"This is New Orleans he is talking about," I said. "It has no relevance to anything involving New York."

The argument then moved to the bench, out of the hearing of the jurors. The defense contended that the torture Lester endured those first few days had a direct bearing on all subsequent statements he made to the police. I countered by reminding the court that absolutely none of Lester's testimony resulted from statements he gave under torture. "The bottom line is this," I said. "This torture, this alleged torture, did it influence him fifteen months later? That's the question. And he is competent to answer it, whether it was on his mind. I have no objection to that question. But I object most strenuously to a blow-by-blow account of outrages allegedly perpetrated on the witness by other agencies at a remote time."

"Look, we are not talking about a slap in the face, slapped around, getting hit a few times," defense counsel insisted. "Assume he says it had no effect. How can the jury evaluate that answer unless they know what happened?"

Back and forth we argued for over an hour, with Justice Greenfield controlling the direction of the debate with his questions and observations. At one point I was greatly cheered when he said, "I am not holding this Court for the purpose of reviewing the actions of the New Orleans City Police Department." But a little later my heart sank when he acknowledged that the jury was "entitled to know if a particular incident had an impact on the witness that it may or may not have left an indelible impression on his mind, such that he would never want to go through that experience again."

Both sides argued desperately, the defense no less aware than myself that the final verdict in this trial might well depend on the judge's ruling here. The defense knew they were losing with the jurors, and they were counting on the New Orleans Police Department to bail them out. I knew I was ahead and could put them away with May's testimony if only the judge wouldn't permit the defense to discredit it with what I felt to be an essentially irrelevant issue.

"All right, gentlemen," Justice Greenfield declared at last, signaling the end of the debate. "I believe I have heard enough. The essential point is that this witness did not come forward at the time of these alleged beatings. He did not at that time reveal the existence or the location of the gun in evidence, People's Exhibit 117. Thus the important thing here is whether his memory of the incidents in New Orleans played on him to such an extent that he decided he would do anything to prevent a recurrence. The precise details have no relevance, except to color the picture and possibly to prejudice the jury with respect to the actions of the New Orleans police. We are concerned with the total impact as it existed in his mind, and therefore I will permit an inquiry in that area and that area alone."

I had won my gamble, although it was still too soon to cash in my chips. There was no doubt in my mind that the cross-examination on torture would hurt us, but now I was confident the damage could be controlled.

> Q: Mr. May, I believe before the interruption you said you were beaten. How long did this beating last?
>
> A: Four or five days.
>
> Q: Every day they brought you back down and they beat you some more, is that right?
>
> A: Yes.
>
> Q: And they used a cattle prod on you, is that right, Mr. May?
>
> A: No, they stopped using the cattle prod. They just used that the first day.
>
> Q: And during the time of this beating, Mr. May, they were questioning you, is that right?
>
> A: Yes.
>
> Q: And you finally told them what they wanted to know, what they wanted to hear, isn't that right?
>
> A: Right, what they wanted to hear.
>
> Q: You told them what they fed you, isn't that right?
>
> A: I told them whatever they wanted to hear.
>
> Q: Mr. May, is it fair to say you would have done anything to stop that beating?

A: Yes.

Q: That you would have implicated anyone to stop that beating?

A: Yes.

Q: That you would have done whatever they wanted to stop that beating?

A: Yes.

Q: Mr. May, will you ever forget that beating?

A: No.

Q: Will you ever forget that torture?

A: No.

Q: Mr. May, when you go to bed at night, do you dream about that torture?

A: Sometimes.

Q: Do you dream about the police who tortured you?

A: Yeah.

Q: And when you dream about them, what do you think?

A: I hate their guts.

Q: And you think about the beatings?

A: Yeah.

Q: Mr. May, are you frightened of the police?

A: Frightened?

Q: Yes.

A: No. I have more hatred than fear.

At the prosecution table, Ken leaned over and whispered to me, "I told you you had to put him on the stand. It's a good thing you listened to me." It was the first time in a long while any of us had felt like joking.

With their questions about torture, the defense had

brought Lester to life. As the memory of those horrible days flooded back to him, his voice took on a new harshness and he snapped off his terse, one-word answers with a snarling ferocity none of us suspected in him before. They had wanted him to talk about fear, they needed him to talk about fear, fear of the police, fear that would make him lie for us. And instead he told them he hated cops, hated them with such transparent bitterness that the jury would have had to be blind and deaf not to believe him.

Twenty-three

AT THE CONCLUSION OF THE PEOPLE'S CASE, the defense filed motions demanding that charges be dismissed against the Torres brothers on the grounds that the state had failed to establish a prima facie case against them. For a full day we argued the issue at the bench. I began by carefully marshaling all the evidence against both Francisco and Gabriel.

According to the evidence of the People's witnesses, Francisco had been present when the plot for "scoping pigs" was hatched in San Francisco. He then left California and came to New York, where the crime took place. On the day before the killings, Christine Rowe testified, he borrowed a stopwatch from her and went out with the other defendants to time traffic lights and police responses. A few hours before the killings, Christine said, she overheard him in a discussion with his brother in which he accused Gabriel of being "chickenshit," "not ready." Christine also testified that he returned to the apartment just minutes after Gabriel Torres and Albert Washington arrived, minutes before Bell and Bottom, and asked that the television be turned on to the news. Christine Rowe swore that later, in San Francisco, he threatened to kill her if she ever talked about what happened in New York.

I went on to argue that against Gabriel the evidence was just as compelling, if not more so. Although he had not been in San Francisco when Albert Washington and the others laid their plans for "scoping pigs," the witnesses testified that he let his apartment be used as the assassination team's command post. It was he who went to the Greyhound station to pick up the gun with which Anthony Bottom killed Waverly Jones. I had introduced into evidence the receipt he signed for the package, and his own lawyer had made it unnecessary to put a handwriting expert on the stand by stipulating that the signature was indeed Gabriel's. According to Christine Rowe, he not only went out with the others to time lights on the 20th and left with his brother on the night of the killings, but he returned, out of breath, with Albert Washington shortly before Francisco Torres and the two gunmen reached the Anderson Avenue apartment.

And of course, the jury had heard sworn testimony that both brothers joined in the celebration that took place the moment the television news bulletin announced that the second police officer was dead. Indeed, in the course of her cross-examination, Alie Horn was asked specifically whether the defendants, during this celebration, were "talking about what somebody had done."

"No," Alie had answered, "they didn't put it like that, in terms of what somebody had done. They were talking about something they had done."

The defense countered that none of this testimony proved anything and that a jury should not be permitted to deliberate in a case where a finding of guilt could be based upon nothing more than "speculation piled on top of speculation."

One by one, they ticked off each piece of evidence and attempted to show that it was either irrelevant or inconclusive. Francisco's participation in the San Francisco discussions was meaningless because the People's witness, Lester May, hadn't recalled what in particular Francisco Torres had said on the subject, whether he favored "scoping pigs" or opposed it. Similarly, Francisco's return to New York was "as consistent with innocence as with guilt," since, unlike the other defendants, he lived in New York and thus had a legitimate reason for going there. Nor had the prosecution shown that Gabriel Torres knew the contents of the package he picked up at the Greyhound station or the purpose for which the gun would be used.

Next, there had been no showing that timing lights the day before the murders bore any relation to this crime. Christine Rowe's account of the conversation between the brothers in the bedroom before they left the apartment on the evening of the killings was too fragmentary and incomplete to show that it pertained to an assassination plot. Moreover, the fact that Francisco accused Gabriel of being "chickenshit" tended to be exculpatory rather than inculpatory.

The fact that Gabriel arrived home with Washington did not necessarily prove he had been with Washington a half hour earlier, when the two patrolmen were gunned down, especially since both Christine Rowe and Alie Horn had testified that he asked Washington, "Why did you leave me?"

Furthermore, the defense argued that the law required a showing that the Torres brothers "actually participated in the crime at 159-20 Harlem River Drive or that they are responsible for the actions of others by having aided and abetted them. There must be proof of some actual assistance rendered. Mere presence at the scene is not enough."

I rebutted by insisting that these defense arguments were fanciful. Although individually true on a point-by-point basis, they ignored the cumulative effect of the testimony as a whole, which, I argued, added up to an unambiguous picture of the Torres brothers' complicity in this crime. Nowhere is there a requirement in law that each piece of evidence in and of itself prove guilt beyond a reasonable doubt. While it is true that jurors should not be permitted to speculate, it is equally true that a jury can and must draw reasonable inferences from the evidence. Not only had a grand jury heard this evidence and found it sufficient for an indictment, but at the first trial Justice Melia had denied a similar defense motion, ruling that the People had presented enough evidence to warrant the jury to attempt to reach a verdict. That was all I asked here. If the evidence did not prove their guilt, it was the jury's prerogative to say so.

At the conclusion of our arguments, Justice Greenfield issued his ruling. "Putting pieces of circumstantial evidence together is not unlike spelling a word," he declared. "One letter in the word may give rise to an inference that it is going to spell what you think it is or many other possible words. The more letters you put together, the more limited you become in the number of words those letters can spell. And so it is entirely possible to have individual pieces of evidence, no one of which points with a moral certainty to a hypothesis of guilt, but all of which, taken together, lead inevitably to that conclusion. The question in this case is whether these individual pieces of evidence, when put together, spell the word 'Guilt.'

"When the State seeks to charge individuals with criminal responsibility for a murder in which they were not the persons who committed the actual acts of murder, it must establish either that they were acting in concert or that there was a conspiracy to kill of which they were an active part.

"To prove that the defendants were acting in concert requires that there be evidence showing the participation of each individual in the entire scheme. The law is equally clear that where there is a conspiracy alleged, the State must first establish the membership of the persons so charged in that conspiracy and must establish that each of them had a part to play in that conspiracy, that there was a common purpose to effectuate a goal and not merely a generalized approval as to what other persons were doing.

"Whatever Gabriel Torres and Francisco Torres may have done, this Court has no way of knowing. The Court must judge on the basis of the evidence which has been adduced here. The evidence shows that they had some awareness of what was going on, and that they had participation in some of the facts which were going on, but it does not, in the Court's mind, rise to the level of establishing that they were part and parcel of a conspiracy to kill. Perhaps they were, perhaps they were not. The Court can only go on the basis of the evidence which has been presented here, and on the basis of that evidence the Court finds it not legally sufficient to warrant a jury to return a verdict of guilt against either of these defendants. Accordingly, the Court will grant the motion of

Defense Counsel and enter a Trial Order of Dismissal with respect to Francisco and Gabriel Torres."

When I got back to my office, numb and angry, the phone was already jangling.

"Mr. Tanenbaum, what's going on down there? You told me I could trust you," a woman's voice complained keenly.

It took a moment before I recognized the voice as Diane Piagentini's. News of Judge Greenfield's dismissal order had been broadcast on the radio within minutes of the decision.

There was an accusation in Diane's tone that I felt I didn't deserve, but I hadn't earned the right to defend myself against it. "I'm sorry," I said weakly. "It couldn't be helped. There just wasn't enough evidence."

"But they killed my husband," she protested.

I tried to think of something to say that would appease her. But I doubted she would find any more consolation than I did in the fact that the Torres brothers were not the actual shooters. "It couldn't be helped," I repeated. "But the trial's not over. I wish there was something else I could say."

There was a silence, and then she said, "I'm sorry, too. I don't blame you, it's probably not your fault. But I feel so helpless. Perhaps I shouldn't have stayed away, at least I would have seen what was happening. I read about it every day, you know, and I try to get a picture in my mind. But it's hard. I want to be there, that's what I called to tell you. I should be there."

"I wish you wouldn't, Diane. It would only make things harder."

There was a catch in her voice. She said, "They couldn't be harder. These men killed my husband, and now it feels like they're just slipping away."

I didn't want her there, I didn't want the defense pointing her out. But it was impossible for me to say no to her. "Diane, listen to me," I pleaded. "Trust me just a little while longer. The defense case is on today, maybe tomorrow. They're only calling a few minor witnesses. Then we begin summations, probably on Thursday. They'll go first, three summations, it will take at least two days. Can you wait until Tuesday? I'll be summing up then, you'll hear the whole case. Just until Tuesday."

"I can wait," she said. "Next month it will be four years. I'm very good at waiting."

The defense case boiled down to little more than two insignificant witnesses. One was Linda Gill's step-father, who claimed the FBI had come to his house to question him about Herman Bell in October 1971. The purpose of his testimony was to show that government witnesses lied when they swore they did not learn Bell's identity until November. On cross-examination, how-ever, I had no difficulty at all in showing that his mem-ory of the date was faulty and that the interview did not occur until well after October.

The second defense witness did them no more good than the first. It was Bill Butler, and for an hour and a half he skillfully parried all their innuendos. Just about the only concession they were able to wring from him was that he flew to California a number of days before the witnesses were flown out to attend the line-up—a petty and totally insignificant inconsistency with Gloria

Lapp's recollection that he was on the plane with her when she went to California. Nevertheless, I was reluctant to let the defense have even that, so on cross-examination I asked him one question: "You said Gloria Lapp was not with you when you flew to California. Was she with you when she flew back from California, Detective Butler?"

"Yes, sir, she was," Bill announced grandly, closing one of the briefest cross-examinations on record.

One of the few advantages the prosecution has under our trial system is the opportunity to sum up last. A few hours Thursday morning were spent at the bench, clearing up some legal and procedural issues that had arisen during the course of the trial. Late in the morning Anthony Bottom's lawyer began his summation. He spoke through the day, spelling out the defense's theory of a frame-up in great detail. I followed him closely, taking notes both on the points he made and on the evidence I would cite when I got my chance to refute him.

Over the weekend I began preparing my own summation. Friday and Saturday were spent entirely with Ken Klein, carefully going over the nine-thousand-page record of the trial and the daily outline Ken had been compiling each night after court adjourned. When Ken went home late Saturday night, he left me with a point-by-point digest of all the evidence in the case, carefully worked out to demonstrate the truthfulness of each witness. On Sunday I began the actual drafting of my summation, knowing I would probably have to make some adjustments Monday night to take into account the points raised by Herman Bell's lawyer and by Albert Washington in their summations.

On Monday morning Albert Washington gave a brief summation that amounted to no less than an attempt to justify the murder of police officers. "The tortures in the police station, they go on," he said. "The murders, they go on. Every day somewhere in this country in the black community, the police shoot somebody. The only time it's a crime is when one of them gets shot. Then they start bawling, they start raising hell, they want stiffer laws. And this is the crime that we're guilty of, because we want to implement laws that serve and protect us. So, in essence, we're fighting for our humanity. Our actions are justified in the sense that as human beings we have the right to defend ourselves."

Bell's lawyer summed up for the rest of the day, concentrating on his theory of a fingerprint switch and his claim that Lester May buried Piagentini's gun in Mississippi. There wasn't a word in his summation I hadn't expected.

Monday night I completed the draft of my summation. My notes ran to approximately one hundred twenty-five handwritten pages, and I felt as I wrote them that each word contained all the anger and frustration of four years of waiting for justice. And mixed in with the passion for justice was something darker, yet no less compelling, I recognized in myself. Like Joe Louis training for his rematch with Schmeling, I was driven by a desire for personal vindication, for revenge. I knew it would take a full day to deliver the summation the way I drafted it, but I refused to hold back anything out of a fear of tiring the jury. I was facing the last day in one of the longest, most expensive, and most far-reaching police investigations in New York State history, the end of one of the lengthiest criminal trials on record anywhere. The jury had been on this case four months. I had been on it twenty-one months, eight of them actually spent in courtrooms. I owed it to the jury and to myself, I owed it to Diane, to the cops who worked on the case, and to the two who died to leave not the smallest defense claim unanswered, to omit the slightest piece of incriminating evidence. I didn't want a clean, neat knockout. I wanted to hold them on the ropes and batter them. I wanted to hit them with everything I had.

"Joseph Piagentini, the evidence shows—he was twenty-eight years old and Waverly Jones was thirty-two. When they died, Piagentini and Jones were doing their job. They were aiding a woman in distress. Because they were policemen. And that is why they died. Jones was not spared because he was a black man. Piagentini was not killed because he was white. Both were slaughtered by these defendants because they wore blue—because they were policemen.

"At no time during this trial, at no time did I bring in the bullet-riddled jackets of Jones and Piagentini, their blood-soaked shirts. Because it is not sympathy that we ask for in this case. We ask for justice. That is why I did not bring in their jackets or their shirts. But I did bring in their guns—these guns. Because these guns—Piagentini's and Jones's guns—it is just as if Jones and Piagentini walked into this courtroom and pointed an accusatory finger at their killers. That is the significance of these guns.

"In a very real sense, ladies and gentlemen, this case starts and ends with these guns. The last piece of evidence found in this case, November nineteen seventy-four, is Piagentini's gun. Mr. Klein and Mr. Fenton found it in Mississippi, where Lester May told them Herman Bell buried it. That is the last piece of evidence. And where did it begin, this trial that leads to Mississippi? It began in San Francisco, when Inspector McCoy learned that the thirty-eight found in the car with Anthony Bottom and Albert Washington once belonged to Waverly Jones.

"Let us go back to San Francisco and think about this a moment. We have Waverly Jones's gun and we have a pearl-handled forty-five, the gun that killed Waverly Jones, Anthony Bottom's gun. Now remember what Washington said in his summation. He told you these men are the guardians of our democracy. So Anthony Bottom is driving around San Francisco with a pouch hanging from his waistband with fifty-nine live forty-five-caliber shells capable of being fired from the murder weapon. And in this forty-five was a clip containing six live rounds of ammunition. And Albert Washington, what did he have? Falling from Washington's waistband is a thirty-eight-caliber pistol with one live round in it. In his pants pockets are twenty-eight thirty-eight-caliber shells capable of being fired from the thirty-eight and there are six loose shells, thirty-eight-caliber live, capable of being fired from this gun.

"Imagine what we are talking about. Bottom has this pouch hanging from his belt. Anthony Bottom, Albert Washington—armed. And what do they tell you? What does the defense say? That the 'armorer,' the armorer of this case is Lester May. The defense throws in Lester May as the armorer. What are they arming themselves for? Are they in Southeast Asia? Is this the Middle East? They are in the City by the Bay, San Francisco. Every day people are leaving New York to move to the City by the Bay. And Anthony Bottom is riding around with this pouch.

"So we have Jones's gun in San Francisco and Piagentini's gun in Mississippi. And the question is asked, Why do the killers keep these guns? Don't they know they are hot? Don't they know they are incriminating? Of course they are incriminating. But remember who you are dealing with here. You heard Albert Washington sum up. I didn't write that summation for him, be sure of that.

"He came here and he argued to you for an hour and a half and he told you some significant things about himself. He talked about justification, about self-defense. Police are pigs to them. They're nonhuman. 'A pig is a pig. Fuck 'em all.' That's what you are dealing with here. They are murdering symbols in their minds.

"Because remember this, that if you kill two human beings and you bother to take their guns, you are delaying your escape. And if you are delaying your escape, you are not taking guns because this is a robbery for guns. You are taking these guns because they are trophies. You are taking these guns because you are dehumanizing your victims. You are taking these guns to show your friends what you did. You are arming yourself from the enemy. That's why you keep the guns.

"So know who you are dealing with in these brazen murders. To these men, Waverly Jones's gun and Joseph Piagentini's gun are the badge of the assassin.

"And if you are brazen enough to pull this murder and take these guns, you are not going to give them away. These guns are the symbols of the eradication of two police officers. And the killers in this case, the killers will know always that these are the guns of their victims and only the killers would keep these guns.

"The evidence in this case, ladies and gentlemen, is overwhelming. The evidence requires that justice be done. Common sense dictates, good conscience commands, and justice cries out that Anthony Bottom be held responsible for what he did, that Herman Bell be held responsible for what he did, that Albert Washington be held responsible for what he did.

"I ask you in the interest of justice and in the name of the people of the State of New York to find the defendant Anthony Bottom guilty of the murder of Waverly Jones and guilty of the murder of Joseph Piagentini; I ask you in the name of the people of the state of New York and in the interest of justice to find the defendant Herman Bell guilty of what he did, guilty of the murder of Waverly Jones and guilty of the murder of Joseph Piagentini; and Albert Washington, guilty of the murders of Waverly Jones and Joseph Piagentini."

On April 8, 1975, the day I delivered my summation, Diane Piagentini was present in court for the first time since her husband's killers had been put on trial. I saw her when I left the courtroom for the lunch recess, but we didn't speak. She merely nodded in my direction, a nod that conveyed a measured approval, but also a disinclination to talk. My rhetoric, good or bad, had no meaning for her, for the only criterion by which she could judge it was the verdict we were all awaiting.

I didn't see her when I left the court at the conclusion of my summation later that afternoon, although I knew she was in attendance until the end. One of the detectives gave her a ride home and promised to call for her in the morning. She wanted to hear the judge's charge.

She came to my office before nine o'clock Wednesday morning. We had coffee and talked for half an hour, but not about the trial. I told her my wife and I were expecting a baby around the end of May.

She seemed pleased. "The end of May," she said, "that's a nice time. It's easier with an infant in the summer."

At twenty past nine Ken came in and said it was time to go. As we walked to the courtroom, Diane tried to apologize for having said nothing about my summation, but I cut her off. "They're guilty," I said. "Let's just pray the jury knows it." The detective who had driven her to court was waiting for us at the courtroom doors. He sat with Diane in the first row of spectator seats, while Ken and I proceeded to the prosecution table.

One of the defense lawyers was already in court. A second arrived a few minutes later. Promptly at 9:30 a cordon of guards escorted the defendants in from the holding pens. The clerk then called on us to rise as the judge entered the court. The defense attorneys, Ken, and I approached the bench, where the defense filed some last-minute motions referring to points of law they wanted included in the charge.

"If that's all, gentlemen, shall we bring in the jury?" the judge asked after responding to all the requests.

The defense lawyers exchanged glances. "Excuse me, Your Honor," one of them said at last. "If I may say something?"

"Yes?"

"Well, Your Honor, I don't want to offend Mrs.

Piagentini in any way," he began with an uncharacteristic show of sensitivity. "But it has to do with her."

My blood boiled. "Look," I snapped, "I don't know what this is all about, but I want this clear on the record. It has never been made known to the jury that Mrs. Piagentini is here. It is certainly her right to be in this courtroom."

"That's correct," the attorney purred. "Except that only police officers are allowed in the first row. Perhaps I'm mistaken and she is a woman police officer, but I assume that is Mrs. Piagentini?"

No one responded.

"Well, is it?" he demanded.

"Yes," I said.

"In that case," he said, "I have an application that she be gently requested not to sit in the first row."

"I'm sorry," I protested, "but if there is one interested party in this courtroom it is Mrs. Piagentini. She wants to hear the Court's charge, and she has every right to be sitting here."

"Oh certainly," the lawyer shot back sarcastically. "She was so interested she was not here during the last trial at all and not here during this trial, not one day. I'm sure Mr. Tanenbaum can arrange it in some way, as gently as possible."

I walked away from the bench. "I'm not arranging anything," I said.

"All right, gentlemen, enough of this," the judge barked. Turning to the defense lawyer who had spoken last, he said, "If you think it will really be that significant, I will ask her to move. Do you make that request?"

"I make that request."

A court officer started toward Diane to carry out the judge's wishes, but Justice Greenfield stopped him with a motion of his hand. Coming around from behind the bench, he walked through the well of the court. She knew what he wanted before he reached her, nodded her understanding as he bent to whisper in her ear. On her face was a look of neither anger nor resentment, for she was above being annoyed by such a petty maneuver on the part of the men who defended her husband's killers. She moved back a few rows while Justice Greenfield returned to the bench. Then the jurors were led in and a court officer locked the courtroom doors, as is customary when a jury is being charged.

It was 10:30. With only two short recesses, the judge spoke for three and a half hours, a magnificent charge that set out the jury's responsibilities in as clear and moving language as I have ever heard. The jury was then sent to lunch and admonished not to begin discussing the case until the judge had an opportunity to supplement his charge after hearing exceptions and additional requests from attorneys on both sides.

The prosecution had none. The defense filed, by my count, seventy-six separate objections to various points in the charge, either omissions or statements they regarded as inappropriate. Justice Greenfield accepted five of these. At 4:25 the jurors were brought back into the courtroom to listen to the final additions to the charge. At 4:45 they were sent from the court to commence their deliberations.

Ken and I escorted Diane Piagentini to my office to await word from the jury room. Bill Butler and Cliff Fenton were waiting for us there. Naturally, we were all tense, and at first we said little, dropping small pieces of unconnected conversation into large silences. At 5:30 Bill went for sandwiches, and when he came back we all began to relax somewhat as we ate. I suppose Diane's presence made it difficult to discuss the case, in the way that mourners find it difficult to begin talking about the deceased at a wake. Yet soon their common memories overcome their reticence as they grow to recognize that sharing their feelings is the reality behind their being together.

Cliff, who is a great storyteller with an infectious, gurgling laugh, helped loosen us up. Even Diane joined in the laughter when he recounted his adventures in the Round Robin Bar and Grille while he and Horace Lukes hunted for Linda Gill. Soon Ken and I were discussing the trial itself, with the two detectives, who had appeared on the stand and thus had been prohibited from attending as spectators, pumping us for accounts of how the various witnesses came through.

At 7:30 I got a call to return to court.

Diane tensed. "What does that mean?" she asked.

I put my arm around her shoulder. "Don't be so nervous," I said. "It's not a verdict, he would have said so. And it can't be a hung jury after just two and a half hours. They haven't broken for supper yet. That's probably all it is. I'm surprised they went so late."

Ken and I hurried upstairs to the court. At 7:35 the jury came in. "The Court is in receipt of an inquiry from the jury," Judge Greenfield announced. He read the question, which concerned a statement from his charge about four elements of the crime the People must prove beyond a reasonable doubt, and then he instructed the court reporter to read back the relevant portion from the transcript.

Trying to divine what is happening in a jury on the basis of the jury's questions is a tricky business, but I was delighted on two counts. The mere fact that the jury was willing to work so late testified to their spirit. I didn't think they'd quit on us the way the first jury did. And perhaps the fact that their question concerned the charge rather than the evidence meant they were already testing to see if they had a basis for a finding of guilt.

Or was that too much to hope? Generally speaking, juries take longer to convict than to acquit. It didn't seem possible they could have come so far in so short a time. Maybe the question meant that some of them were holding out for acquittal and were shopping for a rationale to justify their position.

I cursed myself under my breath for speculating. It only made the waiting that much harder.

Five minutes later Ken and I were back in my office, explaining to Diane, Bill, and Cliff that the jury's question meant nothing.

At a quarter to eight we got another call to return to court. This time the judge sent the jury to their hotel for the night.

The next morning the vigil began at 10:00. We all knew that a verdict could take days. A week or two wouldn't be surprising after a trial so long. Yet the tension of waiting soon became unbearable, and I began to wonder how we would all make it. Noon came and went. At one o'clock Bill again went for sandwiches, which no one felt like eating. Diane was tight-lipped, taut as a kite string. While Bill and Cliff struggled to keep up a semblance of conversation, my mind jumped randomly through months of testimony, playing an involuntary fugue of questions and answers. The silence from the jury room was appalling. I couldn't understand why they hadn't sent down even a single question all day. What was going on up there?

The afternoon passed slowly, painfully. At a few minutes before four o'clock the phone on my desk went off like an explosion. I jumped for it.

"We have a verdict."

"A verdict!" I shouted.

The men grabbed their jackets and ran for the door, Diane right in the middle of them. For an instant she turned her head and looked into my eyes searchingly, as though she wanted me to tell her what the verdict was. Then she was out the door, and I hurried to catch up.

In the corridor we were suddenly in a stream of lawyers racing with us. Word of a verdict in a big trial spreads through a courthouse like panic through a crowd. I ran past Diane and Ken, caught up with Bill and Cliff, and turned them around, heading them for the staircase. "We'll never get on an elevator," I said.

As we hurried up the stairwell to the thirteenth floor, I could hear footsteps gaining on us from behind. When we got to thirteen I pounded on the locked fire door. A patrolman opened it, hesitated a second until he recognized us, and let us through. Behind me as I headed for the courtroom I could hear him telling someone he would have to go back down for an elevator, that no one was permitted in through the stairs.

The hallway was so crowded I could hardly believe so many people had been screened through the metal detectors so quickly. And every few seconds an elevator disgorged another load. Now they were coming too fast for the checkpoint to handle and were piling up behind the metal detectors like a crowd trying to get out of a ball park after a big game. Reporters surging up from the downstairs press room, prospective jurors from the main jury room, lawyers, militants, defendants and witnesses from other courts. And cops, cops, scores of them—uniformed patrolmen, off-duty cops, detectives, the guys who had been writing me letters for over a year now, urging me to hang in there when newspaper accounts gave the impressions of a setback, exhorting me to keep at it when things were going well, reminding me that Joe and Jonesy were two of their own.

We pushed into the courtroom, which was bedlam already and still filling fast. I shouldered ahead to the prosecution table and looked back for Diane. She was in the third row, between Cliff and Bill. At the back of the court, two court officers were struggling to close the doors. Slowly the room came to order, not silence, but a sustained murmur, like a crowded theater before the lights go down. And then the defendants were led in, setting off a rumble of whispers through the crowd, a small but ugly cheer from their knot of supporters clustered behind the defense table.

Bell was smiling broadly, a handsome, powerful young man in his moment of glory, detached, serenely indifferent to the verdict. Washington gestured a black power salute, his face grave and solemn, while Bottom postured like an astronaut in a motorcade. It was suddenly excruciatingly clear to me how easy it would be for them to win, for it would be a victory for them even if only Washington were acquitted. Did the fast verdict mean the jury had taken the easy way, convicting Bell and Bottom but following the judge's lead and freeing the nonshooter?

The jury filed in, and I tried to read their faces. If they look at the defendants it means . . . if they are scowling it means . . . if they are smiling. . . . So many axioms, and I couldn't tell a thing.

"All rise!" the clerk commanded, intoning the formula that set the court in session. Judge Greenfield appeared behind the bench, sat, and there was a rustling of fabric as hundreds of observers slid into their seats.

"Case on trial, People versus Herman Bell, Anthony Bottom, Albert Washington," the clerk called. "Defendants, their attorneys, assistant district attorneys all present. Jury called and all present. Mr. Foreman, please rise."

The foreman stood like a soldier. Which he was.

"Defendants, please rise."

Bell, Bottom, and Washington remained in their seats.

"Mr. Foreman, ladies and gentlemen of the jury, has the jury agreed upon a verdict?"

"Yes, we have."

"How say you as to the defendant Herman Bell?"

"We find him guilty as charged."

I heard a broad rumble of approval. At the defense table, the smile on Herman Bell's face hadn't moved.

"As to which count in the indictment, please?"

"Murder, one, guilty. Murder, two, guilty."

"How say you as to the defendant Anthony Bottom?"

"We find him guilty as charged. To count one, murder. To count two, murder."

The room fell coldly silent, tensed for the last question.

"How say you as to the defendant Albert Washington?"

"To count one, murder, to count two, murder, we find him guilty as charged."

There was shouting. I was on my feet and I felt Ken's arms around me. I turned, looking for Diane. Already the doors to the courtroom were open and reporters were racing out. Hands were reaching toward me, like the pikes of an advancing army. In the middle of the crowd, Cliff Fenton was standing on a chair, his hands clasped above his head. Then he disappeared, pulled down, swallowed up by a mob of rejoicing detectives. Only a few feet from me I saw Bill Butler, tears streaming down his face, pushing his way through to me, Diane behind him, her hand in his. I felt his powerful hand clapping my back, and then Diane's arms around me, hugging me tight, her head on my shoulder as she cried like a lonely child. Bill called out something I couldn't hear and then slipped back into the crowd, disappearing into the circle of detectives, joining Cliff at the center, where they belonged.

By the dozens, lawyers from my office were converging on me, reaching their hands for mine. But the moment was passing so quickly that I couldn't bear to share it. With one arm around Diane, one around Ken, I made my way to the well of the court, where it felt cool and quiet and remote, where it seemed we could be alone, far from the cheers and shouts of joy that still surged across the courtroom. Behind me, the clerk, his voice inaudible more than a few feet away, called over and over for order, which was a long time coming.

Postscript

ON MAY 12, 1975, JUST NINE DAYS SHORT of the fourth anniversary of the deaths of Waverly Jones and Joseph Piagentini, convicted killers Herman Bell, Anthony Bottom, and Albert Washington were brought into Justice Greenfield's packed courtroom for the last time. All three defendants and their attorneys were permitted to make statements, which were followed in turn by statements from Ken Klein and myself on behalf of the People.

The sentencing itself was a foregone conclusion. No one in the courtroom expected the defendants to receive less than the maximum. Taking notice of the fact that a combination of New York State law and Supreme Court rulings precluded capital punishment in this case, Justice Greenfield sentenced each of the defendants to a term of imprisonment from twenty-five years to life on each of the two counts of murder for which they had been found guilty. Because the two murders were essentially part of a single act, and because New York law does not permit the imposition of sentences longer than twenty-five-to-life, he ordered that the two sentences he was imposing be served concurrently, but he specifically directed that his sentences be served consecutively with any time for any other crime in any other jurisdiction.

Before being brought into court that morning, the defendants had been meticulously searched by officers from the Department of Corrections, as had been done every day since the trial began. After the sentencing, which concluded shortly before 1 P.M., they were brought back to their cells in the holding area of the courthouse, where in the normal course of events they would have been served lunch before being returned to Rikers Island. Fortunately, Corrections officers, understandably impatient to be rid of their dangerous charges, decided at the last minute to return them to Rikers Island immediately. Before being loaded into the Corrections vans, they were searched again. This time the search disclosed an appalling assortment of lock picks, knives, and plastic explosives hidden on them. Only the accidental change of plans prevented what might have turned into a bloody escape attempt.

At the conclusion of the Piagentini-Jones trial in New York, Lester Bertram May and the other two New Orleans prisoners who had confessed to participating in the deadly raid on the Ingleside police station in San Francisco were flown to California. All three were at that time under indictment for the murder of Sergeant John Young, and San Francisco authorities intended to put them before the grand jury in order to secure indictments against the other men named in their statements. May already had indicated his willingness to plead guilty to the crime.

Sometime after arriving in California, May changed his mind and decided to fight the murder charge. In response to motions filed by May and the two men indicted with him, a trial judge ruled all three confessions inadmissible on the grounds that they had been given out of the presence of the defendants' attorneys. As a result, the indictments against May and the other two men were dismissed, and no one was prosecuted for this crime, which to this day remains officially unsolved. Lester May was then returned to New Orleans, where he is still in federal prison serving a five-to-fifteen-year sentence for bank robbery.

Gabriel and Francisco Torres both pleaded guilty to the July 1971 robbery of the Fidelity Savings and Loan in San Francisco for which they were given 20-year sentences. Federal authorities saw fit to release them from custody after they served only four years.

Anthony Bottom and Albert Washington were each found guilty of the attempted murder of Sergeant George Kowalski and sentenced to terms of five years to life. Bottom was convicted after trial of the same bank robbery to which the Torres brothers pleaded guilty. For that crime he was sentenced to zero to twenty-five years in prison. In 1977, six years after their arrest, Bottom and Washington were released to the custody of New York penal authorities to begin serving their sentences for the murders of Piagentini and Jones. They will become eligible for parole in 2002.

In addition to his conviction for the murders of Piagentini and Jones, Herman Bell was also convicted of the September 1971 robbery of a San Francisco branch of the Bank of America. For that crime he was sentenced to zero to twenty-five years in federal prison, a term he is still serving as of this writing. He will not become eligible for parole until twenty-five years after he has begun serving his sentence for the murders of Piagentini and Jones.